3369 - Book Warehouse - 2025 (3⁰⁰)

THE EIGHT ESSENTIAL STEPS TO
CONFLICT RESOLUTION

THE EIGHT ESSENTIAL STEPS TO CONFLICT RESOLUTION

Preserving Relationships at Work, at Home, and in the Community

Dudley Weeks, Ph.D.

JEREMY P. TARCHER, INC.
Los Angeles

Library of Congress Cataloging-in-Publication Data

Weeks, Dudley.
    The eight essential steps to conflict resolution / Dudley Weeks.
        p.   cm.
    Includes bibliographical references.
    ISBN 0-87477-656-2
    1. Conflict management. 2. Social conflict. I. Title.
HM136.W38   1992   91-5171
303.6'9—dc20   CIP

Jeremy P. Tarcher, Inc.
5858 Wilshire Blvd., Suite 200
Los Angeles, CA 90036

Manufactured in the United States of America
10 9 8 7 6 5 4 3 2

To you, the reader,
and your potential to resolve conflicts effectively
and to build relationships that use differences
for mutual benefit and growth.

Contents

PREFACE ix

Part I: Understanding Conflict 1

Chapter 1: A New View of Conflict 3
Chapter 2: Five Popular (But Ineffective) Approaches 11
to Conflict Resolution
Chapter 3: The Ingredients of Conflict 33
Chapter 4: The Conflict Partnership Process 63

Part II: The Eight Essential Steps to Conflict 69
Resolution

Step 1: Create an Effective Atmosphere 71
Step 2: Clarify Perceptions 89
Step 3: Focus on Individual and Shared Needs 127
Step 4: Build Shared Positive Power 147
Step 5: Look to the Future, Then Learn from the 161
Past
Step 6: Generate Options 183

Step 7: Develop "Doables": The Stepping-stones   203
to Action

Step 8: Make Mutual-Benefit Agreements   223

Afterword   235

Appendix A: Handling Frequent Problem Areas   237

• Dealing with Anger   237
• When One Party Thinks There Is No Conflict   240
• When You Feel Unsure about Confronting
Someone   242
• When the Other Party Seems Not to Want a
Resolution   247
• Dealing with People Who Only
Want Things Their Way   250
• Dealing with Conflicts Involving Injustices   252
• Dealing with Seemingly Unresolvable
Conflicts   255
• When to Seek a Third-Party Facilitator   257
• Conflict Partnership Third-Party Facilitation
Skills   260

Appendix B: Two Cases That Demonstrate the
Conflict Partnership Process   265

INDEX   286

Preface

Conflict is an inescapable part of our daily lives, an inevitable result of our highly complex, competitive, and often litigious society. Whether it be in our personal relationships or our business interactions, each of us has our own ideas, opinions, and needs, and how we deal with our differences with others can determine the quality of our lives. Whereas some conflicts are simply minor nuisances that we accept as a natural component of existence, others keep our relationships from realizing their full potential, and some become so severe that they do irreparable damage to individuals, families, workplaces, and entire communities. Learning how to deal with conflicts effectively is increasingly an essential life skill needed by every person and every group regardless of one's age, social role, profession, cultural background, or beliefs.

The eight steps I will teach in this book have been developed in the course of my extensive experience as a conflict resolution facilitator, trainer, and teacher in many diverse interpersonal, family, workplace, community, and international situations of conflict. The skills included in this book are those that have proven effective time and again in resolving almost any type of conflict. This book is not intended as a volume of theory to be read once and put on a shelf to collect dust. Rather, it is intended to be used again and again as a guide to improved conflict resolution and relationship-building.

I grew up in the American South in a rather conflict-prone environment. Racism, sexism, ageism, and numerous community and business conflicts were all around me. One of the causes of these conflicts was rooted in a widespread belief that ideas different from the dominant attitudes were wrong or unpatriotic, and should be treated as threats to the smooth operation of society. I noticed how often people allowed their differences to escalate into damaging conflicts. Differences in desires, social and economic status, family and workplace patterns, cultural background, race, gender, and overall views of the way life should be structured and lived— all were used as reasons to build walls between people and create conflicts to be fought with an adversary until one gained an advantage or proved who was right or wrong.

By the time I reached my early teens, I had witnessed enough conflict to realize that *everybody* suffered when conflicts were not dealt with effectively and when individuals or groups were not allowed to contribute their worth and skills to relationships, to the community, and to society. I decided that human beings were letting an important part of their potential atrophy. It seemed to me that many people had become so accustomed to seeing differences as necessarily threatening and adversarial that they were ignoring the potential we all have to use our differences for mutual growth. We were failing to learn from one another, to deal with our differences and conflicts as *partners,* not as enemies in search of victory over another person or group.

As I began espousing these ideas in my relationships, in my community, and then as a youth worker in the civil rights and peace movements, I ran headlong into many obstacles.

It was as though most people had become so comfortable with the "I versus you" pattern of dealing with conflict that all alternative approaches were immediately suspect or viewed as too radical to be considered seriously.

During my years in college, I became involved in several international projects from which I learned firsthand that other cultures also struggle with how best to resolve differences and conflicts in a mutually beneficial way. After college, I served in the Peace Corps for three years, and then worked for several years as a teacher, paramedic, and human rights and social change activist in Asia, Europe, and Africa. In all of these experiences I found that unless conflicts were dealt with effectively, the positive development of personal and societal life was severely hampered. I realized that conflict resolution was a life skill, one that lay at the heart of our potential as individuals and communities. I decided to make my life's work the advancement and teaching of conflict resolution skills.

Conflict resolution had not grown into an accepted "field" at that time. Of course there were the most prevalent, traditional, and accepted approaches to dealing with conflict, such as negotiation, mediation, and arbitration, but as I read about them, talked with practitioners, and tried them out in my work in the United States and overseas, I found these traditional approaches lacking in several important areas. Each approach, in its own way, seemed either to reward the party who could find a way to get more of his or her demands met, who could make fewer concessions, or who could perform better in the conflict resolution "competition." Even when third-party negotiators or mediators were involved, the parties involved in the actual conflict did not seem to be *empowered* by the approach to resolution with skills capable of dealing more effectively with future conflicts or managing their relationship. Although temporary agreements were often reached, the relationship between the parties at odds had not been improved. A subsequent conflict, if indeed the parties even maintained a relationship, would be fought with the same old patterns of "I versus you," "getting what I want," or gaining an advantage over the other party.

I strongly believed that we as individuals, groups, businesses, organizations, communities, and societies could deal with our conflicts in better ways. I began to search for and try out various approaches that would supply parties involved in conflict with skills enabling them to both deal effectively with immediate conflicts and improve their relationship for the future. I tried to find ways to focus on differences and conflicts as potentially positive aspects of relationships, and I began to develop skills that would create a partnership between parties in conflict, a partnership in which they would need each other if they were to resolve conflicts and build a healthier relationship.

In my work in civil rights and peacemaking, in my jobs as community organizer, educator, and development worker around the world, I began to find that people were hungry for alternative ways of dealing with their conflicts. In that theories devised in the safety of the mind often fail the test of the real world, some of the ideas that I had been taught to believe would be broadly successful did not work consistently. For example, I found that simply getting parties to make an equal number of concessions on the demands they had stated did little, if anything, to get to the critical roots of the conflict or to improve the relationship. But there were certain other skills that did prove effective in all types of conflicts, regardless of the age, social role, culture, profession, or other characteristics of the people or groups involved, and so I worked on refining those consistently effective skills.

The result is the *conflict partnership* process you will learn about in this book. The process involves gaining an empowering set of skills. While each of us will need to apply the conflict partnership skills in our own way, the heart and soul of the approach provides the groundwork of an effective guide in resolving conflicts and improving relationships.

I have used these conflict partnership skills in a tremendous variety of conflicts, working with a diverse array of individuals and groups around the world. My work has ranged from interpersonal conflicts, such as two friends involved in a serious battle over how to run a jointly owned business, to a family's devastating conflict arising from drug abuse, to a workplace situation involving two colleagues whose personal conflict threatened to ruin the company for which they both worked. I have applied the skills in community disputes, such as how to deal with a racial crisis and how to build a community center. I have also used the conflict partnership skills to help facilitate institutional conflicts involving universities, hospitals, and social service agencies, and to assist parties involved in international conflicts in such places as South Africa, the Soviet Union, Northern Ireland, Central America, Asia, and the Middle East. In every case, I have been encouraged to see that the conflict partnership process has provided a breakthrough to resolve differences effectively and sustainably.

Resolving conflicts takes hard work and perseverance. Most people with whom you might be in conflict perceive it as a negative experience. They may fear conflict, or don't even want to admit they are involved in one because they somehow feel it means something has gone wrong in their relationship. Others fear dealing with conflict because they assume someone will get hurt or lose power. Many people also feel that dealing with conflicts is usually a rather hopeless exercise, in that both parties will just fight for what they want because they aren't aware of skills that really work. Thus, when we use the conflict partnership skills, we have to persevere because so many people have become accustomed to handling conflict ineffectively.

All of us, I am sure, have at one time or another felt some of these emotions and fears, and that's understandable, for we are still quite undeveloped in what I call our social technology skills. We have spent far more energy and resources on our material technologies than we have in developing the people skills to deal effectively with our differences and with building mutually enriching relationships. But in our complex lives, devoting some time and energy to developing effective resolution skills is now an essential need. This book seeks to be a contribution to that end, for the benefit of your own personal and professional life and for our communities and our world.

PART I

Understanding Conflict

CHAPTER 1

A New View of Conflict

What is this complex phenomenon of human interactions called conflict, this pervasive condition all around us? If you consult a dictionary, you run into such depressing notions as "a prolonged battle or collision," or "the opposition of mutually exclusive impulses, desires, or tendencies." Although you can also find less dramatic definitions, such as "a controversy, a disagreement," most definitions of conflict conjure up rather somber and often frightening associations.

In my conflict resolution workshops around the world, I frequently do an exercise in which I ask the participants to give me the first word that comes to their minds when I say "conflict." Struck by the similarity of the responses regardless of culture, I recently spent a portion of a long, overnight airplane flight doing an interesting task: I compared the word-association lists from workshops representing a sampling of geographic areas (including the United States, the Soviet Union, South Africa, the Middle East, Malaysia, Northern Ireland, Nigeria, Central America, Brazil, and India) to find the most frequently mentioned responses. These were the words associated with conflict:

Fight	Avoid
Anger	Lose
Pain	Control
War	Hate
Impasse	Loss
Destruction	Bad
Fear	Wrongdoing
Mistake	

All of these words appeared on each of the lists from many cultural settings. As you can see, conflict is almost universally perceived as a negative occurrence, a blemish on what most people expect should be the smooth operation of a well-ordered life.

Throughout the annals of human history, our species has found a wealth of ineffective ways to perceive and deal with conflict. In both lore and fact, when there is conflict, people are killed, smote, imprisoned, exiled, beaten upon, segregated, or isolated simply because they differ with others over issues large and small. Today, after thousands of years of human history, we continue to see nations waging devastating and lengthy wars over conflicting ideologies, territory, pride, and perceived national interest; we continue to see communities torn apart over factional strife and ethnic differences; and we continue to see families disintegrate over generational conflicts or spousal disagreements.

Let's look at three typical examples of how conflict is often mishandled and how our negative view of it obstructs us in our ability to resolve differences effectively. In the following cases, and throughout this book, I will use a variety of examples from actual and hypothetical situations in business, family life, and community affairs that I have found effective in teaching the eight steps to conflict resolution. Although the description of the people and issues involved may appear simplistic (it is ironic that conflicts always seem so simple from the outside), I ask that you reflect upon how these cases might parallel complex situations in your own life, even if these examples don't appear to relate to your circumstances immediately.

Rick, an employee at Moto-Corp, a medium-size company, has put in three years of competent work. For the past month, however, he has become somewhat disorganized in his work, showing signs of being short-tempered and unmotivated. Last week Rick finished an important report and sent it to a very respected client whose frequent orders have always been critical to the success of the company. In his present state of mind, however, Rick did a poor job on the report.

Beverly, Rick's supervisor, has always believed she should trust her employees to complete assignments without her having to check every aspect of a project before it is finished and sent to a client. She followed this pattern on Rick's report, not giving it a final review before Rick sent it to the client. Upon receiving the sloppy report, the client called Moto-Corp's president and complained, even going so far as to hint that it might be time to consider ending his relationship with Moto-Corp and taking his business to one of Moto-Corp's competitors. The president was outraged, called Beverly into his office, and ranted and raved about how she "better shape up her division" or look elsewhere for employment.

News of the president's tirade reached other employees, one of whom began to spread rumors that Beverly would be fired by week's end. Beverly heard the rumors, called Rick into her office, and, in a moment of anger and frustration, fired him. The other employees in Beverly's division reacted angrily to Rick's firing. They began to make life miserable for Beverly, and the quality of their work deteriorated rapidly.

A high school teacher attended a six-week summer course called Teaching Controversial Issues at a well-known university. When she returned to her high school for the fall term, she taught a two-week lesson focusing on several controversial issues. The students in her class felt the lesson was valuable and shared some of the content with their parents. Four of the parents who held strong opinions about a couple of the issues called the principal of the high school and complained that the teacher was preaching her own views rather than teaching, and demanded that the teacher be either severely disciplined or fired. The complaining parents were all quite powerful in the community, a fact that caused the principal to tremble. He had always prided himself on maintaining good relations with the stalwarts of town, and wanted to keep things that way. The principal called the teacher into his office and greeted her with, "I will not have my teachers using the classroom to preach their subversive ideas!" The teacher was so taken aback she reacted angrily, accusing the principal of "caving in to influential parents who have no idea how balanced my lesson was on these controversial issues!" With that, the teacher stomped out of the principal's office. She then organized a group of teachers who agreed to boycott classes the next day to protest the principal's autocratic methods. The school board, parents, teachers' union, and students all got involved in a battle that damaged the semester for everyone.

A community is arguing over whether or not to build a new hotel complex downtown to help revitalize the area and attract jobs. One community faction favors the hotel; an opposing faction believes the community should build low-income housing instead of the hotel. The two factions remain rigid in their respective points of view, seeing the conflict as a battle between the *correct* idea (ours) and the *wrong* idea (theirs). As the battle intensifies, people in the opposing factions who had been friends for years allow their friendships to suffer, the community begins losing some of its former spirit of unity, and some of the other projects needed by the community fall by the wayside as the adversarial atmosphere drains away the vital energy needed to get about the business of developing the community and meeting its needs.

As these three cases show, when we fear conflict or perceive it as a negative experience, we harm our chances of dealing with it effectively. The truth is, however, that conflict is neither positive nor negative in and of itself. Conflict is an outgrowth of the diversity that characterizes our thoughts, our attitudes, our beliefs, our perceptions, and our social systems and structures. It is as much a part of our existence as is evolution. Each of us has influence and power over whether or not conflict becomes negative, and that influence and power is found in the way we handle it.

Many conflicts can serve as opportunities for mutual growth if we develop and utilize positive, constructive conflict resolution skills. Indeed, conflict can serve as one of the engines of personal development and social evolution, generating opportunities to learn from and adapt to the diversities and differences that are natural and healthy characteristics of our society. Conflict can bring out into the open alternative ways of thinking and behaving. It can challenge us to manage our lives in ways that utilize our differences for mutual growth and benefit.

Thus, one of the first steps in becoming more effective at resolving conflicts is to understand the positive potential that awaits in all situations of discord. In other words, we need to transform how we think about conflict. The chart on the following page summarizes how we might transform our perceptions of what conflict really is.

The first perception in need of transformation is that conflict is always a disruption of order, a negative experience, an error or mistake in a relationship. However, we need to understand that conflict is actually an outgrowth of diversity that can be utilized to clarify a relationship, to provide additional ways of thinking and options for action that you may

A New View of Conflict

From perceiving conflict as always being . . .	*To perceiving conflict as often being . . .*
1. A disruption of order, a negative experience, an error or mistake in a relationship	1. An outgrowth of diversity that might hold possibilities for mutual growth and for improving the relationship
2. A battle between incompatible self-interests or desires	2. One part of a relationship, a part that involves needs, values, perceptions, power, goals, feelings, and so on, not just interests or desires
3. An isolated event we allow to define the entire relationship	3. Occurrences that punctuate a long-term relationship and that can help clarify it
4. A struggle only between right and wrong, good and evil	4. A confrontation between differences in certain aspects of a relationship, but not to the exclusion of other aspects that are still there to build on

not have considered, and to open up possibilities for improving a relationship. Perceiving conflict in this way encourages constructive behavior, whereas viewing it as always being a negative experience encourages us either to avoid dealing with the conflict or to do battle with the "adversary" who caused this negative experience to burden us.

The second perception in need of transformation is that

conflict is always a battle between competing and incompatible self-interests or desires. Thinking of conflict in this way leads us to feel that the other party is trying to block our getting what we want. We then often try to block their getting what they want, and both parties become more and more stubborn as they pursue their own desires and ignore the presence of needs or goals the two parties might actually share.

The third perception is also common. Many people view a particular conflict as defining their entire relationship with another party. In other words, they allow one conflict to become so dominant that the overall long-term relationship is ignored. A far more effective perception of conflict is that it is but one part of a complex and useful relationship. A conflict often punctuates the long-term relationship, bringing to the surface something that needs to be addressed. If dealt with effectively it can even help clarify and improve the relationship.

The fourth perception in need of transformation is that conflict usually involves a struggle between absolutes, such as right and wrong and good and evil. Some conflicts do indeed concern differences over deeply felt values. But far too often, people allow themselves to attach good-versus-evil and right-versus-wrong labels to a conflict so that they can convince themselves that their position is beyond question. Rather than jumping to the conclusion that a conflict involves *absolute* differences, we need to explore the possibility that a particular conflict may be over subjective preferences rather than values (and at that, only in certain aspects of the relationship), and realize that there are other aspects of the relationship that we can build on positively.

THE CONFLICT PARTNERSHIP APPROACH

This book is about resolving conflicts in a way that is both effective and *sustainable*. The way a particular conflict is both perceived and resolved must take into consideration the future of the relationship. Many of the traditional books on conflict resolution try to show readers how to win in negotiations or to gain and keep an advantage over an adversary. Even the more progressive negotiation books that focus on what is called a win-win solution to a particular conflict put little, if any, emphasis on improving the overall relationship for the future.

The conflict partnership approach focuses on both the immediate conflict *and* the overall relationship, of which a particular conflict is but one part, providing skills that are not only conflict resolution skills but also relationship-building skills. Such an approach provides us with the power to reach what I call the top level of conflict resolution. Let's look at the various levels and see the differences.

The top level is reached when parties in conflict come to a resolution that meets some individual and shared needs, results in mutual benefits, and strengthens the relationship. This is what conflict partnership is designed to do.

The middle level is reached when parties at odds come to some mutually acceptable agreements that settle a particular conflict for the time being, but that do little to enhance the relationship beyond immediate concerns. Traditional negotiation, mediation, and arbitration patterns tend to reach this middle level of conflict resolution.

The lower level is reached when one party conquers the other, when one party submits to the demands of the other party, or when the relationship is dissolved with mutual damage.

Throughout the remainder of this book, I will explain how the conflict partnership process can help you reach the top level of conflict resolution. It is my hope that you will be able to take the skills demonstrated in the examples, combine them with the discussion and explanations, and then apply these skills to your own conflicts and relationships. These skills are effective and sustainable in any interpersonal, family, business, community, or international situation.

CHAPTER 2

Five Popular (But Ineffective) Approaches to Conflict Resolution

As people seek to improve their conflict resolution abilities, one of the most important preparation tasks is to look inside themselves to gain a better understanding of their own tendencies, patterns, and beliefs. By doing so, people can focus on particular skills they need to work on as they learn to replace their ineffective approaches with improved conflict resolution behavior.

Appraising one's personal methods for dealing with conflict need not be a threatening or self-critical task. It can be a valuable, enlightening, and even fun experience. Several exercises that can help you clarify how you tend to deal with conflict follow.

After each conflict scenario below, look over the choices provided and check the one(s) you feel most closely resemble what you might be tempted to say or do. Although these cases are hypothetical, try to put yourself in the situation and imagine your reaction. After you have completed all of the exercises, we will explore the ineffective conflict resolution approaches represented by the responses. (Note your responses to each of the exercises either on a piece of paper or in the book. We will be using them shortly.)

CASE ONE

Vivian and you work at the same advertising agency and share an office and a budget. The current project the two of you are working on involves producing a magazine ad for a client Vivian attracted to your firm. Vivian feels she should be in charge of the project in that she recruited the client. She envisions an elaborate ad, complete with expensive artwork and many colors. You think a simple ad is better suited to the product being advertised (a new line of diapers), but your main concern is the cost. You don't want to blow your entire quarterly budget on just one overdone ad. As your conflict with Vivian drags on, the boss becomes more and more agitated over the slow progress of the work and the bickering between the two of you.

At the end of an especially tiring day, the boss marches into your office and forcefully orders the ad finished by to-morrow night. After the boss leaves, Vivian turns to you and says, "See what you've done? I'm getting blamed for your stubbornness. I got the client, so I'll decide the ad! Stop fighting me on this!"

What would you probably say? Which of the responses below would you most likely be tempted to make?

1. You counter, "I'm not going to give in on this, and that's final! There's no way I'm going to let you win on this thing! My ideas on the ad are better, and I think the boss will agree."
2. You respond, "Well, if you're going to get so uptight about this, go ahead and do it your way."
3. You say nothing, and wish Vivian a good evening and go home.

4. You retort, "Look, Vivian, I've been working here
   longer than you have and I know what's best for this
   company. When you've been here a few more years,
   maybe you'll be able to see things more clearly."
5. You offer, "Well, if you'll cut out four of the ten colors
   I'll go along with your idea of having tennis shoes on
   the baby while he's getting changed."

CASE TWO

Two weeks ago you started a new job. You occupy an office
with Tom, a pleasant, hard-working man who has been with
the company for several years. The only thing you don't
like about Tom is that he smokes, and the smoke from his
cigarettes bothers you considerably. The company employs
a lot of people who smoke, and their resistance to a no-
smoking policy has been successful. As the newest employee,
you don't want to begin making demands your first week,
so you try to accept Tom's smoking as an unavoidable negative to an otherwise positive work environment.

By the end of the second week the smoke has begun
taking its toll on you. You know you must do something.

Look over the choices below and select the one(s) you
feel most closely resemble what you might be tempted to do.

1. Start smacking gum loudly (or some other obnoxious
   behavior), in order to get back at Tom by doing
   something that irritates *him*. Then, when he complains,
   say, "Okay, I'll stop smacking my gum if you'll stop
   smoking those cigarettes."
2. Begin placing on Tom's desk various articles containing
   frightening statistics about the hazards of smoking.
3. Go to the supervisor and ask to be moved to another
   office.
4. Say to Tom, "If you really cared about me, you'd stop
   smoking."

5. Suggest to Tom that he should buy a big fan, put it on his desk, and turn it so that it blows the smoke away from your desk.

CASE THREE

Your fifteen-year-old daughter has suddenly become *very* interested in boys. She feels that most of the boys her age are too immature for her and begins spending time with a college sophomore. She comes home late from school every day, and tells you she has joined the high school's jogging club.

Late one afternoon you have to drive by the local college on your way to an appointment. You see your daughter and a young man sitting in his car kissing passionately. Although you are sorely tempted to take your daughter home for severe punishment, your important appointment cannot be delayed. When you finally get home and find your daughter studying in her room, you have to decide what to do.

Which of the following choices do you feel most closely resembles something you might be tempted to do?

1. March into her room and say, "You have been lying to me, and if you don't stop seeing that boy, you will be grounded for a month!"
2. Tell your spouse what you saw and tell him or her to "assume some responsibility around here and go talk to your daughter."
3. Say nothing directly to your daughter about the incident but find yourself being silent with her, or given to angry, hurt looks, or even to a sudden demand that she do more of the household duties she hates the most.
4. Tell her that if she agrees to stop seeing the young man, she can have that new sweater you have been refusing to buy for her.
5. "I'm your mother [father] and you will do what I say! Stop seeing that boy!" You then begin an exhaustive

search for a nice boy her age and invite him over for dinner.

CASE FOUR

Your city has a large number of homeless people. The mayor has just given her support to a plan to build a homeless shelter in your neighborhood. You support the plan, but many of your friends are opposed. Last week you debated the issue on local television with one of your longtime friends; the debate became heated, and the friend stomped out of the studio and hasn't spoken to you since. The local newspaper ran an article on the debate that further inflamed passions in the neighborhood. You have received calls from several people blaming you for causing conflict in what used to be a lovely community. You feel you must do something, but what? What would you do? Which of the possibilities below do you think you might be tempted to do?

1. Complain to your spouse that you are being blamed for everything, but do nothing else.
2. Call the reporter who wrote the article and demand that she retract some of the more libelous comments made about you or else you will bring a lawsuit against the reporter and the paper.
3. Take some food to the homeless people on Elm Street.
4. Use your position as the president of the Neighborhood Projects Committee to try to ram through a vote in favor of the shelter at the next meeting, a meeting you know your debate opponent won't attend because of a business trip.
5. Talk to a leader of the adjacent neighborhood to try to get that neighborhood to house the shelter in return for your neighborhood's offer to host the deficit-ridden Founders Day Fair the next two years.

Although these four cases may provide a glimpse into your conflict resolution tendencies, they cannot, of course, fully reveal how you deal with conflict. As you explore the conflict partnership skills in later chapters, it will be helpful to continue asking yourself about your own tendencies in situations of conflict. But for now, let's see what particular ineffective conflict resolution approach each of the responses demonstrates, according to the following categories: conquest, avoidance, bargaining, bandaid, and role player. Each of these ineffective approaches is discussed in detail after the following table, which arranges the responses under the approaches each demonstrates.

Case	*Conquest*	*Avoidance*	*Bargaining*	*Bandaid*	*Role Player*
One	1	3	5	2	4
Two	4	2,3	1	5	3
Three	1,3	2,3	1,4	4,5	5
Four	2,4	1	5	3,5	4

THE CONQUEST APPROACH

Scoring a victory, defeating the opponent, proving how right you are and how wrong the other party is—these are the goals of The Conqueror. A conflict becomes a battle to win, a struggle to gain advantage in the relationship or to attain dominance in the relationship. The person using the conquest approach tries to weaken the other party, assuming that the other party's weakness will somehow make his or her own strength greater.

The behavior exhibited in divorce settlements often follows the conquest approach. Both parties, through their lawyers, do everything they can to create the perception that the

other party is at fault, and that the settlement should reflect this fact by greatly penalizing the offending party and rewarding the offended party. The divorce becomes not only a means of dissolving the marriage but also a way of defeating and often punishing the other person.

The conquest approach is also evident in many workplace conflicts. Take, for example, the case of Marge, an administrative assistant, and two supervisors, Hanna and Roland. Marge had been Hanna's assistant for two years when the company began experiencing financial problems, so she became the administrative assistant for both Hanna and Roland when Roland's administrative assistant was laid off.

Marge did her best to adjust to the difficult task of working for two quite different supervisors. Hanna resented having to share Marge with Roland, and Roland remained angry for having lost his own administrative assistant. Roland decided that he could get Marge all to himself by weakening Hanna's credibility in the company to such a degree that the company's president would fire her.

Roland either fell into or intentionally used the conquest approach. Even nice people sometimes find themselves doing mean things when faced with conflict if they have had no constructive experience with conflict resolution. Roland tried to intimidate Hanna, belittling her in front of their colleagues and constantly reminding Hanna of his personal friendship with the president of the company whenever Marge's time was required simultaneously by both Hanna and Roland. Roland saw the situation as a battle between himself and Hanna that he was determined to win, a conflict in which he foolishly perceived that weakening Hanna would somehow make him strong. Roland's conquest behavior soon began to poison the atmosphere of the office, obstruct the effectiveness of the company, cause severe problems in his working relationship with Hanna, and make Marge's life miserable.

What's Wrong with the Conquest Approach?

- By depending on bullying, dominance, and manipulation to weaken the other party, the conquest approach sets a pattern in which power is understood and used in destructive ways. Once this pattern is set in a relationship, it is often difficult to see power in more constructive ways.
- When the conquest approach is used, the party who already has the most coercive and dominating power in the relationship usually has a distinct advantage in determining the outcomes. However, this perpetuates an unhealthy relationship in which one party controls the other. Not only is the subordinate party prevented from making future contributions to the relationship, but the dominant party deprives himself or herself of the contributions the dominated party might make.
- The conquest approach polarizes positions and greatly restricts options for resolving conflicts.
- A "loser" is necessary to the conquest approach, and, therefore, not only is a desire for revenge created, but the conquered party is disempowered and demoralized in her or his ability to contribute to the relationship in the future.
- The conquest approach does nothing to improve a relationship, whether in friendships, families, work relations, communities, or even among nations. The more this approach is used in dealing with conflicts, the more likely it is that the parties in the relationship will seek dominance rather than cooperation in other aspects of the relationship.

All parties ultimately suffer from the conquest approach. The loser is limited in his or her potential to contribute to the long-term relationship. The winner may enjoy a short-term advantage, but usually either has to deal with the revenge factor or is cheated out of the benefits the loser would otherwise be able to contribute to the relationship. If the conflict is within a family, the family unit suffers a blow to its cohe-

siveness and to the full participation of its members. If the conflict is within the workplace, the conquest approach creates needless and damaging power struggles and overall inefficiency.

THE AVOIDANCE APPROACH

Avoidance behavior is both seductive and complex. It is tempting to believe that conflicts will just go away if we pretend they do not exist. Because we want to believe that avoiding conflicts works, we often come up with creative strategies in trying to make this possible.

One type of avoider is so fearful of conflict that great energy is expended on trying to avoid getting into relationships with people who differ in values, ideas, life-style, and a host of other characteristics. This type of avoider not only cheats himself out of the potential enrichment and expanded possibilities that diverse relationships can provide but also perpetuates the misperceptions that conflict is negative, and that there are no effective ways to deal with conflict skillfully and positively.

Other avoiders simply pretend that there is no conflict because they have no confidence in being able to deal with it, or because they think admitting there is a conflict at all is somehow demeaning in that nice and competent people manage not to have conflicts. Or, like many of us, they mistakenly assume that time will heal all wounds. By ignoring the problem, they think it will disappear.

Other people use the avoidance approach by sidestepping confrontation with the other party. Unlike the people who pretend there is no conflict, these avoiders inwardly acknowledge that there is a conflict, yet they refuse to confront the other party. There are several reasons why such people don't like confrontation. One reason is that confrontation is sometimes narrowly perceived as strictly unfriendly behavior. A

second reason is that people sometimes fear that once they confront the other party, a battle will ensue, a battle in which someone will come out the loser—and it doesn't matter whether it's them or the other person. A third reason is that they may feel they wouldn't belong anymore if they confronted someone else in their office or social group.

Another quite prevalent way people use the avoidance approach is by focusing on diversions. If enough peripheral or unrelated matters can be used to divert attention from the actual conflict, these types of avoiders feel that they can get by without having to deal with their real problems.

Let's examine one case illustrating avoidance. Consider Susan and Donna. The two women had been friends ten years until a mutual acquaintance told Donna that Susan had actively opposed her nomination for chairperson of the local women's group. Hurt and angry, Donna canceled her date with Susan for lunch the next day. Afraid Susan would telephone, Donna kept her answering machine on throughout the next week, refusing to return Susan's numerous calls. When they bumped into each other at a PTA meeting, Susan insisted that they sit and talk. The conversation went something like this.

"Donna?" Susan said with concern. "Is something wrong? I've tried to call you all week."

"Nothing's wrong," Donna replied, fiddling nervously with her hands. "I've just been busy."

"Well," Susan sighed, "it seems to me there's something wrong. Is there trouble at home?"

"Nothing's wrong!" Donna said gruffly, then looked away. Soon she took a deep breath and turned back to Susan. "What did you think of the PTA meeting?"

"It was okay, I guess," Susan said without much enthusiasm, "but I want to talk about—"

"I didn't realize the drug problem had reached all the way down to the elementary school level," Donna said, shaking her head.

"Me, neither," Susan replied. "I heard they caught one of the seventh-graders selling drugs on the playground. But, Donna, I think we need to talk about—"

"Well, I hope they expel the boy," Donna said and got up. "I've got to go. See you around."

" 'See you around'? That's it? Donna, something's wrong, and I wish—"

"Look, Susan," Donna said harshly. "If you don't know what it is, then I'm not going to tell you. I shouldn't have to! Oh, never mind! I've got to go."

Donna left and, during the ensuing weeks, continued to avoid dealing with Susan. She allowed her anger and feelings of being treated unfairly to increase, and with each passing day dreaded even the thought of having to confront Susan. Whenever Donna's daughter wanted to go play with Susan's daughter, Donna told her she should try to find a new friend. Eventually, Susan gave up on her attempts to reestablish a friendship with Donna.

Why did Donna keep avoiding a confrontation with Susan over her alleged role in the women's group election? Perhaps it was because Donna wasn't sure Susan really did try to block her election, and so she didn't want to appear a fool by falsely accusing Susan. Perhaps it was because Donna did not want to appear to be whining. Or maybe it was because Donna, who hates to get into arguments and feels she has no skills to deal with anger, feared she would get into such an argument with Susan.

Regardless of why Donna avoided confrontation, the results were clearly disastrous for the relationship. Not only did Donna fall prey to the avoidance tactic of nonconfrontation, she allowed herself to use the tactic of diversion. In her brief conversation at the PTA meeting, Donna diverted attention from the conflict by trying to talk about what went on at the meeting. Although an important topic, discussing drugs in elementary schools was not relevant to the conflict between Donna and Susan. If she had used the drug problem to work with Susan on a shared concern, bringing the subject up might have been a healthy step in moving beyond the one area of their relationship in which a conflict existed. In the cooperative spirit of addressing that common concern, she might have been able to talk to Susan about the election, but Donna used the topic of drugs as a means of avoiding the conflict.

Why the Avoidance Approach Doesn't Work

- When people avoid putting themselves in situations or relationships in which conflicts might arise, they may be depriving themselves of opportunities for important personal growth. We often learn when faced with the obstacles that force us to reevaluate our ideas and feelings.
- Avoidance merely postpones dealing with the conflict and usually allows it to worsen. This is not to suggest that you must jump on every difference of opinion. Not all differences are significant enough to be considered real conflicts, and should be accepted as part of our human diversity—not made into issues that separate people. Furthermore, it may be wise to temporarily postpone dealing with a conflict if the timing, location, or mood of one or both parties involved might not be conducive to healthy dialogue. But if a real conflict does indeed exist, it will need to be addressed eventually. To avoid it will compound the problem. Time does *not* heal all wounds.
- Frustrations are usually exacerbated by avoidance, and misperceptions go unclarified. For example, Donna doesn't actually know if Susan did indeed try to block her election as chairperson. She simply accepted the word of a mutual acquaintance as fact, and continued to feel wounded because of it.
- Avoidance denies parties in conflict the opportunity of using their differences to clarify their relationship and to open their minds to the possibility of improvement. If Susan really did oppose Donna's nomination, perhaps she

had legitimate reasons her friend should know about so that she could try to improve her behavior or skills.

THE BARGAINING APPROACH

Picture an outdoor market in just about any country of the world as a seller and buyer haggle over the price of the goods. This age-old custom doesn't hurt anyone, and can even be fun. But when people or groups use only the bargaining approach in dealing with conflicts involving needs, values, and personal feelings, effective conflict resolution is not served.

The bargainer sees conflict resolution as a game in which portions of demands and interests are traded and success is defined by how much each party concedes. A good example of the bargainer can be found in two workers who share an office. One worker likes the temperature at an invigorating 65 degrees, the other at a warmish 80 degrees. Both workers tend to use the bargaining approach when dealing with conflict, so, predictably, the "solution" they came up with was as follows: the thermostat would be set at 65 in the morning and at 80 in the afternoon! Never mind that the 80-degree person was miserable and ineffective during the mornings, and that the 65-degree person was lethargic, grumpy, and ineffective during the afternoons, the workers compromised—each gave up the same amount, and to the bargainer, that is what conflict resolution is all about.

Another example of this approach involves a conflict over how to spend a community organization's money. The organization had two people who always seemed to take the lead in suggesting projects, yet who always seemed to disagree on which projects to pursue. Factions usually formed around these two leaders. In this particular case, one faction of the organization argued forcefully that the money be spent on turning a large vacant lot into a park with a swimming pool and tennis courts. The other faction wanted the money to go for the construction of a community center and an outdoor amphitheater.

The two factions argued the issue for weeks. Then, in the traditional bargainer approach, the leader favoring the park said, "Well, I still think this community needs a large park, but I guess I'll have to compromise. You accept a much smaller center and give up the idea of the amphitheater, and I'll accept a smaller park and scratch the idea of the swimming pool and tennis courts. Then we'll put the center in the park." Tired of the conflict, the other leader agreed to the compromise.

When the agreement was made public, those members of the opposing factions who also normally employed the conquest approach were upset that their leader gave in. Other members accepted the compromise as a good resolution of the problem. One especially wise member of the pro-center faction pointed out that "once again this community has taken the easy way out. We agreed on something, but nobody is happy about it. The park will be too small to be a functional park, and the community center will be totally inadequate and vulnerable to vandalism since security will be almost impossible in an open park area."

Effective and sustainable conflict resolution is not assured because the parties involved compromise. Bargaining is often glorified by calling it compromise or traditional negotiation. It has become a widely accepted approach to conflict resolution, whether in divorce settlements, management–labor problems, organizational conflicts, or international relations. However, the bargaining approach can have many negative effects.

Why Not Bargain?

- The bargaining approach focuses on the demands each party is making, in effect seeing the other party as what

they have demanded while ignoring the needs, perceptions, values, goals, and feelings that are the heart and
soul, the core identity of people involved.

How do you compare the worth of one person's
goal, or feeling, or value to another person's? The bargaining approach would have us believe that as long as
both parties in a conflict trade somewhat equal portions
of their demands, effective conflict resolution has taken
place. Such is usually not the case, and when we look at
value conflicts in Step 3, and at related material in other
steps, this point will become clearer.

- The bargaining approach defines power in terms of what
  one party can either coerce from or get the other to give
  up. For example, I have been involved in many situations
  in which one party works hard to get the other party to
  give up a particular demand or to give the opposing
  party something they want. When the strategy works,
  the successful party then brags about how powerful they
  were. However, this is an unhealthy pattern for relationships, and can drain valuable energy from the alternative
  of trying to cooperate by doing such things as emphasizing mutual benefits rather than what each party can
  wrest away from the other.

- Spin-off conflicts are often created by the bargaining approach as each party maneuvers for advantage and continues to make unrealistic demands that they know will
  not be accepted. Such demands create the appearance that
  the other party is unwilling to compromise because they
  never agree to any of the demands. As this strategy is
  continued, the person or group being asked to do things
  they cannot realistically do becomes increasingly angry
  and thereby refuses to discuss the conflict further or
  strikes back.

- The bargaining approach often obscures the *relative* value
  of needs, interests, and so on held by the parties in conflict. The bargainer often focuses more on the arithmetic
  of concessions than on the relative value of those concessions. Why? Often this is because it is easier to bargain
  with numbers than it is to get to the heart of a conflict

and take positive steps to resolve it. This mindset may be easier, but it damages the relationship in the long run.

THE QUICK-FIXER OR BANDAID APPROACH

Many people are so uncomfortable with conflict that they reach for whatever quick-fix solution they can find. I call this the Bandaid approach because the net effect is similar to putting a bandaid on an infected wound.

Why the quick-fixer slaps ineffective bandaids on conflicts varies from person to person. Perhaps the quick-fixer has little confidence in conflict resolution skills, or perhaps he or she is worried that if the true nature of a conflict is allowed to emerge, the threat of emotions becoming heightened also increases. Others use bandaid solutions to avoid getting into areas they fear will expose their personal vulnerabilities that might suggest a definite need for improvement in some aspects of their behavior.

The bandaid approach is rarely effective. Take, for example, a conflict involving George and Robert, colleagues who allowed their political differences to cause great difficulty for both of them. Their supervisor, Ms. Gray, realized that the effectiveness and profitability of the company was being undermined by the frequent and loud political arguments between George and Robert throughout the workday. The two would start arguing at the least provocation wherever they happened to be in the office.

Ms. Gray tried several bandaid approaches. First, she had George's desk moved as far from Robert's desk as possible. That didn't work because the two men found ample opportunity to keep up their loud debates during coffee breaks and the normal walking back and forth during the workday. She then tried to alter working hours, having Robert work 11 A.M. to 7 P.M. and George 7 A.M. to 3 P.M. All that did was hamper the flow of business deadlines and add more stress to the family lives of the two. Her third bandaid was even less effective: she ordered George to take a two-week vacation the first half of the month and Robert to take a two-week vacation the last half of the month. The result was chaos in the office as the other workers tried to adjust quickly to the change in vacation plans. Furthermore, both George and Robert spent part of their vacation time devising new ways to make life miserable for each other once they got back to work. Not once did the three of them ever devote a concerted period of time dealing with the brunt of the conflict; namely, that political discussions should not be conducted during work hours, and that the work performance of both men and the effectiveness of the entire office were being damaged by such discussions. But they all preferred to tiptoe around the issue by putting bandaids on what was increasingly becoming a serious wound for all concerned.

Why the Bandaid Approach Doesn't Work

- The bandaid approach creates the illusion that the fundamental problems of a conflict have been addressed, or that things will now be fine, thereby allowing some important matters to go unclarified and unresolved. This usually results in a worsening of the conflict.
- This approach often produces or heightens a lack of confidence in conflict resolution as the parties experience no lasting improvement in either the conflict at hand or in their overall relationship. Each party remains entrenched in blame and holds rigidly to its own point of view.
- This approach often temporarily rewards the quick-fixer, who can cleverly create the illusion that the parts of the conflict he or she is able to put bandaids on are actually the gaping wound. When Ms. Gray instituted the first bandaid solution, she told her boss she had fixed the problem, and she received praise. When the bandaid quickly proved inadequate, her boss criticized her for misleading him into thinking the problem had been solved. The quick-fixer's temporary reward will be fleet-

ing as the other parties affected by the conflict realize what has happened, and the conflict worsens.
- The bandaid approach disempowers all parties because they do not develop a *process* they can use effectively in future conflicts.

THE ROLE-PLAYER APPROACH

During your lifetime, you will probably fill many diverse roles. Child, family member, student, friend, spouse, parent, worker, boss, member of groups: the list of the various roles a person may play is endless. Although there are certainly many situations in which people must make decisions and deal with issues using their role responsibilities, far too many people unnecessarily hide behind their roles in dealing with conflicts. Rather than relating to others as people, they relate only from a persona: boss to employee, teacher to student, parent to child, and so on.

However, when people deal with conflicts in a way that depends on roles to determine the outcome, they may be falling into a trap. The boss who sees an employee only as a subordinate worker is failing to take an interest in the *person* who fills that role; spouses who see relationship responsibilities only in terms of rigid gender roles are putting up barriers to a more flexible, fulfilling relationship; and parents who respond solely in their role as parents when they always answer "Because I told you so!" when their children ask that most wonderful of questions, "Why?," are not helping their children to grow and develop. In each case, this approach often creates worse conflicts later because the needs of the entire person, who is much more than just the characteristics of a particular role, were not considered and specific problems were not resolved.

Society gives each social role a certain status, expectations, power, and rights. But frequently this assignment is

not done equitably. Racism, sexism, ageism, and other dis-
criminatory patterns lock members of these groups into disadvantaged roles and positions of lesser power. And some
roles are accorded enormous advantages and power.

In a conflict, when people act only from their roles, those
in roles of lesser status and power will usually be further
disadvantaged. This inequality is a fertile environment for the
emergence of damaging conflict and ultimately a disintegra-
tion of the relationship.

For example, let's look at a situation involving a professor
and a student named Jan. On the first day of class the professor announced that there would be three exams and that any
student who missed an exam would fail that exam. Jan made
good grades on the first two exams, then, the night before
the third exam, she got a call from her mother explaining
that a crucial family problem required Jan's presence at home
that night. Being close to her family, Jan immediately hopped
in her car and drove the three hours to her home. She was so
concerned she forgot to leave a message for her professor
explaining she would miss the exam. She wasn't able to return
to school until the next day, some five hours after the exam
had been completed by the rest of the students. The professor
had given her an F on the exam.

Jan tried to get in touch with the professor. Seeing her as
yet one more student who had missed an exam and was
calling him to make some lame excuse, he did not return her
call. Finally, Jan waited for him for three hours outside his
office the next day and caught him as he was returning from
another class.

"Professor Sanders," Jan began, "I need to talk with you
about the exam I missed. I had a family problem and—"

"You missed the exam, Ms. Adams," the professor said
as he entered his office. "You know my policy."

"But I had to go home," Jan protested. "It's not fair."

"Universities aren't run on fairness, Ms. Adams. Professors have their roles to play, and students have theirs. I can't

make exceptions for everyone. You did not live up to the responsibilities as a student. It's as simple as that."

Extremely frustrated, Jan blurted, "If you won't be understanding of my situation, I just may have to go to the dean!"

The professor smiled condescendingly and said, "And the dean will support me because I'm a faculty member and you're a student."

Eventually Jan was able to make up her exam by presenting her case to the dean and getting her mother to write him. But what is important here is the way the professor used only his role in dealing with the situation. His role gave him the authority to ignore all of the pertinent facts and all of Jan's needs.

What makes the role player act this way? Sometimes it is the fear he will lose the protection he perceives his role provides if he deals with the other party as a person, not just a role. If the professor had acknowledged Jan's problem and seen her as a person with family responsibilities and not just as a student, the conflict could have been resolved without the damage done both to Jan's nerves and the professor's standing with the dean. Sometimes the reason may have to do with feelings of insecurity the role player has about his or her inadequate conflict resolution skills.

Some role players seem to believe that their role gives them the right to dominate people in lesser roles, especially in situations of conflict. They use their roles to tryannize others.

Negative Effects of the Role-Player Approach

• The role-player approach can perpetuate an unfair relationship or system and block needed changes in that relationship or system.
• This approach cheats the conflict resolution process out of the valuable contributions a person in the less socially powerful role can make.

- When the role-player approach is used, the options for resolving the conflict are greatly restricted.
- This approach creates an adversarial relationship that can damage the positive possibilities for both parties in the future.

I have seen these five approaches appear time and again in family, workplace, community, and many other types of conflicts. In reading about these approaches, I hope you were looking for patterns within them that you may have a tendency to fall into when dealing with conflict—for understanding what our tendencies are is an important step in identifying those things we need to work on and improve.

CHAPTER 3

The Ingredients of Conflict

To gain a clearer understanding of conflict, exploring the major components operating in situations of opposition is a critical task. Although there are others, in this chapter we will identify the seven basic elements that characterize most conflicts. Examples of how these ingredients can cause conflict will be given, but we will wait until Part II to discuss the specific skills helpful in dealing with them.

DIVERSITY AND DIFFERENCES

Diversity is a healthy aspect of human society. Diversity can open up possibilities, challenge us to consider alternatives, and keep us from allowing ourselves to stagnate. We need to celebrate diversity, not fear it or perceive it as a threat.

Within our diversity as humans there are differences in perceptions, needs, values, power, desires, goals, opinions, and many other components of human interaction. These differences often lead to conflict. Depending on the way we deal with these differences and disagreements, conflict can either be positive or negative.

In dealing with conflicts, the point is not to remove the differences but to use those differences to (1) clarify our understanding of each other and the relationship, (2) consider ideas and possibilities we may not have thought about, and (3) see if there are aspects of the relationship on which we can build effectively to improve the relationship.

People often choose to feel threatened by the mere existence of a differing point of view, or they let the differences they have with someone define their entire relationship. In the short scenario related in the previous chapter, George and Robert allowed their political differences to dominate their entire relationship. They became so caught up in the conflict over politics that they allowed it to obscure the good working relationship they had as employees of the same company. Rather than looking for new insights that may have existed in the other person's point of view, the two closed the doors to their minds and allowed their differences over politics to create such anger that they ended up ruining their jobs. They did not have to *agree* on politics, nor did one have to change the other's beliefs. How much better it would have been had they been able to (1) affirm the fact that the country they both respected was better off because diverse opinions kept the nation searching for improved possibilities, (2) agree to disagree on politics, and then (3) concentrate on their shared goal of making the company they worked for as effective as possible.

Diversity is such an integral part of conflict that more needs to be said about its positive value. Examples are everywhere. The various members of a work force hold diverse jobs. This diversity allows each worker to develop a certain degree of expertise in a particular function, and the diverse functions combine to make the overall work effort of the business or organization more effective and efficient. The value of diversity can also be seen in the variety of ideas the work force can contribute. Many vital ideas for improvement often come from the wealth of ideas put forth by the quite different people who do the work. If only one person with only one field of vision makes all of the decisions, many fertile ideas can be lost.

The family is another area in which diversity is important. Although a family provides a similar environment for all of its members, each member, whether it be the mother, father, or child, experiences and perceives situations in a unique way. In the rather extensive work I do with families, I have learned that many damaging conflicts are caused and worsened because some members are not able to make their special contributions to the family. Many of the diverse perspectives and suggestions each member has can enrich the possibilities for the entire family. Families that actively cultivate diverse interests and do a range of things together also seem to stand a better chance of keeping their minds and their family relationships growing and productive.

Friendships might also be cited as a rallying point of diversity. If people surround themselves only with friends who are very much like themselves, it is easy for them to become trapped by the illusion that all one needs to do to understand the community, the society, or the world is to look in the mirror. Children who are surrounded by a rich environment of friends while young may have a much better chance of functioning effectively in the diverse world once they become adults.

On the larger scale of communities and societies, if a community or society has diversity, the economic health of that community or society will be enhanced. When a city or nation has only one or two major industries or exports, it is quite vulnerable to economic downfall when that one industry or export suffers hard times.

These and countless other examples make clear the fact that diversity is positive, that humans should promote diversity rather than stifle it. As has been pointed out, doing so will often stimulate conflict, but if we transform the way conflict is perceived, and if we employ effective conflict resolution skills, differences can be used to explore a wealth of possibilities, work for mutual benefits, and clarify and improve relationships.

NEEDS

Needs are conditions we perceive we cannot do without, or that we believe are critical to the well-being and development of a relationship. The most fulfilling and mutually beneficial relationships are those in which the needs of both parties are met. In that the meeting of needs is essential to survival and development, conflicts over needs can be quite serious. Discord arises when one or both parties either ignore needs, obstruct the meeting of needs, confuse needs with desires, or experience incompatibility over certain needs that one or both parties define as essential.

When Needs Are Ignored

Conflicts can arise when we ignore the needs of the other party, our own needs, or the needs of the relationship.

Ignoring the other party's needs. We harm relationships and often cause damaging conflicts when we ignore the needs of others. They feel that they are not being treated as valuable people or groups, and their contribution to the relationship suffers.

The case of an assembly-line worker, Charlotte, shows how conflicts can arise when needs are ignored. Charlotte has not had much formal schooling, but has a natural intelligence and wisdom from years of experience. She wishes she had a higher-paying management job, but has accepted her role on the assembly line and wants to do that job as best she can. In order to fulfill that goal, however, she has certain needs she feels must be met. One of Charlotte's needs is to feel appreciated both as a valued worker and as a human being with intelligence. Betty, the manager of the plant for which Charlotte works, sees Charlotte primarily as a body on the assembly line among many other bodies. Betty's perceived need is to make sure that the assembly line produces its quota of products per day, and preferably more. Her job depends on it.

Betty feels it is a waste of time to mother the workers by being concerned about anything other than how many products roll off the assembly line. Charlotte never said she needed to be mothered. What she does need is to be appreciated as a human being who has some good ideas about how to improve assembly-line procedures.

Charlotte asserts herself and writes Betty a memo focusing on several suggestions. Betty responds by telling Charlotte, "You only need to concentrate on doing the work." The other workers hear Betty's remark, share Charlotte's bitterness, and thereafter perform their work functions with less commitment and efficiency.

The conflict that arose between Betty and Charlotte resulted in large part from Betty's inability or unwillingness to understand and accept what Charlotte needed. The resulting conflict obstructed Betty's primary need as well, in that the assembly line's efficiency deteriorated. Failing to clarify and act on other people's needs *as they perceive them* creates conflict and damages all parties involved in the relationship. If one party feels the other's needs lack validity, it is important that both parties articulate their points of view.

Ignoring one's own needs. Some people become so concerned with not appearing selfish that they deny their own needs in relationships. Although much less frequent than ignoring other people's needs, there are cases in which what I call the selfless syndrome creates serious conflict.

One such case involved a caring, giving person named Burt. He lived with Rachel, a woman who was also caring and giving. Burt spent most of his time trying to make Rachel happy, always going out of his way to be sensitive to Rachel's every need. The ideas they discussed, the groups they joined, the house they bought, and the activities they engaged in were all determined by Rachel's needs and interests.

Rachel tried to get Burt to say what he needed, but he always managed to let Rachel's needs determine decisions. Soon Rachel began to question how much she was giving to the relationship and whether or not she was actually the caring and giving person she had always strived to be. Both Rachel and Burt became depressed, and found themselves getting into a series of confusing conflicts. In ignoring his own needs, Burt had inadvertently denied Rachel her need to contribute fully to the relationship.

Ignoring the needs of the relationship. Relationships also have needs. Sometimes the needs of the relationship outweigh some of the individual needs that one or both of the parties perceive they have. More on this matter will be covered later.

When the Satisfaction of Needs Is Obstructed

Conflicts may also arise when needs are obstructed either by another person, by the way the relationship is structured, or by the systems and dominant patterns of a family, workplace, or society. Sometimes there is no malicious intent to block the meeting of needs, but the effect on the person or people deprived of their needs is damaging nonetheless. In other cases, there is a purposive attempt to deprive someone else of the satisfaction of their needs.

In the conflict involving Betty, Charlotte, and the other workers, the fact that Betty had established no process through which assembly-line workers could contribute their suggestions for workplace improvement obstructed the workers' need to feel respected as intelligent and valuable people. Betty may have respected the work force as workers making a product, but that was not the only, or the most important, need they felt. The conflict was caused not only by Betty's ignoring Charlotte's needs, but by a system and policies that gave workers no significant channel through which to exercise the need they felt to offer suggestions.

Many family conflicts also result from needs being obstructed. For example, teenagers have the need to discover their own identity and values. When parents insist that their teenage children rigidly follow the dictates of the parents' approach to life in every matter, damaging conflicts can occur because the teenagers feel their need to be their own person is being obstructed. On the other hand, teenagers can also obstruct the needs of their parents. Many parents have a need to feel that they are still a part of their teenagers' lives, that they are still needed. When teenagers consistently shut parents out of their lives, never sharing even brief discussions of their activities, the teenagers are obstructing the needs of their parents.

When Needs and Desires Are Confused

Needs and desires are not the same. Needs are more critical to a person's life than are desires. Desires are not needed, they are *wanted*; they are not essential to the well-being of a person or group. People often desire something so strongly they interpret that desire as a need. Understandably, people become much more intense and uncompromising when pursuing needs than when trying to satisfy desires. By perceiving so many desires as needs, we increase the likelihood that damaging conflict will erupt as we struggle to make sure that those needs are met.

The confusion between needs and desires often plays a major role in creating and perpetuating conflict. People frequently allow themselves to see the other party as wanting certain things, while seeing themselves as needing certain things. Such a perception makes it easier to convince oneself that his or her goals in dealing with a conflict are more important than the other person's goals. In effective conflict resolution, focusing on needs is essential, but so is clarifying which issues are needs and which are desires.

When Needs Seem Incompatible

The most serious conflicts involving needs usually arise when the respective needs of the parties seem incompatible. In other words, if one party gets what she needs, the other party cannot get what he needs because the needs appear to be opposite. Even when the needs are not as opposite or incompatible as they may appear, if the parties perceive them to be incompatible, the type of conflict that results can be extremely frustrating and potentially damaging to a relationship.

A wife and husband live in Greenville, a small town in the Midwest, and both work. He has put in fifteen years for the same company and is on track for seniority promotions, bonuses, and an excellent pension plan if he stays with the company. She has been with a local affiliate of a national company for twelve years and has advanced as far as she can in the local affiliate. She is suddenly offered the position of second vice president of the national company, but must move to the national office on the East Coast. The husband feels he needs to stay with the company in Greenville; the wife feels she needs to take the job on the East Coast if she is to further her career. If they move east to meet her employment needs, he gives up his promotions. If they stay in Greenville to meet his employment needs, she has no chance for the type of career advancement she feels she needs. Thus, we have a classic example of a conflict arising from incompatible needs.

Suggestions on how to deal with incompatible needs will be covered later, but for now, you might want to explore in your own mind some ways you might deal with the conflict involving the Greenville couple.

PERCEPTIONS

People interpret reality differently, but does that mean there is no true reality? Well, yes and no. A particular event may indeed happen in a certain way, but people can have different perceptions about how and why the event happened and what the event means. Some of these differing perceptions may actually be incorrect, or, to use another word, they may be misperceptions; but if the perceiver believes the misperceptions are true, in effect, they become reality to that person.

Many conflicts are the direct result of perceptions and misperceptions. Some conflicts grow out of *differing* perceptions. One party sees a particular situation or event one way, the other party sees it another way. A daughter named Vicki wanted to go away to a distant college noted for its expertise in her chosen profession. What she said to her parents was, "I want to go away to school." Her parents perceived Vicki's motives as being to get away from her parents and sow her wild oats, yet all they said to her was, "We want you to go to a school near home." Neither Vicki nor her parents *clarified* their individual perceptions, and simply argued throughout Vicki's senior year in high school, making life miserable for everybody.

People in conflict might disagree on how something should be perceived, but unless they first clarify how each is actually perceiving the situation, effective conflict resolution is unlikely. I have seen many potentially damaging conflicts fade away when the parties involved clarified their perceptions and found that the conflict was based on certain misperceptions.

How to clarify perceptions and misperceptions will be covered in Chapter 6, but let's examine here four types of perceptual conflicts: conflicts arising from (1) *self*-perceptions, (2) perceptions of the *other party*, (3) differing perceptions of *situations*, and (4) perceptions of *threat*.

Self-Perception Conflicts

Although conflicts arising from self-perceptions can take many forms, two major categories of self-perception conflicts can be noted. The first category contains conflicts occurring because people base their self-perception on the perceptions or expectations others have of them, or on the way they are treated by others. People who, in order to know or define themselves, must constantly check how they are being seen by others or treated by others, or what others expect of them, are creating a breeding ground for damaging conflict.

Jon is the twenty-year-old son of an executive father and a lawyer mother. Jon has always been provided with every material advantage a young man could possibly desire, and, on the surface, his is a life many peers might envy. On closer examination, Jon's life can be seen for the conflict-laden struggle it really is.

Jon's perception of himself is borrowed directly from his parents and from his peers. He is "the son of Clarence and Marian who must fulfill his destiny and find happiness by becoming a corporate lawyer millionaire by age thirty-five." That is the way his parents and peers see him. Adopting those perceptions of himself, Jon is majoring in business in college and sending applications to law schools. He is also alone a lot of the time, primarily because he is often sullen, depressed, and, in general, a most unlikeable fellow. On those rare occasions that he is with people, he is doing drugs.

I asked Jon, "When are you happiest?"

He replied, "Ol' Jon's happiest when he's driving his sports car or when his stock broker tells him he just made a killing."

I asked, "Why do you talk about yourself as he instead

of I? It makes it sound like the real you is a spectator watching yourself go through life."

I waited, he thought, then he sighed, "Yeah, that's about it. I *am* somebody else. I'm not really that Jon they all tell me I am. I'm really happiest when I'm working with kids, when I'm doing something for disadvantaged kids. But I should have been born somebody else if I want to live that kind of life."

The mind, heart, and potential of this twenty-year-old man were all trapped in the *image* others had of who Jon was and should be. He had allowed himself to define himself according to what his parents and society perceived he should and could be—a self-perception that was contrary to what he really felt and wanted to be. Trying to live a lie led to an internal conflict that inevitably spilled over into his relationships. Thus, his life of conflict grew out of how he dealt with his self-perception.

Another expression of this first category of self-perception conflict comes when a person or group adopts a self-perception based on the way they are treated by others. The most prevalent examples arise in relationships in which one party is treated as though she or he is inferior, or is oppressed or persecuted. If victimized people focus only on their victimization and see themselves as inferior or only as victims, conflicts usually arise. Why? Because the relationships become dominant-submissive, with the victim adopting a submissive role and sometimes lashing out at others in pre-emptive self-defense.

A second type of self-perception conflict occurs when a person's perception of his own values is unclear, or when his behavior is inconsistent with his values. Once again Jon's case serves as an example. Even though Jon felt that one of the priority values in his life was helping less fortunate kids, his perception of how important that value was to him was not clear enough to give him the confidence to act on that value. He allowed that value to get trampled by the values of his parents. Furthermore, his belief in that value was contradicted by his behavior, and severe conflict was the result.

Conflicts Involving Perceptions of the Other Party

How we perceive the people and groups with whom we have relationships plays an important part in conflict. Several manifestations of this ingredient can be easily identified.

One manifestation arises from the way a person or group perceives conflict itself. If one or both of the parties tends to see the existence of differences as a battle between adversaries, the other party is usually seen as a foe. When dealing with foes, there is a great temptation to perceive the other party in their most negative aspects, often to the exclusion of their positive potential. This pattern often turns what could be healthy differences into potentially damaging conflicts.

Another way perceptions of the other party can contribute to conflict centers on images *of others that we allow to develop in our minds.* Perhaps the images stem from rumors or gossip people accept as fact without finding out whether or not the rumors are actually true. Perhaps the images stem from judging the other party on only one especially disliked act, ignoring all of the more positive acts that person or group has committed. Or perhaps the images stem from stereotypes based on perceptions of race, gender, profession, socioeconomic class, political or religious preference, or a host of other rigid categorizations of people and groups. Whatever the source, these images can cause serious damage.

Images obstruct the opportunity to get to know other people for who they really are, and in so doing block the development of what might be mutually beneficial relationships. Dealing with others as rigid images also tends to create within those people and groups a degree of frustration and anger because they feel they are being judged unfairly. That feeling often leads to and perpetuates conflict. Furthermore, perceiving others as rigid images makes conflict resolution extremely difficult. No matter what the party being perceived as an image says or does, that party is not allowed to break free from the rigid box the image has constructed. All of these examples of seeing others as stereotypes should help us understand that creating images is not only a lazy way of conducting relationships but also a potential producer of conflict.

Yet another manifestation of conflicts caused by perceptions of the other party comes from intentional distortions of how the other party is perceived. Some people create false perceptions of others in a self-serving attempt to make the other party appear of lesser value. Usually based on the illusion that "I can make myself seem better by making someone else appear wrong, weak, or of lesser value," misperceptions of others are sometimes formed and promoted in spite of evidence to the contrary. Before long, the person or group creating the misperceptions often loses touch with reality and actually begins to believe that the misperceptions are indeed fact. Serious conflict emerges from such a pattern.

Why some people and groups seem to feel a need to create misperceptions of others will probably occupy psychological research for decades to come. In my experience, one insight into the question seems pervasive: negative misperceptions of others often stem from the insecurity of the one creating the misperceptions. Rather than working on oneself to build a strong, positive personal life through identifying core values and living those values consistently, some people and groups devote their energy to trying to create negative perceptions of others as a means of making their own personal life appear more valuable.

Let's look at an example of a conflict involving perceptions of the other party. Kathy has worked under a supervisor named Paul for three years. Kathy's job performance has been good, and she has received positive evaluations from the clients she has served. She has long felt that Paul's treatment of his subordinates is rather rigid and bossy, a sentiment shared by some of her co-workers. Kathy has tried to talk with Paul about the situation several times, but Paul always tells her, "My job as supervisor isn't to be a nice guy. It's to run a tight ship."

During the past several months, Kathy's perception of Paul as an autocratic boss with no real understanding of his subordinates has intensified, as has Paul's perception of Kathy as a whiner. Just last week one of Kathy's clients, the Calley Corporation, who had done business with the company for four years, switched its business to a rival company. Paul was furious, partly because the loss of Calley made him look bad in that he supervises Kathy. Paul called Kathy to his office, and the following conversation took place.

"I knew this was coming," Paul said sternly. "You have devoted all your energy to criticizing me rather than keeping our clients happy. Losing Calley is inexcusable!"

"Don't you want to know why Calley left us?" Kathy asked. "It wasn't my fault. If you cared more about your employees and met with us regularly you would have found out Calley has been looking for a less expensive company for some time now."

"Clients like Calley don't just up and switch companies unless the person handling their account does something to disappoint them. I'm afraid you've become a troublemaker, Kathy. If you were really a team player and would stop demoralizing the other employees by criticizing me, this would never have happened."

Kathy rolled her eyes in exasperation. "As usual, you're not listening to me, Paul. You're bringing this trouble on yourself. You're just too rigid with all of us. You and I are both parents, Paul. Are you this autocratic with your family? If you are, I'm sure you have the same problems with them."

"That was way out of line!" Paul said angrily. "Why have

you become such an argumentative and vindictive person? You're making our work relationship impossible!"

The perceptions Kathy and Paul have of each other are completely negative. They are putting each other into the convenient, stereotyped boxes of autocratic, rigid boss and whining, argumentative troublemaker. Paul has allowed the particular conflict arising from the loss of the Calley account and his negative perceptions of Kathy to become his sole focus. In so doing, he is ignoring some crucial issues, such as Kathy's positive job performance for the past three years, finding out the possible reasons why Calley switched to another company, and the troubling possibility that perhaps he should alter his supervisory patterns and listen more carefully to his subordinates' comments about emerging problems with various clients. Paul misses all of these important factors, factors that could help resolve the conflict and improve the workplace, because his negative perceptions of Kathy and her being at fault block his need to clarify his perceptions of Kathy and the conflict.

Kathy is doing the same thing. In her rush to perceive only the negative aspects of Paul, she ignores the possibility that he may indeed have a point about her letting her dislike of him drain energy from servicing Calley adequately. She could have organized a meeting between her co-workers and Paul to try to improve their work relationship, but once Paul became perceived as a completely negative boss, such a meeting would seem useless to her.

Conflicts Involving Perceptions of Situations

When people perceive situations differently, conflict can result. Take the case of Elliot and Paul. Elliot is Paul's boss in the company example we just reviewed. When Paul and Kathy lose the client, Paul is called into Elliot's office and subjected to a tirade on how much the company will lose because the important client has defected to the competition. Elliot knows Paul has been a good employee, but the loss of the client becomes his sole focus. He asks several executives why Paul lost the client, and receives a number of self-serving opinions from people who consider Paul to be a hotshot who has been given more credit than he deserves over the years. Elliot then builds his own perceptions of Paul (perceptions of the other party) and his own perceptions concerning the loss of the client (perceptions of the situation) on the rumors and gossip he hears.

Elliot never clarified these perceptions with Paul. If he had, he would have understood that Paul felt Elliot's policies had never allowed him the flexibility to respond to some of the client's new needs over the past few months, a policy that led directly to the client's defection. But if Elliot can perceive that it's all Paul's fault, he can convince himself of his own innocence in contributing to the problem. A conflict occurred in part because the two men perceived the *situation* of the client's defection in quite different ways. When such major differences in how the parties perceive a situation go unclarified, conflict is likely.

Conflicts Arising from Perceptions of Threat

A threat is an intention to inflict pain or injury, or a person who is regarded as a possible danger. We all know that there are events, situations, and people that do indeed pose a real threat. But people often choose to see threat where it does not really exist, or to view anything that differs from their own way of thinking as a threat. Such perceptions often cause conflict. Why we allow ourselves to feel threatened in such situations is complex. Such reasons include the following:

- One is insecure in his or her beliefs and cannot allow the test of differing beliefs.
- One feels that to be powerful he or she must be in total charge of a situation, and any divergent opinion or behavior threatens that power.

- One may feel there are no effective skills to deal with differences and conflicts, and that every conflict is thus a potential disaster.
- People have been weaned on the false notion that a conflict is a battleground, with an opponent out to do one harm.

All of these explanations no doubt hold some validity, depending on the situation and the people involved. Although we may never fully understand all of the complex factors involved in our perceptions of threat, we can do a much better job of sorting through perceived threats to see if they really do constitute a threat. Simply because the belief or behavior of others differs from our own or makes the satisfaction of our own desires more difficult does not mean we are threatened.

Let's look at an example of a conflict caused by perceptions of threat. Bart and Michele work for the same company and both are in contention for the same promotion. Bart chooses to perceive Michele as a threat and begins to complain that she is frequently favored by the male boss because she is a woman and the boss doesn't want to be accused of sexism. Bart and Michele work on projects together, and depend on a good working relationship to do their joint tasks effectively. As Bart starts to treat Michele more and more as a threat, conflicts arise between them and their work suffers. Furthermore, regardless of who receives the promotion, the two will have to work together closely in the future. Bart's perceptions of Michele as a threat thus damages both their current and future relationship, and it damages a common need and goal they share—namely, the production of effective work.

Is Michele really a threat to Bart? To be sure, she is a competitor for the promotion, but if Bart focuses on the needs and goals they share and on his own need to keep doing quality work, he will not be as tempted to perceive Michele as a threat. Once he views her as a threat, unnecessary conflicts are sure to arise.

POWER

Another essential ingredient of conflict is power. How we define power, and how we use it, greatly influence the number and nature of conflicts within our relationships and the way we deal with those conflicts.

I define power as the capacity to act effectively and the ability to influence. Many people, however, behave as though they see power as the ability to make others behave as they want them to, to exert control, or to gain advantage over someone. When this definition of power guides behavior, damaging conflicts are inevitable, primarily because one of the parties in the relationship is, in effect, being disempowered and made dependent on the other person's agenda for the relationship.

Many examples of the power component of conflict come from the workplace. Take the example of two salespeople who work for competitor companies and who are eager to gain new clients, primarily because the companies they work for have announced that they will give a bonus to the salesperson who acquires the most new clients in the next month. One prospective client is especially attractive financially, so both salespeople go after that client vigorously. Each becomes obsessed with trying to make both the other salesperson and the competitor company look bad in the eyes of the client, dropping hints of slovenly work, personal-life embarrassments, and unethical business practices. The prospective client becomes fed up with such behavior and refuses to do business with either company. Both salespeople lose, the companies lose, and the two workers end up being demoted because they directed their energies at blaming each other for the debacle instead of concentrating on their job performance. The mistaken belief that power would come from weakening the position of the other person and the other company caused a damaging conflict that hurt both workers.

In my work with families I see many conflicts caused by

sented in Step 4. For now, I'd like to emphasize three major points: (1) how power is defined and used plays a role in almost every conflict; (2) when power is used as a tool to control or to gain advantage over others, damaging conflicts are often the result; and (3) dealing with conflicts using the "power over" pattern proves ineffective and usually exacerbates the conflict.

VALUES AND PRINCIPLES

A value is something we consider to be of significant importance, such as the value of always being honest with a relationship partner, or not trying to belittle someone else as the way to try to make oneself seem better, or a moral value such as fidelity in marriage, or, for some people, being a vegetarian. A value can involve a belief, a principle, or even a pattern of behavior we have come to perceive as extremely worthwhile. Some values are of such critical worth to a person that there is little, if any, chance that the value will be changed or sacrificed, regardless of the situation. Other values are of lesser importance and may be altered or changed for the sake of a relationship. Values can influence the creation of conflict in several ways.

Values and principles can lead to conflict when people jump to the conclusion that the conflict they are involved in is one of values or principles. Believing that the conflict is about values and principles gives people a greater justification to defend their position and to go after what they want with fierce, self-righteous, unyielding energy. In reality, however, the conflict may be over *preferences*, not values or principles. Values and principles often involve ethical and even moral beliefs, which take on more importance in a person's life than do preferences. In much the same way that needs and desires should

a similar pattern. The Bailey family has two paren
teenage daughters. The father is very religious,
of society is immoral, and wants to protect hi
from temptations of sin. He sees the role of prote
of the most important duties a father must fulfill.
to allow his daughters to date any male outside t
religious faith, constantly tells his daughters that n
be trusted, and even puts a time limit of five secon
long a goodnight kiss can last at the door.

The eldest daughter, who is seventeen, gave up
reason with her father long ago, and simply began
his restrictions. Their relationship has been full of c
the past three years, and the other daughters are als
stant conflict with their father. With the help of her
the eldest daughter finally decides to have a long
her father. When she asks him why he feels he mus
every aspect of her life, he responds, "I'm just t
protect you."

She replies, "I think you are trying to protect y
power, Dad . . . your power *over* me. If I can make d
on my own, and some of those decisions turn out re
for me, then I get the feeling you think you aren't a
father or that I don't need you. But that's not the point
I need right now in my life is to have a healthy social l
to make some of my own decisions. Dad, if you'll h
meet those needs, then to me you'll truly be a strong fa

As the father and daughter discussed the issue over
the father became impressed with the way his daughter
about power and strength and how well she seemed to u
stand her own needs. He gave her view further though
told her one night, "I think you've taught me somethi
that being a strong father may involve having the coura
let his children make some decisions on their own. If y
work with me, I'll try to ease up on thinking I have to co
you so much."

Details on how to use power constructively will be

be understood as different entities, values and principles need to be understood as standing apart from mere preferences. Many conflicts are caused when parties exaggerate the importance of preferences to such a degree that they become perceived as values and principles. Take, for example, the conflict involving Rick and Roberta.

Rick and Roberta work for a small advertising firm. They are in conflict over a particular television ad they are writing for Walliby Industries, a company that makes a host of products, including dentures. Rick's idea for the ad reads, "When you whistle and then smile at an attractive jogger on the jogging path, do your dentures protrude from your mouth in a Bugs Bunny smile? If so, switch to Walliby, the dentures so natural, nobody will ever know."

"That's crude, Rick," Roberta scolds him. "And it's also sexist. You are implying that the characteristic of women joggers that's most noteworthy is their sexual attractiveness, not their athletic ability or the fact they are trying to keep in good health."

"I think it's funny," Rick defends himself.

"C'mon, Rick. We can't sacrifice principles for the sake of humor."

Rick has never been one to take criticism well. He starts drumming his fingers on his desk, a sure sign he is getting annoyed. "Look," he finally says. "It's just a matter of preference. You prefer less humorous ads than I do."

"It may be a matter of preference to you," Roberta responds, "but to me it's a matter of principle. Sexist innuendos are just plain wrong."

Rick immediately jumps on the word *principle* and tries to come up with his own principle to fight Roberta's. "Look! I am the senior ad man in this agency. Senior employees must have the final say when there's a deadlock on ideas or else there's no order in an organization!"

Rick elevated his preference to the level of a principle

when he confronted Roberta's criticism of his ad, thereby trying to give his preference more power. Roberta wouldn't succumb, however, and, feeling abused, increased her own stubbornness. They continued to fight over the ad until they missed the deadline. Had Rick been able to understand that a preference is not as critical as a principle, perhaps he could have worked things out with Roberta in a way that kept their important work relationship a lot healthier.

Another way values lead to conflict occurs when one party refuses to accept the fact that the other party does indeed hold a particular idea, goal, or behavior as a value or principle rather than merely as a preference. Changing the Rick–Roberta conflict a bit, let's say that a rigid hierarchy of decision-making really is one of Rick's major workplace principles. Roberta, on the other hand, strongly believes in the principle of nonhierarchical, everyone-is-equal decision-making. Roberta simply can't believe, or refuses to believe, that anyone can still hold as a value the archaic notion that senior employees should always get their way. Therefore, Roberta sees Rick's position as simply a matter of preference, not a value, and treats Rick's opinion with much less respect than Rick feels it deserves.

Whether or not Roberta believes Rick's position *should* be a value or principle is not the point. If it is indeed a principle to Rick, Roberta must accept that fact and deal with Rick's position in terms of a value. She could then say, "Well, we obviously have a conflict over principles here. Maybe we should scrap both your Walliby ad and mine and work on a totally new one together. At least now we know each other better. It's important for co-workers to know something about each other's principles, don't you think?"

Rick and Roberta will still disagree on some ideas in the future, but perhaps they will be better able to understand the real conflicts facing them, in part because they will be more conscious of clarifying whether preferences or principles are at issue.

Still another type of value conflict arises when the parties hold seemingly incompatible values. The key question becomes, How important is that particular value to the overall relationship? It may be crucial, or it may be of lesser importance than other values in the relationship.

Finally, conflicts can emerge when one or both of the parties is unclear about its own values. Being wishy-washy or inconsistent about one's own values can cause great frustration and conflict in relationships. Clarifying one's own values—which are priorities and which are not—becomes a critical step in the process of effective conflict resolution. Because conflicts over values and principles are among the most difficult we face, specific attention is given to dealing with such conflicts in Chapter 6.

FEELINGS AND EMOTIONS

Most conflicts involve some investment of feelings and emotions. There are many ways in which people deal with their emotions when embroiled in conflict. In many cases, people let feelings and emotions become the primary determiners in dealing with a conflict. In other cases, parties in conflict do the opposite, trying to ignore feelings and emotions, usually because they fear that if they express them, they may seem out of control or may obscure what the conflict is really about. In yet other cases, people acknowledge that feelings and emotions are involved, yet try to intellectualize them to the point that the other party never realizes the intense feelings a particular conflict is causing. All of these approaches to dealing with feelings and emotions can cause and exacerbate conflict. Here are some examples to show you what I mean.

Sammy and Trish are brother and sister, Sammy twelve years old, Trish ten. Trish cries a lot, and Sammy wants to cry a lot but has been taught that it is not manly to cry. Their parents are divorced, and the two children live with their mother. Trish likes to have her girl friends over for slumber parties, and Sammy hates having all of those "dumb girls" around. For the past year, the conflict has raged incessantly, following the same old patterns. Trish invites her friends over, and Sammy tries to sabotage the party by letting his pet snake, docile yet large, slither through the house. Trish screams at Sammy, cries, and implores her mother to "Do something!" Sammy screams, tries out all of his new curse words on Trish, and also insists that Mom "Do something!" Mom allows Trish and Sammy to deal with the conflict with only their emotions and feelings, and the result is disastrous.

Kevin and Debra work at the same organization, Kevin serving as Debra's boss. Kevin feels Debra is a good worker, a big help with the new employees, and, above all else, a very physically attractive woman. Debra feels that Kevin behaves as a good boss except for his frequent comments about how great it is that such an attractive woman is the first thing clients see when they enter the office, and the even more frequent times when she catches Kevin looking at her, followed by a wink and a smile he thinks are irresistible. Debra finds her frustration and annoyance becoming a detriment to her work, and she feels the treatment of her as an "attractive thing" is demeaning and insulting. Fearful she will either be seen as a radical feminist or will cause Kevin to get angry, Debra ignores her feelings and locks them inside. Feelings and emotions, however, have a way of seeping out through even the most tightly closed shells, and soon Debra's negative feelings toward Kevin express themselves in angry looks, stacks of work being dropped loudly on his desk without so much as a "here's the material you wanted," and a few well-placed comments to the other women in the office questioning Kevin's decisions and job performance. Kevin, although not usually perceptive, cannot help but sense the change both in Debra's behavior toward him and her work performance. As often happens with people who are not confronted clearly and directly, Kevin's assumptions soon become facts in his mind, and he decides Debra is losing interest in her job. He, too, has a tendency to keep his confrontational feelings and emotions bottled up inside, so he then begins to treat Debra's work with a rather curt attitude. He decides the only contribution she brings to the office is her stunning physical appearance, and he increases his visual attention to that part of her presence. Needless to say, the situation worsens as both Debra and Kevin avoid expressing their feelings concerning the conflict.

Finally, let's say that Debra really does confront Kevin, but adopts the third pattern previously mentioned: she overly intellectualizes her feelings and emotions.

"I have figured something out and want to talk with you about it," Debra says to Kevin. "I think you must have had a father who saw women only as sexual objects."

Kevin stares at Debra with a kind of "where did *that* come from" look, and can only manage a "Huh?"

"You are probably just unconsciously mimicking your father's attitudes," Debra continues. "I'll bet you could sort it all out if you and a therapist talked about your father."

"*What* are you talking about?" Kevin says, and frowns.

"Why, the way you treat women, of course," Debra says matter-of-factly. "Men *are* capable of seeing women as something other than sex objects, you know."

"I know that," Kevin says, still somewhat confused. "But what does this have to do with you? You come into my office and start talking about my father's attitude toward women. Then you tell me to go see a shrink. Are you taking some kind of mind-altering drug or something?"

"Just take some time tonight to think about what I said," Debra says without emotion. Then she gets up and leaves, proud of herself for having kept her emotions and feelings concerning Kevin's treatment of *her* totally submerged.

Kevin watches her leave, frowns at his desk for a second, then shakes the strange conversation out of his head. At home that night he does *not* think about what Debra had said, partly because he is still unaware that Debra was *feeling* anything. To be sure, Kevin should have been sensitive enough to pick up on the message hidden in Debra's intellectualized approach to the conflict, but *his* feelings were never touched by Debra because she only intellectualized her own.

Human beings are feeling, emotional creatures, and thus feelings and emotions often play a role in conflict and conflict resolution. When people suppress emotions and feelings, as Debra did at first; when they use emotions and feelings as the primary means of dealing with conflict, as happened with Trish and Sammy; or when people overly intellectualize feelings and emotions, as Debra did when she finally confronted Kevin, conflict will likely occur and worsen.

We cannot leave our discussion of the most important factors in conflict without giving at least some attention to a type of conflict often overlooked: internal.

INTERNAL CONFLICTS

Many people mistakenly believe that conflict always involves another person. Some of the most severe conflicts I have witnessed have been *within* a person. If the conflict is not recognized as internal, or if the internal conflict is not dealt with effectively, it will probably create conflicts within relationships. That the initial conflict is sometimes internal is important to understand.

Internal conflicts can be caused (1) when people are not sure what their values are, or of who or what they want to be; (2) when people are not sure what type of relationship they want with another person; and (3) when people have diverse internal voices urging them to respond in various ways, and deciding which voice to follow becomes a conflict-producing dilemma. One of my recent cases offers a glimpse into the first two types of internal conflict.

Twenty-five-year-old Sidney married Marcia a year ago. He almost decided not to marry—partly because he believed that marriage had become a license for society and the wife to exploit the husband to make up for all of the past exploitation of women by men, and partly because he wanted to be a world traveler and felt such a life-style was inappropriate for raising a family. But he loved Marcia and didn't want to lose her, and she wanted to get married. Eventually, Sidney agreed to marry.

But after a year together, Sidney was miserable. He saw himself as trapped in the suit of a small-town businessman when he wanted to be exploring the mountains of Nepal in wool cap and hiking boots. He felt his values were in prolonged battle with each other: the value of being a good husband fighting with the value of being a global ambassador promoting protection of the environment. He wanted to be with Marcia, but he wasn't sure he wanted to be married, and he knew she would never enjoy traveling, not even to another town, much less to Nepal.

Sidney's conflict was internal: being married and living in a small town versus being free to travel and to do what to him was more important work. But he did not discuss this internal conflict with Marcia and soon began to take out his frustration on her by exaggerating minor differences they had. Where to eat out, what type of toothpaste to buy, and other trivial issues became substitute conflicts for the real conflict he felt inside. Marcia did her best to tolerate Sidney's behavior, but found herself increasingly frustrated. When he began getting home late at night, she incorrectly accused him of having an affair, which prompted him to think *she* was having an affair. After eighteen months of a very strained marriage, Marcia filed for divorce.

Conflicts can also arise from what I call internal voices.

How many times have you been in a relationship and felt inside yourself a variety of voices competing for dominance? Controlled anger, pity, understanding, vindictiveness, calm reason, irrational rage, assertiveness, a desire to escape, an urge to punish—these and many other potential responses to another person sometimes tempt and confuse us. Sometimes we even reach the point of spectator to the circus inside and simply let whichever voice is loudest at the moment take over until one of the other voices gains the upper hand. To many people, this phenomenon sounds all too familiar, and within this pattern can be found seeds of conflict.

A good example involves our friend Debra, who, you will remember, is the secretary who felt her boss, Kevin, was being sexist. Many conflicts were fomenting inside Debra. For one thing, she wasn't sure how to interpret Kevin's behavior. One of her internal voices was telling her that Kevin *was* being sexist. Another voice was telling her that Kevin was genuinely appreciating her physical beauty in addition to her value as a person and employee. Perhaps another voice wondered if she wasn't a little attracted to Kevin.

Debra couldn't decide what to do. Should she confront him with the fact that his comments and looks were bothering her? Should she swallow her pride and quietly accept the situation as just one more example of male obsession with female attractiveness? Should she punish him by purposely failing to notify him of an important meeting? Should she just let it go, or maybe ask him out for a drink at the local fruit juice bar? All of these choices were available, some much more appropriate than others, but Debra let the internal conflict paralyze her, which soon tied her in knots and made it difficult for her to deal with the conflict effectively. Kevin may have provoked the conflict by his remarks and glances, but Debra allowed her internal struggle to make it worse.

Among the various types of conflicts people become embroiled in, perhaps none is more complex than internal conflicts. Often people do not want to admit that the source of the conflict they are having with someone else is actually within themselves. They find it much easier to blame the other party, thus creating a damaging conflict with that person instead of taking responsibility for and working on their internal conflict. In cases in which there is a combination of an internal conflict and a conflict with someone else (as in Debra's situation), dealing effectively with one's internal conflict first can greatly assist in dealing well with the other party.

CORNERSTONES FOR UNDERSTANDING CONFLICT

Here is a summary of the main ideas in understanding conflict.

- How we understand conflict influences how we approach conflict resolution.
- Conflict is an outgrowth of diversity and differences. As such, conflict is not always negative. Conflicts can be used to clarify relationships, open up alternative possibilities, and provide opportunities for mutual growth.
- Conflicts are not always limited to battles between interests and desires. Needs, perceptions, power, values and principles, feelings and emotions, and internal conflicts are critical ingredients of our relationships and the conflicts that punctuate relationships. Understanding which components are involved in a particular conflict is essential to resolving the conflict effectively.

Now that you have examined the seven ingredients of human conflict, you are ready to delve into the skills that can help you resolve conflicts effectively. The next chapter introduces these important skills.

CHAPTER 4

The Conflict Partnership Process

*C*onflict partnership is a process consisting of eight skills, or steps, that can empower people and groups to build mutually beneficial relationships and to resolve conflicts effectively. Each of these steps will be discussed in detail in the following chapters. First, however, let's explore the basic principles behind the process.

At the heart of the conflict partnership process are five basic principles concerning how we can deal effectively with conflict.

WE, NOT I VERSUS YOU

Conflict partnership establishes a foundation on which the people or groups involved in a conflict can transform the adversarial, combative I-versus-you pattern usually found in conflict into a healthy attitude, one in which the tone is: We are working together to improve our relationship and to deal with our differences. The interaction then becomes a partnership in which each party needs the other if the conflict is to be dealt with successfully. Virtually all of the eight steps in conflict partnership help to establish this "we" relationship, but the skills and examples discussed in Steps 1–4 and 7 can be especially helpful.

CONFLICTS ARE DEALT WITH IN THE CONTEXT OF THE OVERALL RELATIONSHIP

The conflict partnership approach deals with specific conflicts in the context of the overall relationship. Conflicts usually punctuate a relationship rather than define the entire relationship. However, people often lose sight of the needs, goals, and other positive aspects of the overall relationship when in a conflict. A single conflict, in effect, is allowed to *become* the relationship. Whereas most people understand that conflicts are important and must be dealt with, how a particular conflict fits into the overall relationship is often neglected. The skills discussed in Step 2, especially those that focus on clarifying what a conflict is about, can help people keep the needs and goals of the relationship in mind as they deal with particular conflicts.

EFFECTIVE CONFLICT RESOLUTION SHOULD IMPROVE THE RELATIONSHIP

In order for conflict resolution to be truly effective, according to the conflict partnership approach, the process employed must also improve the overall relationship. Some conflicts can be "negotiated" in the short term, yet the process used might do nothing to improve the long-term relationship. Indeed, some apparent solutions to a specific conflict can actually harm the future relationship. In that conflict partnership is an effective way of responding to conflict and is a relationship-building process, all of the eight steps and their accompanying skills address this important principle. The actual cases discussed throughout the remaining chapters provide clear examples of how we can improve relationships in the way we deal with specific conflicts.

EFFECTIVE CONFLICT RESOLUTION RESULTS IN MUTUAL BENEFITS

If conflict resolution is to be effective, all parties involved in the conflict must feel they have received something of benefit from the process. The benefit they receive may not be the one they expected when the process began, but they must have some need, value, or feeling satisfied if they are to support whatever resolution is eventually agreed upon. Each party, therefore, needs to be concerned not only that she or he receives something of benefit from the conflict resolution process but also that all other parties receive something of benefit. We will be learning specific things that can be done to promote mutual needs, power, and benefits.

RELATIONSHIP-BUILDING AND CONFLICT RESOLUTION ARE CONNECTED

As mentioned earlier, one of the additional benefits of conflict partnership is that its steps and skills can be used to both resolve specific conflicts and establish and nurture healthy relationships. Thus, conflict partnership combines relationship-building and conflict resolution. Damaging conflicts often occur because a relationship has not been developed and maintained well. If conflicts are dealt with effectively, the process can be used to rebuild relationships on a more mutually beneficial foundation, and even to avoid future conflicts.

Now that we have summarized five basic principles underlying conflict partnership, let's compare this approach with the traditional conflict resolution/negotiation patterns widely used in situations of conflict.

The traditional approach usually brings the parties in conflict together so that they can present their demands, which usually include everything each party desires from the other, even though each party probably knows that the other cannot or will not agree to the extreme conditions of the demands. The plan, of course, is to compromise on lesser demands if the other party refuses to budge. There are several inadequacies in this traditional approach.

First, the parties are often angered that their "opponent" knows so little about them as to make such unrealistic demands. Thus, a get-all-you-can, maybe-I-can-slip-something-by-you atmosphere is immediately established. I have seen conflicts that were not involved in the original conflict created by this demand-based approach.

Second, once the parties have focused on demands, those demands often become the substance of each party's view of the other. In other words, the parties allow the competing demands to define each other. Lost in the process are the needs, perceptions, values, concepts of power, and feelings that are crucial components of conflicts and relationships.

Third, the energy of conflict resolution is negatively focused on the give-and-take of negotiation, rather than on what the parties might build together positively. Making concessions and compromises might be better than remaining intransigent, but it falls far short of a conflict resolution process that uses the mutual positive power of the parties toward improving their relationship. I have seen many people and groups walk away from a negotiating table with an agreement in hand yet feeling frustrated, skeptical, and even angry because their energy had been devoted to making concessions rather than building an improved relationship. The temporary agreement might contain the conflict for awhile, but the parties are usually itching for the time the agreement will have to be renegotiated, with the chance of conceding less. The relationship has not been improved, and the next conflict will be dealt with in the same demand–concession pattern.

Conflict partnership, on the other hand, focuses on the needs, perceptions, goals, potentially shared power, and possible commonalities of the conflict partners, not on their combative, competitive, and often unrealistic demands. Each party learns more about the other and becomes more aware of the other party's needs and potential positive power. Thus, conflict partnership stands in stark contrast to the traditional approach, which often rewards the party who can somehow maneuver the negotiations so that the other party gives up a comparatively greater portion of their demands, a classic use of negative power.

Another difference between conflict partnership and the widely used traditional approach is that whereas the latter often lets the conflict define the relationship, conflict partnership, as already pointed out, sees the specific conflict as just one part of the relationship. The task then becomes one of dealing with the existing conflict in a way that opens up possibilities for improving the relationship as well as resolving the conflict at hand. The goal is not to defeat the other party and seize a temporary advantage, but to develop a sustainable resolution of the conflict, made possible in part because an improvement in the relationship has been established.

Thus, the conflict partnership process transforms the way we perceive and use conflict resolution, as the chart on the following page shows.

From	*To*
An I-versus-you battle for victory and/or advantage over adversaries	A shared *we* responsibility and opportunity to clarify and improve the relationship while resolving, with mutual benefit, particular conflicts arising within the relationship
Solely a rescue-squad reaction aimed at putting out conflict fires or temporarily fixing them	Both a proactive process through which healthy relationships can be built and strengthened *and* a process to deal effectively with conflicts once they occur
An event that begins when parties in conflict sit down to negotiate and ends when a temporary agreement is reached on a conflict	A process consisting of skills and steps taken both alone and with the other party before, during, and after working out a mutually, beneficial resolution to a conflict
A way of dealing with conflicts that focuses on making demands and then on trading portions of those demands to gain advantage	A process based on needs, both individual and shared, on clarified perceptions, on improving the relationship, and on mutual benefits, not domination

PART II

The Eight Essential Steps to Conflict Resolution

THE CONFLICT-PARTNERSHIP PATHWAY
TO EFFECTIVE CONFLICT RESOLUTION

Conflict partner A	THE RELATIONSHIP	Conflict partner B
needs	conflicts	needs
values	commonalities	values
perceptions	differences	perceptions
goals	shared needs	goals
feelings		feelings
interests		interests

1. Create an effective atmosphere.

2. Clarify perceptions.

3. Focus on individual and shared needs.

4. Build shared positive power.

5. Look to the future, then learn from the past.

6. Generate options.

7. Develop "doables"—stepping-stones to action.

8. Make mutual-benefit agreements.

Conflict partner A	Improved relationship patterns in which differences and conflicts are dealt with in ways that nurture mutual development.	Conflict partner B

Create an Effective Atmosphere

Creating the atmosphere in which the conflict resolution process takes place is an important, and yet often neglected, skill. The atmosphere is the frame around the canvas on which we paint how we will agree, disagree, and build an improved relationship.

People often set, sometimes unconsciously, an ineffective atmosphere, and then seem surprised that they are unable to develop an effective outcome. Just as it is difficult for trees to grow in an atmosphere devoid of needed nutrients, it is difficult for effective conflict resolution to occur in an atmosphere that obstructs rather than promotes positive interaction.

Creating an atmosphere for effective conflict resolution includes attention to, among other things, your personal preparation, the timing, the location, and the initial opening statements the parties in conflict make once they are together.

PERSONAL PREPARATION

The mindset people bring to the conflict resolution process influences the way they deal with conflict. Although additional aspects of personal preparation will be covered in Step 2 under the heading Clarifying Perceptions of the Self, it is important to offer two initial suggestions as we begin our look at how we create a partnership atmosphere.

First, remind yourself that conflict is not always negative, that conflict can help clarify and improve a relationship. Second, remind yourself that an I–versus–you atmosphere obstructs effective and sustainable conflict resolution, and that you and the other party need each other as partners in working on the conflict.

Third, go through a brief review of the conflict partnership steps, taking special note of the skills most pertinent to the relationship and to the conflict at hand. Doing so helps empower a person not only with confidence but with the reminder to pay special attention to key skills and to be careful of certain negative tendencies. Even though I have been involved professionally in conflict resolution for many years, I still try to go over the conflict partnership steps each time I deal with a conflict.

Fourth, avoid locking yourself into rigid demands of what the solutions must be. Remind yourself that you and the other party can develop options together. I advise having a few mutual-benefit options in mind, but not spending a lot of time thinking out the details before meeting with the other party.

TIMING

Although some conflicts erupt so suddenly that we must deal with them immediately, most conflicts offer a chance to choose *when* we begin the conflict resolution process. Rarely will timing make or break conflict resolution, but it can influence the process negatively or positively. If the conflict partnership skills are applied, bad timing can usually be overcome, but why create unnecessary difficulty either by ignoring timing or choosing an ineffective time?

Although some people may argue that astrology, visions, and certain supernatural phenomena can guarantee a perfect time for just about anything, there is no fail-safe, magical moment for conflict resolution. What we *can* do is make sure we have tried our best to choose an effective time for opening the conflict resolution process. Several criteria can help us make the best possible choice.

Rather than jumping into an intense conflict resolution process prematurely, do some groundwork. Conflict resolution works best when all parties involved recognize that in order for some of their individual needs to be met, the other party must be involved in a dialogue. Resolving the conflict will be difficult, although not impossible, if one of the parties seems to feel there is no conflict, or that the conflict is the other party's problem.

Let's take the example of two neighbors, Jane and Mary. Jane feels she has a conflict with Mary over the dead tree in Mary's yard, primarily because a sudden storm may cause one of the large limbs to fall in Jane's yard. Mary shows no signs of recognizing a need to deal with the problem. Rather than trying to force Mary to sit down for two hours to discuss the problem, Jane might want to say to Mary, "Do you think we need to talk about the dead tree? I'm worried it could hurt one of our children if it fell during a storm."

Mary responds, "Don't worry, Jane. That old tree has been there for years."

"Well," Jane says, "I'm still worried. You and I have always been able to work things out when one of us has been bothered by something, and I think we need to put our heads together and see what we can do."

"Well, I don't think it's a problem," Mary replies, "but if my best friend is bothered by it, sure, let's discuss it."

"When would you have a couple of hours?" Jane asks.

Rather than barging into Mary's house and starting to deal with the particulars of the potential conflict, Jane communicated that she felt there was indeed a problem and that she and Mary needed each other to work it out. She established solid groundwork and a partnership atmosphere, and used timing effectively.

Choose a time that is long enough and free enough from outside distractions to allow for effective interaction. In other words, there needs to be an agreed-upon commitment to a time that is as free as possible from ringing telephones, a favorite television show, a parade of human traffic, and, in more public conflicts, the often sensationalist and intimidating intrusion of the media. A recent workplace example shows what can happen when this seemingly obvious criteria of effective timing is ignored.

Rita, the office manager, is upset because Carl, one of the secretaries, has been coming in late all week. Rita has thrown Carl a number of very obvious, angry glances. Carl, who doesn't like Rita very much anyway, has responded by ignoring Rita, even to the extreme of pointedly not speaking to her when they pass each other in the office. Rita knows that the busiest time in Carl's work schedule is from 10:00 A.M. to noon, but she is so determined to get the conflict resolved that she ignores the "timing" skill and, at 11:00 A.M., tells Carl to come to her office. During the discussion, Carl's telephone is ringing off the hook, his temporary helper keeps motioning to him through the glass window of Rita's office to answer the important calls, and Rita herself keeps being interrupted by co-workers who need her to sign documents. If Rita had considered the issue of timing, she might have realized that waiting until a time both she and Carl were less distracted would have been wise.

Based on the characteristics of the individuals involved in the conflict, try to choose a time that maximizes concentration and communication skills. Nate and Celia's marriage is experiencing serious conflicts. Nate calls me on the phone one night and says, "I keep trying to work things out, but we're getting nowhere. We've sincerely tried to talk about our problems, but Celia just doesn't seem to understand or communicate."

When I ask him to describe one of their discussions, I find out that the only time they discuss their problems is at the breakfast table at 6:30 A.M. Celia is one of those people who is not a functioning human being until about 10:00 A.M. She talks and moves and even goes to work, but her powers of concentration and communication do not get into gear until mid-morning. No wonder she seemed to not understand or communicate over early-morning orange juice and pancakes. Deep problems in the marriage may indeed exist, but the seemingly simple matter of poor timing in when to talk about the problems makes conflict resolution more difficult.

Choose a time that does not give an advantage to one party over the other, but maximizes the positive skills of all parties. In the ineffective conquest approach discussed in Chapter 2, one party will likely try to find a time that will be of disadvantage to the other party. Even some professional negotiators I know attempt to gain advantage by purposely maneuvering to set negotiations for a time period incompatible with the *adversary's* best level of performance.

Realizing that conflict resolution works best when all parties are functioning at effective levels of cooperation, concentration, and communication, conflict partnership urges the conflict partners to choose a time all parties agree is conducive to effective performance.

As mentioned earlier, timing is not usually the most crucial factor in conflict resolution. It can, however, make the
process much more difficult, or, if chosen wisely, contribute
positively to the atmosphere. Be wise about how long you
and your conflict partner talk without a break. Usually keeping at it for more than two hours diminishes effectiveness.

PLACE

Except in cases for which there is no choice, determining
where a conflict will be worked on should be a conscious
decision. Far too often people simply do not think about the
place conflict resolution will occur. As is true with timing,
the *place* at which a conflict is dealt with will rarely make or
break the process. Location can, however, have either negative or positive influence. Although each situation is obviously unique, it is helpful to keep in mind several guidelines
in the choice of location.

*Choose a place that is nonthreatening to all parties, one that helps
all parties feel positively empowered to work effectively on the
conflict.* For example, if one of the parties is in an obvious
position of lesser power (such as a child dealing with a parent,
or a worker dealing with a supervisor), we need to take
great care to set the conflict resolution process in a physical
environment that helps the party presumed to have lesser
power feel as secure as possible. Let's look at two contrasting
examples of this guideline.

A father has his office in his home. During the past year
he has had numerous conflicts with his teenage son. Every
time the father and son have dealt with their conflicts, the
father has chosen his rather imposing office as the location.
The son, although feeling confident that he is not totally to
blame for the difficulties, immediately feels intimidated when

he goes into his father's territory. The father's diplomas and awards are visible on the wall, subtle reminders of his maturity and success. The son, feeling himself shrink in importance and power compared to his father, usually becomes defensive or even finds himself accepting a lower self-image. Consequently, he becomes less able to deal with the conflict effectively.

A recent conflict at a factory provides a positive example. The factory workers and management had been experiencing a conflict over several matters, including the dangerously slippery conditions on the factory floor. Each time they met to discuss the problem, management would invite the workers' representatives into the boardroom of the administrative building. At the discussions, the workers seemed ill at ease and somewhat ineffective in presenting their needs and concerns. After little progress, I was called in to help with the conflict. One look at the workers sitting uncomfortably in the plush boardroom told me that they were feeling all of the power of management displayed against them, symbolized by the excessive trappings of management's home turf. After checking out my perception with a few of the workers, I urged management to consider calling an end to the workday two hours early, taking off their coats and ties, and holding the next discussion on the factory floor. Management complied, and although the two parties still had disagreements on the issues, the workers felt much more confident in explaining their concerns effectively. Furthermore, the management representatives experienced firsthand just how unsafe the slippery floor really was. A new floor was installed within two weeks, and the improvement in the attitude of the workers and the increase in worker productivity quickly made up for the expense of the new floor.

Choose a place that promotes a relationship of being connected in a partnership rather than being divided in an I-versus-you battle. The following are examples of settings that might promote connected partnership.

1. A place relatively devoid of distractions or diversions, such as a window looking out onto tension-producing traffic jams, a bed where a couple might be tempted to rely on physical embrace to temporarily soothe over problems that eventually must be confronted, or a place so crowded that it feeds mental and emotional feelings of having no room for creative thought.
2. A room in the house usually associated with cooperative activities rather than a room either associated with one of the family members more than the other members or where some of the more damaging arguments have taken place.
3. Dealing with especially difficult school, workplace, or even family conflicts in a designated "dialogue room" rather than in the office of the principal, boss, or parent. (I have urged the creation of dialogue rooms in a number of schools and companies, with much success.)
4. A circular seating arrangement rather than tables facing one another, or in some cases even having a circle of chairs without any tables at all, thereby removing at least one of the symbols of rigid division.
5. Using the neutral tranquility of nature rather than more confining settings which may have past associations and images unsettling to one or both of the parties.

In conflicts involving differing cultural or socioeconomic parties, choose a place that does not offend cultural mores or favor one party over the other. One glaring example of how mistakes can be made if this guideline is ignored occurred in a recent neighborhood conflict involving two ethnic groups. One well-meaning resident of the neighborhood worked hard to get the leader of each of the groups to meet with her to begin a dialogue on the conflict. She did everything well, except for the choice of the location where the discussion would take place. Oblivious to the fact that location can influence the atmosphere in which conflict resolution takes place, she set the meeting in a church whose religion had historically been seen as an oppressor by one of the ethnic groups. Needless to say, the leader of that group refused to participate, and convinced himself that the well-intentioned woman trying to bring about a resolution to the conflict was on the side of the other group and had purposely chosen the church to intimidate his group.

Another case involved a wealthy parent whose daughter, Mollie, was dating Randy, a young man in her school who came from a very low-income family. The father learned that Randy had been arrested a couple of times during demonstrations supporting the creation of a shelter for the homeless. Every time Randy came over to Mollie's house, her father "picked a verbal fight" with Randy—or at least that was the way Mollie expressed it to her father after one especially embarrassing evening had mercifully ended and Randy had gone home, angry and feeling victimized.

Mollie strongly advised her father that he should resolve his conflict with Randy because Randy was very likely to become her husband in the not-too-distant future. The father reluctantly called Randy and invited him to meet somewhere to resolve the issue. Where did Dad tell Randy to meet him? Why, at Dad's country club, of course. Randy went, kicking himself all the way there for agreeing to the country club venue. Once there, the socioeconomic divisions between Mollie's father and Randy were painfully emphasized by the country club's opulence. As he sat on the country club's terrace, Randy felt himself getting more and more angry and out of control. Every time he looked at the huge golf course stretching before him, he saw land that could be used for housing the homeless. Every time he looked at Mollie's father, Randy saw the symbol of all of that waste.

Some might want to criticize Randy for not being able to look past all of the divisive socioeconomic symbols, but the location of the meeting blatantly accentuated those symbols in his mind. How much better things might have gone that night if the father had suggested they meet in a diner, take a walk, or meet *anywhere* other than a country club.

INITIAL COMMENTS OR OPENINGS

Although dialogue can indeed be constructive, there is nothing automatically productive in having parties in conflict meet to deal with their differences. They may bring attitudes and behavior patterns that will be damaging. If people follow the personal preparation, timing, and location suggestions just discussed, they will create the best possible atmosphere in which two parties can meet. Once the parties come together, the rest of the partnership atmosphere needs to be created, and it needs to be maintained throughout the conflict resolution process.

The initial comments, or openings, people make once they begin the conflict resolution dialogue constitute an important part of the atmosphere. By the time parties meet, a lot of potentially damaging words, emotions, and perceptions have already filled the air. That makes it even more important for the opening comments to help create a more positive and potentially effective atmosphere. They help set the tone and direction for the dialogue that follows.

Just as there is no magical time or place that can guarantee success in conflict resolution, there is no one perfect opening for every conflict. However, there are some openings that have consistently proven effective. There are a few general openings that can be effective in getting a positive conflict resolution process started, regardless of the type of conflict or the people or groups involved. Other conflicts, however, may be served better by certain specific openings, based on what has already been tried, on the characteristics and tendencies of the people involved, or on the immediacy of resolving the conflict. Specific examples of both general and specific openings will be given later, but we first need to look at the basic functions openings should serve.

What Opening Comments Should Do

If your opening can do at least one of the following, it will be a first step in the conflict resolution process.

1. Try to establish a partnership atmosphere of "we are dealing with our relationship and with our conflict," and dispel the fear that you are viewing the process as an I-versus-you battle for conquest, advantage, and/or a weakening of your conflict partner.

> EXAMPLE: "I just want you to know that I'm not looking at this as some sort of fight to determine a winner. I believe we are in this together, and we need each other to work it out."

2. Try to let your conflict partner know that you are interested in improving the overall relationship while dealing with the particular conflict at hand.

> EXAMPLE: "This conflict is just one part of our relationship. By working well together to deal with this particular problem, I believe we can improve how we handle other problems that may come up in our relationship."

3. Try to affirm the belief that options and feasible steps to improvement can be generated through a shared effort, and that you are open to suggestions. This should be done without gushing forth unrealistic expectations or magical cure-alls.

> EXAMPLE: "I'm sure we've both thought of some things we might do to deal with this conflict, but I'll bet there are some good options we can come up with together that we haven't thought of individually."

4. Let your conflict partner know that you believe it is both possible and healthy for people in a relationship to agree to disagree on certain points, and that there are other aspects of the relationship that remain strong even though you may be in conflict on a particular matter.

> EXAMPLE: "Maybe we can use this disagreement to make our relationship better. I can learn from you and you can learn from me. Just because we disagree on this problem doesn't mean we have to let it make us forget the other things we share in our relationship."

Now that we have seen what openings should do, let's look at some examples of both general and specific openings I have found to be effective. Please remember that the precise wording is *my* preference and may not necessarily be the wording you feel is best for you.

GENERAL OPENINGS

The openings as typified by the following examples are effective for almost any conflict.

1. "How much time do you have? Good. I think we can take some positive steps in that amount of time if we work together. I want you to know I'm not looking at this as a struggle for who comes out ahead, or who is more to blame. I want us *both* to feel some of our needs are being met and that our relationship will be better because of what we do here."

This opening promotes positive, realistic expectations; clarifies the amount of time available; helps establish partnership; and tries to relieve any fears of your trying to defeat your conflict partner.

2. "I know we both have strong opinions and feelings about our situation, and I want you to know I will try to listen to and understand your point of view. I see us as needing each other to work through this particular conflict and to help our relationship grow. So, I'd like to hear what you think the conflict is, and any suggestions you have about steps we might take to resolve the issue."

This opening promotes partnership, listening, clarification, and mutual empowerment. It would be good for situations in which you might not have discussed a lot of the specifics of the conflict or in which you aren't sure how well you know your conflict partner.

3. "I know that we've both said some angry things and made some demands, but I'd like for us to work together to try a more effective way of dealing with our differences. Just because we disagree on this or that point doesn't mean we have to let such things make us forget the strengths in our relationship. [An example of a strength would be good here.] Let's look at what we really need, and maybe we can use this conflict constructively."

This opening tries to move beyond rigid demands, perhaps made in anger, to focus on the needs and strengths of the overall relationship—strengths which show that you and your partner do have a relationship capable of dealing with this particular conflict. It also tries to affirm that disagreements don't have to be seen only as negative. Such an opening would be especially effective in conflicts and relationships in which past anger and demands have significantly affected dealing with them.

SPECIFIC OPENINGS

The following examples are openings applicable to typical, yet specific, situations.

1. For situations in which your conflict partner seems to have little confidence in conflict resolution and in which avoidance is a problem:

> "I think we're both strong enough to deal with this in a way that helps us both. Maybe we can try a couple of things we haven't tried before, things that have helped a lot of people. For example, [then you might want to give a very brief description of one of the conflict partnership steps/skills you think is a good one with which to begin]. Want to try it?"

2. For situations in which the conquest approach has been the pattern usually employed in dealing with conflicts:

> "I get the feeling we've been trying to defeat each other when we've dealt with our conflicts. Maybe we've spent so much energy working *against* each other we haven't had any energy left for working *with* each other. We've both got a lot of *positive* power to use in dealing with this problem, so maybe we can use that power *together*. [If your conflict partner asks what you mean by positive power, it opens the way for you to give an example from Step 4 in the conflict partnership process.]

3. For situations in which there has been a tendency to get trapped in the past and only fight the same old battles with the same old patterns:

"I don't know about you, but I feel we've gone 'round and 'round about things we've done or should have done in the past. Maybe if we focus first on some steps we can take *now* to improve things, we can see that we don't have to let ourselves get trapped in the past. Then maybe we can deal more positively with *learning* from those past incidents."

4. For situations in which people seem to be reluctant to or afraid of expressing important feelings and emotions involved in the conflict:

"Maybe we haven't let each other know how we *feel*, how deeply each of us may feel affected by what's been going on. If we can agree to express our feelings, and to be listening for what we can *do* about those feelings, maybe we'll appreciate each other's needs more and can open up some possibilities we haven't seen before. I think it shows strength if we can express our feelings to each other."

5. For situations where one or both of the conflict partners have certain tendencies that obstruct effective conflict resolution—tendencies such as interrupting, personalizing rather than focusing on the behavior, labeling or name-calling, not listening or clarifying, and so on:

"I know I sometimes let myself get so caught up in getting my own point across, I don't listen to what *you* are saying and meaning. Can we agree to really listen to each other, and to make sure we have clarified what each other is saying and meaning at the time we say it?" [This example holds for whatever the negative tendency is, although the lack of a listening and clarifying skill is the negative tendency here.]

Needless to say, a list of possible specific openings could go on for pages, depending on the characteristics of a particular relationship or conflict. The point to remember is that some situations might call for a specific opening that addresses the particulars of a given relationship or conflict. When in doubt, one of the general openings would probably be a wise choice.

You can come up with some openings that will be just as good, or better, than the ones suggested here. I have learned, however, that the functions described under the heading What Opening Comments Should Do, and the examples of both general and specific openings provided here, can help begin the conflict resolution process in an effective atmosphere.

Additional Points to Remember About Openings

- Try to choose an opening that is tailored to the specific conditions of both the conflict at hand and the individual characteristics of you and your conflict partner.
- If you aren't sure what opening might best suit a particular relationship or conflict, use a general opening that serves at least one of the functions discussed under the heading What Opening Comments Should Do.
- Whatever opening you use, it should feel natural and be expressed in language you feel comfortable with; language that does not sound memorized or resemble cue-card statements.
- Try not to give such a long opening that it turns into a speech. Such openings usually set a monologue pattern for the rest of the conflict resolution process, rather than promoting the valuable pattern of dialogue and asking questions. Lengthy openings can also sound like preaching.

In our discussion of this first conflict partnership step, we have seen that personal preparation, timing, place, and openings all contribute to the creation of a true partnership atmosphere. I am sure we all know that some people will resist seeing conflict resolution as a partnership. However, if we persevere in trying to create, maintain, and demonstrate such an atmosphere in our attitudes, words, and actions, the other party begins to feel invited into a process they soon see has positive possibilities for meeting personal needs and for improving the relationship.

Although critical at the beginning, working to create a partnership atmosphere is a task one needs to repeat throughout the conflict resolution process and into the future of the relationship. Within such an atmosphere, the other conflict partnership skills we will now discuss are given even more power.

Clarify Perceptions

Perceptions are the lenses through which we see ourselves, others, our relationships, and the situations we encounter. As such, perceptions wield enormous influence over our behavior. If we perceive something to be a certain way, even if we are incorrect, in our minds it *is* that way, and we often base our behavior on that perception.

We form our perceptions from many sources. The formal and informal learning provided within our family or nurturing unit plays a role. The learning provided by a society's educational systems contributes. Social pressure and a society's reward systems are other sources, sometimes coercing, sometimes encouraging people to accept and perpetuate those perceptions and patterns dominating their society. Some perceptions are also formed through what I call education by absorption, a process akin to osmosis, in which the dominant patterns of a person's environment are gradually internalized subconsciously. Other perceptions are formed when certain desires, interests, or goals become so fixed and intense in a person's mind that he or she perceives things only in a way that justifies those desires, interests, and goals. And, of course, perceptions are formed by the way we interpret the effects of the experiences that fill our lives.

Looking at all of the influences that contribute to the formation of perceptions, it is tempting to conclude that we are putty in the hands of these influences, that we are but powerless spectators watching our perceptions rule our lives. Nothing could be more misleading.

We *choose* our perceptions; *we* have the power to determine what they are and how they influence our behavior. We do not have to be slaves to our own desires, or the pressure of other people, or the patterns of a society or culture. We can take charge of our own perceptions, and strengthen our skills in clarifying them.

Perceptions greatly influence the way people and societies mold their attitudes and much of their behavior, and therefore play a major role in the causes of conflict and in the way we deal with it. The conflict partnership process focuses on clarifying perceptions in three critical areas: perceptions of the *conflict*, of the *self*, and of the *conflict partner*.

CLARIFYING PERCEPTIONS OF THE CONFLICT

As we move into a discussion of this important skill, we need to reemphasize a most essential understanding within the conflict partnership process: a particular conflict is but one part of the overall relationship, revealing an area of the relationship that, if dealt with effectively, can help clarify the partners to each other and to themselves. Thus, we should take great care not to let a particular conflict define the entire relationship in our perceptions.

I often find that people involved in a conflict automatically assume they know what the conflict is about. If effective conflict resolution is to occur, we need to work with our conflict partners to clarify perceptions of the problem, not simply assume that one's own assumptions correctly explain what the conflict is about. People often feel angry, hurt, or mistreated by certain things the other party has done or failed to do, and then focus only on their own interpretation of those particular actions or inactions. In reality, conflicts usually involve a lot of factors arising from the overall relationship, not just from a particular thing that was or was not done, and the perceptions of what happened can vary greatly.

Important Questions to Ask First

In clarifying perceptions of a conflict, we need to deal with several important questions.

Is the conflict over one rather isolated event that shows little consistency with the rest of the relationship, or is it but the latest in a series of conflicts revealing problems within the relationship as a whole? For example, in a household in which one spouse does most of the housework and the other works outside the home, let's say the latter comes home from work one day, finds the house a mess, and angrily berates the spouse for being irresponsible and lazy. If the outburst is inconsistent with his or her usual response in similar situations, the extreme behavior and the conflict about to explode probably stems from a horrible day at the office, not from a major problem in the relationship. If the outburst is but the latest in a series of intolerant and abusive acts, the conflict over the messy house may indeed be a symptom of a serious relationship problem.

Am I sure this is a conflict with the other party and not a conflict within myself? Ben is tied in knots because he wants to be in a job that challenges his mind more than his present employment. He begins to argue with his boss over the slightest disagreements, displays a short temper with other employees, and decides the conflict is with a tyrannical boss and incompetent co-workers. Is that what the conflict is really about, or does it stem from Ben's internal conflict over feeling he should change jobs but not wanting to go through the long process of job hunting and maybe even a period of unemployment?

What do I think the conflict is about? What is it not about? If Ben had seriously asked himself this question, he probably would have clarified his own perceptions. He could have realized that he had liked his boss and fellow employees during the first two years of his employment, and that they had not changed. In the earlier example, if the person surrounded by the messy house asks, What is this *not* about?, he or she might discover that the conflict is *not* over being married to an abusive, irrational spouse who always rants and raves at every inconvenience, but over an isolated incident that particular day.

Is the conflict over values or just preferences? Tom, Dorothy's new secretary, always comes to work dressed in a suit and tie. Dorothy hates to dress up, and thinks heels and hose are too uncomfortable and confining. As Dorothy leaves every day dressed in her functional skirt and blouse, the sartorially splendid Tom gives her disapproving glances. Tom even makes comments to the other secretaries in the office, such as, "You would think a boss would try to be more professional." These comments eventually find their way back to Dorothy, and she realizes the differences she has with Tom over proper dress may be the cause of his unfriendly behavior toward her.

Does the conflict over clothes involve a value or a preference? To Dorothy, the conflict definitely does *not* involve a value. Her clothes don't get in the way of her work performance; indeed, she works better when wearing comfortable, functional clothes. But if Tom *treats* the situation as though a value is involved, Dorothy had better sort out with Tom whether or not he is turning a preference into a value and thereby needlessly creating a more difficult conflict.

Is the conflict really over needs or desires? As defined earlier, needs are conditions we perceive we cannot do without, or perceive as being critical to the well-being and development of a relationship or of one or both parties in a relationship.

As has been pointed out, people often choose to perceive something they *want* as a need, partly because doing so seems to add strength to their argument that they have to see a certain outcome in a situation of conflict. Another aspect of the question, Are needs involved?, has to do with understanding that a *relationship* has needs, too. Some conflicts may not involve critical *personal* needs, but they may involve steps the parties need to take if the well-being or development of the *relationship* is to occur. More on clarifying needs will be covered in the next two sections of this chapter and in Chapter 6.

Is the conflict over goals or methods? A supervisor and one of her employees both shared the goal of efficient productivity. The conflict they are having is over which methods can best meet that goal. If they look more carefully at whether the conflict is over goals or methods, the supervisor might understand that the employee shares her goal of efficient productivity, and will then not be as likely to accuse the employee of not caring about efficiency. Using that shared goal as a foundation for productive discussion, the supervisor might come to the realization that the shared goal might be better served by incorporating some of the good ideas on methods the employee suggests.

What are the components of the conflict? Which do I feel most strongly about? Which parts should be dealt with first, and which can be addressed more effectively if we consider them after dealing with other parts first? The Campbells are a family of four. The father works as a schoolteacher, the mother as a business executive. Gina, the seventeen-year-old daughter, is a cheerleader, and Bob, the fifteen-year-old son, is a high school athlete. Although seen as an all-American family by their community, all is not well in the Campbell household.

All year, the parents have been arguing repeatedly. Their arguments started over what college Gina would attend in the fall, with the father strongly favoring the local community college and the mother even more strongly favoring the state university. That conflict has now reached shouting-match levels, and, as so often happens, has spread ill will to other parts of the family dynamic.

Other matters are also creating mayhem at the Campbell house. Gina is dating a young man both parents dislike immensely, and she wants to go away with him for the weekend. Bob is angry at his parents because they never come to any of his baseball games, and he's mad at Gina because she treats him like a little kid at school, and because she "spends half her life" in the bathroom they share.

One evening just after dinner, the verbal fighting finally reaches an explosive level. Mom's toughest business executive patterns suddenly erupt, and she takes charge by yelling, "This family is falling apart! Leave the dishes and gather in the den ready to resolve this conflict once and for all!"

Where do the Campbells begin? What part of the family conflict do they tackle first? Well, sadly to say, nobody asks that critical question. They sit for two hours trying to deal with the family conflict and, predictably, get nowhere.

If they had looked at the components of the family conflict, they could have (1) taken turns expressing what each felt needed to be discussed, then (2) tried to focus on the component of the family conflict they had the best chance of resolving that night, or on one they all agreed was a problem, and then (3) decided on the next part of the conflict they would address the next night. By failing to look at the *compo-*

nents of the conflict, the Campbells trapped themselves into making the conflict one entangled "it." The various parts of the conflict they could have worked on effectively became lost in the poorly defined, elusive "family conflict."

Now that we have considered some of the effective questions helpful in clarifying perceptions of a conflict, let's go into more detail on several critical skills.

Sorting the Components of a Conflict

In failing to employ this valuable skill, the Campbells were not alone. When people come to me seeking assistance with a conflict, I often hear, "We've got to do something about our relations with group X," or "We need to do something about our failing marriage," or "Our company is in terrible conflict." My response will eventually emphasize the point that we cannot deal just with relations, or a marriage, or a conflict. We have to begin by dealing with specific components of the relationship or conflict. When people and groups view the conflict in vague, general terms, they have no handles to hold onto and utilize.

Although a conflict may sometimes seem to be one huge, monolithic entity without discernible points of entry, conflicts do indeed have various components we can identify. Some components must be dealt with immediately; some may be simply one party's wish list; some may be outside the power of the parties to do anything about; some may be based on wild misperceptions and heresay. The possibilities are limitless.

In sorting the components of a conflict we are attempting to do several important tasks.

We are attempting to find components we can use as starting points in the conflict resolution process. It is usually wise to begin with a conflict component that stands a good chance of being resolved. Why? Because the conflict partners may not yet have developed enough trust in each other or confidence in being able to work together to allow them to deal effectively with the tougher issues.

We are attempting to identify parts of the conflict one or all parties feel are priorities. For example, the parents of a three-year-old child both have such time-consuming jobs that the child gets little attention during the day. The parents get into a conflict, each blaming the other for the child's neglect. They focus on which of their respective jobs is most important, which brings in more money, and who is at fault. If both parents focus on *child care* as the part of the conflict both feel to be a priority, possible solutions become more apparent (such as the parents taking turns in bringing the child to the excellent daycare center at their respective companies) than if the focus is on which parent is to blame. Identifying the priority components of a conflict makes a mutually beneficial resolution much more possible.

We are attempting to identify parts of the conflict in need of clarification. For example, the job performance of a worker named Debbie has recently begun to slip. Her boss looks only at the job performance and gives no attention to clarifying why Debbie's performance is inferior to a former level. If the boss had been utilizing the skill of identifying parts of the conflict in need of clarification, he would have learned that another worker had been purposely obstructing Debbie's work in an attempt to gain an advantage over her, as a promotion they both desired was about to be decided. The boss incorrectly assumed it was Debbie's fault because he failed to clarify his perceptions.

We are attempting to identify components that will need to be dealt with eventually, but that should not be dealt with first. The most solid reason for waiting to deal with a particular component of a conflict is that due to its volatile nature, the parties in conflict would never be able to work together on it until they had built some trust and confidence by working successfully on more feasible components of the conflict. Once those more feasible components are resolved, there is a foundation of trust and momentum on which the more difficult components can be addressed.

We are attempting to sort out what is primarily an internal conflict within one of the parties but that is being perceived (or selfishly used) as a conflict between the parties. One case exemplifying this involves Millie and Roger, who work in the same department at a small company. For the past month, their work relationship has become increasingly antagonistic. Roger snaps at Millie for seemingly trivial things; Millie becomes increasingly frustrated, and she eventually allows herself to treat Roger with the same adversarial attitude. Their work suffers; Roger blames Millie, and the conflict worsens as the company's president reprimands them both.

Roger's conflict is not really with Millie. He is going through a difficult divorce and child-custody dispute. Millie is good friends with Roger's estranged wife, and he automatically assumes Millie sides with his wife, although that is not the case. The conflict is within Roger. Although he knows it is unwise, he allows his personal problems to harm his work relationship with Millie. If both Roger and Millie would look at the various parts of the conflict, they could clarify that their relationship as co-workers is not the real conflict, nor is Millie's alleged siding with Roger's estranged wife. Not clarifying that the source of the conflict is within Roger's personal life causes a conflict to develop between Roger and Millie at work.

Recognizing and Avoiding Ghost Conflicts

Ghost conflicts are minor problems we allow ourselves to elevate, in our minds, to the level of serious conflicts. When the actual problem is one we either understand poorly or wish to avoid altogether, we sometimes try to focus attention on ghost conflicts as the heart and soul of the problem.

Falling into the trap of ghost conflicts takes many forms. Take, for example, a young man and woman who, after five years of marriage, have grown apart because each has developed quite different personal life goals. Each feels good about her or his own personal growth, but their new goals are not compatible. Rather than affirming the valuable growth each has experienced, and working out whether or not they can reach those valuable goals while still being together, they begin fighting over ghost conflicts. He fights with her over the wet laundry hanging on the shower curtain rod, which hits him in the face when he goes to shower; she fights with him because he has the television on too loud; and so on and so forth through a long list of rather petty concerns. As is usually the case when ghost conflicts are allowed to obstruct perceiving what the conflict is really about, the relationship worsens as the real conflict goes unresolved.

Dealing with Value Conflicts

Conflicts over values are often the most difficult to resolve. As mentioned earlier, we should try to make sure values really are involved, rather than simply preferences. When values *are* involved, several important steps can be taken.

Clarify how important the value is to you and how important it is to the worth of the relationship. When Deni and Burt got married five years ago, Deni was working as a waitress. Burt was, and still is, working at a plant that makes parts that eventually fit into nuclear weapons. Deni saw Burt's work as a job he did well, a job that paid a decent wage.

Three months ago Deni became friends with a person

who had been extremely active in the peace movement for years. Deni became exposed to facts and ideas she had never known, and soon became an active worker in the drive to rid the world of nuclear weapons. Deni loved Burt and their life together, but she could not escape the fact that his work now violated one of her values.

Deni must clarify several critical questions. "Are there enough *other* values Burt and I share in our relationship to keep the relationship alive?" "Is the value of a denuclearized world so important to me that I cannot, in good conscience, stay married to a man who helps make nuclear weapons?"

Without clarifying these questions, Deni will have a hard time moving forward in her attempts to resolve the conflict. She thinks long and hard, and decides that she and Burt desperately need to sort things out. This brings us to the next step in dealing with value conflicts.

Clarify how important the value in conflict is to your partner. Deni has avoided talking with Burt about her growing discomfort over his job, primarily because she feared she would learn that he was strongly in favor of nuclear weapons as a major part of national security. Before going any further, Deni needs to clarify whether Burt is working at the defense plant simply because it is a job, or if he considers nuclear preparedness an important political value. They talk, and Deni learns that Burt does indeed believe he is contributing to national security, that he considers nuclear preparedness necessary. Deni must now go to the third step in dealing with value conflicts.

Understand that there are at least three options in dealing with value conflicts.

1. The parties do battle until one of them gives in and changes positions on the value in conflict.

2. The parties agree to disagree on that value, and because that value is so critical, one or both parties end the relationship.
3. The parties agree to disagree on that value but find other parts of the relationship important enough to continue the relationship.

Deni and Burt both realize that neither will change beliefs; therefore, option 1 seems fruitless. They consider options 2 and 3, and decide that even though the value is important, they have a lot of other values they share, they enjoy life together, and they do not want to go their separate ways. Using the other conflict partnership skills, they work on the other parts of their relationship based on other values while disagreeing on the nuclear weapons value. They even reach a point at which they go together to a peace rally, then to a defense industry program, and then, while at home, discuss the issues raised at the quite diverse meetings.

In value conflicts, the one option often assumed to be the only option is number 1: do battle until the other party gives in. Rarely will that option bring anything but destruction. To be sure, there are some values each of us holds that we will not compromise. In no way does conflict partnership advocate that successful conflict resolution requires a person or group to give up its values just to reach some sort of reconciliation. But if the parties want the relationship to continue, or if the parties have no choice but to continue the relationship, they need to agree to disagree on the particular value in conflict and try to build on the shared needs, values, and goals that are also part of their relationship.

As we bring to a close this section on clarifying perceptions of the conflict, it is important to emphasize again that our first assumptions of what a conflict is about are not always accurate. We need to sort through the various perceptions and components of a conflict to make sure we are not allowing ourselves to miss the heart of it. Without both parties having a clear perception of what the conflict involves, effective and sustainable conflict resolution becomes extremely difficult. We now turn to the second dimension of the conflict partnership skill of clarifying perceptions: clarifying perceptions of the self.

CLARIFYING PERCEPTIONS OF THE SELF

Clarifying our perceptions of the conflict is not enough; we must also clarify our perceptions of *ourselves*. Several questions, a kind of pre–conflict resolution self-awareness checklist, can help accomplish this task.

Important Questions to Ask First

How am I perceiving the conflict and its resolution? The importance of transforming the way we perceive conflict and conflict resolution has already been discussed. The key is to make sure that we are perceiving conflict not as a negative battle overshadowing all of the relationship, but as a chance to clarify the disagreements and to work together to resolve them in a way that also improves the overall relationship. If a person realizes that he or she is perceiving conflict as a negative, conquer-or-be-conquered battle, it may be better not to jump into dealing with the conflict until a more effective attitude can be energized.

What are my needs? Which are most vital and immediate? As stated earlier, needs are conditions we perceive we cannot do without, or are conditions critical either to the well-being and/or development of the relationship or to one or both parties in the relationship. Identifying and understanding our own needs is not as easy as it might appear. Exploring several key questions can be helpful in perceiving needs more clearly.

- What does the relationship need if it is to be improved?
- What do I need as an outcome in this particular conflict?
- If I don't get what I say I'm needing, how will I be damaged? How will the relationship be damaged? Do any of *my* perceived needs obstruct some of the needs of the *relationship*?

Dealing with these questions forthrightly can help differentiate between needs and desires, and can encourage people to see not only their own needs but also the needs of the relationship.

Mick and Meg have three children, all under the age of ten. Carrie, the youngest, is only nine months old, and requires a lot of attention. Meg is becoming increasingly frustrated because Mick rarely changes Carrie's diapers, feeds her, or gets up in the middle of the night when Carrie starts crying. Meg is feeling a real conflict with Mick, and whenever she confronts him, the conversation usually goes like this.

> MEG: "I need help with Carrie, Mick! You're not doing your share!"
>
> MICK: "You're better with her than I am. You can meet her needs better."
>
> MEG: "That's not fair, Mick!"
>
> MICK: "Hey, I'm just wanting what's best for Carrie."

Mick's perception of the needs involved in the conflict leave something to be desired. If he were to ask the questions previously mentioned, he might clarify his perceptions.

What does his *relationship* with Meg need? Well, for one thing, it needs a mutual feeling that the relationship is a partnership if peace and tranquility are to exist. Mick wants a partnership relationship, not just where Carrie is concerned, but in all parts of the relationship.

What does *Mick* need? He needs a good relationship with

Meg and the children, of that he is sure. Is he meeting one of his needs by *not* taking more responsibility for Carrie? Well, he doesn't *like* to change diapers or get up at 3:00 A.M., but is there really a need involved? Taking a larger role in Carrie's care will not really damage Mick, so perhaps he should understand that his dislike of diapers is far less significant when compared to the needs of the relationship and to his own need to be a true partner.

Mick's situation leads us to the other part of our initial question: Which needs are most important and immediate? Let's say that Mick really does require more sleep than Meg. With inadequate sleep, Mick drags through the next day, making troublesome mistakes. Carrie needs care, Meg needs help with Carrie, the relationship needs partnership, and Mick needs sleep. What to do? Which needs are most important and immediate?

Mick and Meg must answer these questions for themselves, but one possibility might be the following. Carrie's needs are critical and she can't meet all of them herself. The need for Meg and Mick to have a partnership relationship encompasses all they do, so it is a critical need as well. Mick needs sleep, and Meg needs help. Perhaps Mick might become more responsible for Carrie during his waking hours, and Meg can respond to Carrie's cries at night. This might not be the best resolution of the conflict, but at least it would show that Mick is trying to clarify perceptions of the needs involved.

What are my goals for the relationship, and how do my goals for this particular conflict affect them? Many labor–management disputes seem to ignore this very important question. Often both parties focus intently on their own goals and never ask if some of those goals are actually harming the relationship for the future. Getting a short-term personal goal can sometimes obstruct long-term relationship goals.

Take, for example, a conflict over health benefits at ADCO Industries. The labor union's goal is a fifteen-percent increase in benefits; management's goal is to keep benefits where they are so that last year's increase in profits can be used to add a new product as part of ADCO's expansion. Both parties feel strongly about these conflicting goals.

Each party, however, is also keenly aware that its own well-being depends on a cooperative relationship. If they remain rigid in their personal goals on this one conflict, not only will other issues become more adversarial, but both labor and management will suffer as their relationship becomes more bitter.

By clarifying their perceptions of the critical *relationship* goal (cooperation), they may be able to see that a rigid adherence to a specific *personal* goal (fifteen-percent increase/no increase) might obstruct the long-term relationship goal. Focusing on the relationship goal might allow the parties to reach agreement on providing a smaller benefits increase, or on finding other ways some of the needs of workers might be et.

An important footnote to the ADCO conflict deserves mention. If the process the parties use to come to an agreement focuses on concessions, it is unlikely the relationship will be improved for the future. The conflict partnership process focuses on coming to an agreement based on a recognition of the critical relationship goal of improved cooperation. This is an important distinction, one which may have a powerful influence on whether or not the relationship will be improved. Defining agreements as being the result of concessions usually produces reluctant agreements and battles involving strategies to see who can concede less.

Are my expectations positive yet realistic? What one expects to accomplish in dealing with a conflict also needs clarification. Several questions can help clarify expectations.

- Are my expectations based on a conquest view of conflict and conflict resolution in which I must either win or consider myself a loser?
- Are my expectations so rigid that they won't allow the conflict resolution *process* I will be sharing with my conflict partner a chance to work?
- Are my expectations for the immediate conflict resolution get-together realistic given the time we have available to us right now?
- Am I letting my own expectations be shaped or distorted by other people or groups not involved in the conflict?
- Are my expectations taking into account the *other party's* needs, values, history, constraints, and so on?
- Am I expecting the other party to behave in ways I *want* them to, or think in ways I think they *should*? If they don't behave or think as I want them to, will I make the serious mistake of interpreting that as meaning they cannot be trusted?

These questions can be very helpful in clarifying our expectations. Because people often confuse expectations with trust, the differentiation between these two concepts needs attention.

I often hear one party say of the other, "They just can't be trusted. How can we resolve this thing if I can't even trust them?" When I ask, "What's an example of their not being trustworthy?," I'm often given no specific example, or I'm told of a situation in which the other party failed to do something expected of him or her.

If a person or group can be trusted only if they are what we want them to be, or do what we want them to do, we are using trust as a weapon to get our own way. We can say, "They did not live up to my expectations," but that is not the same thing as "They can't be trusted."

Clarifying expectations can help people sort out what they are really needing, what is feasible, and which functions the conflict resolution process might serve. *Un*clarified expectations complicate matters more than we often realize. Furthermore, having too many inflexible expectations will greatly disempower both the conflict resolution process and the mutual benefits such a process can provide.

Are any of my values or principles involved in this conflict? As previously discussed, people sometimes erroneously convince themselves that a particular conflict involves deeply held values or principles. Understanding whether a conflict involves values or just preferences thus becomes another step in clarifying perceptions of the self.

How do we clarify whether something is one of our values or principles? One way is to ask questions similar to the one we asked about needs: "If this value or principle goes unfulfilled or is violated, how will my *self-respect* be damaged? Will I feel something that seems like shame? Will I feel embarrassed around those people whose values and principles I most respect?" Granted, it may be difficult to answer these questions definitively, but we have all felt the difference between a loss of self-respect and a loss of something we *wanted*. Perhaps the best we can do is to be aware of the importance of not letting preferences be exaggerated into values, and then to try to answer the foregoing questions the best we can.

I know of a recent case in which a real estate agent got into a conflict with his boss. When the agent was assigned a particular house to sell, he was told by his boss that the house had a few construction flaws that, if not mentioned by the agent, would not be noticed by prospective buyers. The agent wasn't sure why, but he felt uncomfortable. He confronted the boss, saying, "I don't like to mislead people."

The boss admonished the agent with, "Are you afraid the buyer will find out after they've lived in the house for a year, and then they'll not like you? Everybody does this. Don't let your fear of not being liked get in the way of making a sale."

The agent did not allow himself to accept the boss's perception that the conflict stemmed from a desire to be liked.

The agent looked inside himself and realized that an important value or principle was involved, and that he must be true to that principle. Bolstered by a clearer understanding of himself and of the conflict, the agent decided to be honest with the prospective buyers. They did not buy that particular house but, admiring the agent's honesty, contacted him two months later to show them another house, which they bought.

Clarifying perceptions of one's own values involves other considerations. For some people, certain conflicts involve more than one value or principle. Let's say that Jay, the real estate agent featured earlier, believes not only in the principle of honesty, but in the principle of being a good team player in whatever job he holds. The boss and the other agents put a top priority on making a sale even if they have to hide flaws in the houses they sell. To the agency, being a good team player means following the priorities of the agency. Jay has two values or principles operating in his conflict, and they contradict each other. Jay must clarify which principle is most important.

For other people in certain conflicts, one or more *relationship* values may not be compatible with certain *personal* values. This problem played a large part in a conflict involving the Bartlett family. Andy, the father, had always been a fiercely private person, believing that everybody in the world should mind their own business, especially *his* business. He valued the personal strength he felt came from dealing privately with one's own troubles. When Andy got married and had a family, he never talked with the family about things that were troubling him. He would withdraw into himself, and his depressed behavior would have a negative effect on the rest of the family.

The other members of the family increasingly felt left out of Andy's personal troubles and helpless to offer assistance and support to a person they loved. Andy began to realize that another value was becoming clear to him: that one of the foundations of a strong family is trusting one another enough to discuss personal problems that are sure to affect the way one behaves within the family. That relationship value was being obstructed by his own personal principle of "my personal problems aren't anybody else's business." Andy struggled with the problem for several years. Finally, after clarifying the value conflict within himself, he realized that the relationship value was more important than his personal value. Slowly, he began to allow the family to share in dealing with his personal problems.

What have I done to contribute to the cause and perpetuation of the conflict? As simple as this question sounds, I am amazed at how many people and groups never ask it when dealing with a conflict. The desire to get more than the other party in settling a conflict, and the temptation to justify one's own desired outcomes by blaming the conflict on the other party, often lead people to ignore their own contributions to the cause and perpetuation of a conflict.

For some people, simply asking this question can start them on the road to answering it. Other people, however, need a more specific way of identifying their own negative contributions to the conflict. One conflict partnership technique that has proven effective for many people is to trace the conflict back to the point at which the conflict emerged and ask, What could I have done differently to take us in a more positive direction? In the conflict discussed earlier, Roger and Millie could have traced back and discovered that their work relationship began to worsen when Roger's divorce occurred. They could then have clarified their perceptions about the situation and probably have avoided the conflicts at the office.

What are my "buttons" and how might I recognize them and deal with them effectively? Not long ago I was asked to facilitate a conflict over what a community would do with some vacant land in the downtown area. Some very respected, powerful community and business leaders were embroiled in the conflict. As we discussed some of the behavior that had doomed to failure a recent negotiation session they had convened before I got involved, one of the leaders said, "Well, I know I went crazy at the meeting, but I go berserk when people preach vegetarianism!"

The source of the berserk behavior was a "button" in that leader that, when pushed, sent currents of negative electricity into his mind and behavior. Most of us have buttons that, when pushed, create an atmosphere in which we end up thinking, saying, or doing things we know will obstruct effective conflict resolution. Recognizing our own buttons is an important step in clarifying perceptions of ourselves.

What are *your* buttons? What words, behavior, topics, nonverbal communication, and so on tend to make it easy for you to think, say, or do things you know will only complicate attempts at conflict resolution?

One way to identify your buttons is to go back over recent situations in which you lost control of yourself. Can you pinpoint a particular button? Is there a pattern that seems to repeat itself? Or you may want to ask someone who knows you well. Perhaps they have seen some of your buttons that you have been unable to recognize.

Another helpful approach is to be aware of certain physiological warning signals that are telling you that you are about to lose it. Perhaps it is a sudden knot in the stomach, a twitch, sweating, or a flushing of the skin. It could be any number of things. Because we don't always know when one of our buttons has been pushed, being sensitive to these physiological warning signals can help us recognize that this has occurred.

We *can* learn to recognize our buttons and warning signals. We can also take charge of ourselves and not let those buttons lead us into negative behavior. We do not have to let someone else's behavior gain power over us just because they have pushed one of our buttons.

If we allow our buttons to gain control over us, they become a locomotive-like force building up power and speed until our more rational capabilities soon get left behind. There are ways to keep the buttons from gaining control over us, but each person must find those ways that work best for her or him.

Some people find that taking deep breaths can derail the locomotive. Others use visualization, painting a mental picture of either a relaxing scene, such as a sailboat moving over water, or a picture of themselves as a calm, rational, effective person dealing with a specific task. Others might find it helpful simply to excuse themselves and get away from the situation for a bit. Some people can use a quick muscle tensing–relaxation exercise in which they tense their muscles and then relax them quickly, letting the good feeling of relaxation flood over them.

Something I have taught and found especially helpful for a lot of people involves rechanneling energy. When we react to a button being pushed, a lot of energy begins to well. Take that energy and, instead of letting it become negative behavior, direct it to saying something positive, or asking a question, or concentrating on the other parts of what the person said—parts that were obscured by the part containing the button.

One important aspect of rechanneling energy occurs when someone is expressing anger directed at you. There is a temptation to respond to that anger with your own anger, by taking the attack personally, and by becoming defensive. If we can rechannel that energy into clarifying the meaning involved in the other person's anger, if we can immediately concentrate on finding something in their message of anger that we can do something about together, we can turn a potentially negative moment into something positive.

Both before and during the conflict resolution process, we will be well served by knowing our own buttons and being prepared with the means to control them.

In what ways do I need the other party? One of the messages of the conflict partnership process is that parties in conflict need each other as partners if they are to resolve their differences effectively. Admitting this need sometimes proves difficult, however, because many people in situations of conflict focus only on the divisions separating them from what they perceive as their conflict adversaries. Difficult or not, a key step in clarifying perceptions of the self is recognizing that conflicts are resolved most effectively when the parties admit that they need each other as partners in the conflict resolution process. There are many ways in which relationship partners need each other, yet situations of conflict are often allowed to obscure those ways.

What misperceptions might the other party have of me, and how has my behavior contributed to those misperceptions? What have I done that makes it easy for the other party to see me or my behavior as a threat? Have I set up an ineffective atmosphere for conflict resolution? Has the other party interpreted a past action of mine incorrectly, and how can I best clarify that incorrect interpretation?

Dealing with these and other questions can help us move beyond misperceptions. Misperceptions often cause conflict and obstruct effective conflict resolution. Once people ask themselves the foregoing questions, they can then work more effectively with their conflict partner to clarify misperceptions.

Am I dealing with the conflict only in a role? Many people adopt the role player approach in dealing with conflict. They let whatever power, expectations, regulations, threats, fears, and stereotypes that are associated with certain roles become the rules within which a conflict is handled. In so doing, the role player not only ignores the people behind the roles but also limits the development of creative options for dealing effectively with a conflict.

We all know that in order to resolve certain conflicts, someone in an authority role must make a decision. If a son or daughter starts a conflict by stringently insisting on taking the family car for a pleasure drive in a raging snowstorm, the parents may have to use their role authority and say No. If students rigidly insist on having a loud party in their classroom in a school with very thin walls, teachers use their role authority and tell the students the party cannot be held in the classroom. If two employees working for the same company submit quite different proposals for the use of a special project fund, and only one project can be funded, the supervisor might use her or his role authority either to choose one of the proposals or to ask the two employees to come up with a joint proposal.

However, people often use roles as the *first* recourse in dealing with conflicts rather than initially trying to work things out through a partnership process. Many conflicts never have to reach the stage of having role authority serve as an arbitrator or resolver if the parties in conflict employ conflict partnership skills. Thus, people need to make sure they are not jumping prematurely to the use of role power, hiding behind their roles, or using their roles as a substitute for the more effective partnership process.

How can you clarify whether or not you are locking yourself into unnecessary role playing in dealing with a conflict? Several questions might help, depending on the situations and people involved in a particular conflict.

• If I weren't in this role, and the other party weren't in that role, what process and skills would we likely use to deal with this conflict?

- What do I know about the other party as a *person*? Have I taken the effort to learn about him or her as a person?
- Am I ignoring *feelings*? Maybe if we share some of our feelings about this conflict, we can become people to each other and open up more options for dealing with this conflict.
- What commonalities do we share that have nothing to do with our roles? (We both like sports, have children, eat at the same deli during lunch hour, and so on.)
- Are we trying to deal with this conflict in a location that accentuates our roles? (the boss's office, the parent's room, and so on)
- Am I afraid to deal with this conflict person-to-person rather than role-to-role? If so, why? Frequently this is so because a person feels she or he has no reliable conflict resolution skills and thus falls back on role power. Learning the conflict partnership skills will make acting only within roles less likely.

Exploring these and other key questions can assist people in clarifying perceptions of the self. Depending on the particular conflict, some questions are more important than others. All, however, deserve attention, as a clear and honest self-view empowers people and groups to deal with conflict more effectively and with greater confidence.

We have now explored how we can clarify perceptions of the conflict and of the self. The remaining perceptions in need of clarification are our perceptions of the other party.

CLARIFYING PERCEPTIONS OF THE OTHER PARTY

Even if we clarify perceptions of the conflict and of ourselves, we have not effectively accomplished Step 2 of the conflict partnership process until we have clarified perceptions of our conflict partner.

I find it surprising that I am sometimes asked, "*Why* is it important to understand the other person or group involved in a conflict? I know what I want. I understand the conflict. Isn't that enough?" No, it is not enough. Resolving a conflict is a *shared* process, not a battle between two or more parties who have their minds already made up as to what the outcome of the process will be. Effective conflict resolution is indeed a partnership, and understanding your partner in the process empowers both of you to deal with your shared conflict effectively.

Clarifying perceptions of the conflict partner involves two sets of perceptions: your perceptions of your partner, and your partner's perceptions of you. We will explore specific ways to accomplish these tasks, but first we need to look carefully at two general factors that frequently obstruct our ability to clarify the perceptions we have of others.

Stereotyping

To get a clear picture of what stereotyping is and does, imagine yourself being locked into a large box and then hearing the person who has put you there throw the key down a deep well. As you crouch in the darkness of the box, you hear crowds passing by reading aloud the label your captor has put on the box: "Here lies a person who has always been, is now, and forevermore shall be an enemy" (or a thief, or an idiot, or a sexist, or a liar, or any number of other stereotypes). You feel violated, misunderstood, and somewhat helpless to show the world who you *really* are.

As awful as that picture seems, many people, in effect, lock individuals and groups in stereotyped boxes every day, especially in situations of conflict. In a very real sense, those who do the stereotyping are also locked in a box, a perceptual box of their own making that distorts reality.

Why some people let themselves stereotype others is complex. One reason seems to be that stereotyping can delude people into thinking they can control others by creating a negative image of them. If the stereotyped person or group can be declared irrational, inferior, greedy, or whatever, they can be seen as powerless in the face of *your* rationality, superiority, and other characteristics you attribute to yourself.

Another reason is that stereotyping is an easy and convenient way of dealing with people. Or, to put it more bluntly, it is a lazy way of dealing with people and groups. You don't have to make the effort to see who the person really is or might become.

Another reason people stereotype is that they often define others based on what they *want* the other person to be, in order to make themselves feel more worthy, or to make the other party appear less worthy, or to gain what they perceive as an advantage.

Still another cause of stereotyping stems from the tendency to define the people you are in conflict with only on their most negative behavior. Doing so allows you to ignore the other person's positive possibilities and focus only on the bad things they did to cause the conflict.

Whatever the reason, stereotyping can create conflict, escalate it, and obstruct effective conflict resolution. Following are some of the negative effects caused by stereotyping.

Stereotyping damages both parties. Offenders are damaged because they (1) lose the contributions to conflict resolution the victims could make if freed from the labeled box, and (2) lose their own power to clarify perceptions. The victims of stereotyping are damaged because they (1) lose the power that could come from being able to use those positive parts of themselves obscured by the stereotyped label, and (2) lose the positive contributions the offenders could provide if they freed themselves from their own limited perceptions.

Stereotyping can sometimes make both parties prisoners to a process in which the false, stereotyped image becomes the misperceived reality both parties use to deal with the conflict. The one being stereotyped may try diligently to show the lie of the stereotype, but when ignored by the offender time and again, sometimes gives up trying and does exactly what the stereotyped image suggests. Without being given the recognition that they are better than the stereotype, some victims accept that lower self-image and end up perpetuating the stereotype.

Stereotyping also limits the options for resolving a conflict and for building a mutually beneficial relationship. The offender sees the victim as a category and, almost like punching a computer key for that category, identifies a certain way that person must be handled.

Before leaving the topic of stereotypes and moving along in our discussion of how we can clarify perceptions of the other party, it is important to reemphasize that stereotyping greatly harms effective conflict resolution. The conflict partnership process helps people to avoid stereotyping and to clarify and move beyond stereotypes.

Ineffective Communication Skills

There are also three communication skills that operate throughout the process of clarifying perceptions of the other party—listening, sensing, and asking clarifying questions—which often interfere with the conflict resolution process.

Listening. Most people seem to think that they listen quite well. However, whereas they might hear well, that does not mean they listen well. Effective listening requires more concentration and clarification than people usually give to the daily routines of life. This is especially true in situations of conflict in which pressures and emotions run high.

We rarely listen in the manner in which we are capable. Sometimes people are too busy thinking of the brilliant thing *they're* going to say next. Sometimes people let a pushed button interfere with their ability to listen. Sometimes people don't want to appear dumb and so pretend that they have listened carefully. Some people even purposely listen poorly so that they can avoid an unpleasant truth or have an excuse to misperceive.

Whatever the reason for poor listening, we need to increase our powers of concentration and listening while involved in a conflict, and we need to keep clarifying what the other party is saying and meaning.

Sensing. Sensing is our eyes, ears, and other means of sensory perception taking into our brain the nonverbal communications given by a conflict partner. I find that people often ignore sensing when dealing with a conflict. The conflict partner may be fidgeting, grimacing, staring into space, showing shock or pain, or communicating nonverbally an entire range of reponses to what we are saying. We need to sense those communications if we are serious in our efforts to understand the other party clearly.

Sensing can be overemphasized, of course. Books have been written claiming that one can infer precise messages from particular nonverbal cues. Crossed arms are supposed to mean a certain thing, crossed legs something else; a pattern of avoiding eye contact is always sending a certain message. The list goes on and on. Devoting too much attention to nonverbal communication, and convincing ourselves that certain expressions or movements always mean a particular thing, can lead to stereotyped and often incorrect assumptions.

The point of effective sensing is quite simple: we need to realize that not all people feel comfortable expressing themselves verbally, and that we should be aware of any nonverbal signals that might help us understand how the other party is reacting to our own behavior and to the conflict resolution process.

Asking clarifying questions. Many people try to deal with conflicts by making more statements than questions asked. We must state our concerns, needs, goals, values, and feelings as clearly as possible, but we also need to ask clarifying questions.

The question "I hear you saying [thus and so]. Is that what you meant?" is an effective way of clarifying your perceptions of what your conflict partner is saying and meaning. It is a far better way than stating, "You said" thus and so, or, "what you really mean is . . .", and then stating what you may *want* the other party to be saying or meaning.

Asking questions can help the conflict resolution process in several ways. It shows your conflict partner that you are really interested in what they are saying and meaning and that you don't want to make misleading interpretations. It can give you vital information the other party might not offer. It can also give you a moment to regroup if you reach a point at which you don't know what to say, or if a pushed button is about to take control of you.

Important Questions to Ask First

Clarifying perceptions of the other party involves asking some of the same questions you focus on in clarifying perceptions of yourself.

Is the conflict partner perceiving conflict negatively and perceiving conflict resolution as a threatening battle? We need to be aware of how our conflict partners are perceiving conflict and conflict resolution. If they are seeing conflict only as a negative experience, and if they are treating conflict resolution with one of the ineffective approaches discussed in Chapter 2, we *can* do something about it—we can actively demonstrate an alternative by consistently applying the conflict partnership skills.

As mentioned earlier, I have learned through experience that conflict partnership is extremely inviting. In most cases, the process usually shows the other party that the conflict can be dealt with in a more effective way and can be used to improve the relationship for the future. People may resist becoming involved in the process at first, but if we are consistent in our use of the conflict partnership skills, the benefits usually feel positive enough and effective enough to our conflict partners that they become a part of the process.

In understanding how the other party is viewing conflict and conflict resolution, we need to look at ourselves to see if, perhaps unintentionally, we are creating an atmosphere or doing things that make it easy for our partner to fall into one of the ineffective patterns. I am not saying that you bear responsibility for making the other party behave in a certain way. What I *am* saying is that you can help create conditions in which your conflict partner will be more likely to become actively involved in a more effective approach to conflict resolution. You can help affirm that the current conflict needs to be seen in the context of the overall relationship, demonstrate the importance of clarifying perceptions, and be a model of effective conflict resolution by using the rest of the conflict partnership steps.

What are their *needs?* We have already dealt at length with the nature of needs; we will now focus on three special considerations in clarifying perceptions of the conflict partner's needs.

First, there is a fine balance between accepting the other party's needs as they state them and working with a conflict partner to make sure that the stated needs are not just demands or desires. Care must be taken not to discount their perceived needs because you feel the other party *shouldn't* need them. What to you may be a low-priority desire may to them be a need. Two helpful questions or statements are:

• I'd like to understand why you say you need that.
• If we can't agree on that, how will that cause you problems or how will that hurt our relationship?

A second consideration focuses on taking the other party's stated needs and asking yourself, "Might that need be one I also have, or that our relationship has?" People involved in conflicts sometimes reject considering another person's needs because of the familiar misperception that "if they get what they need, *I* won't get what I need." Far more *shared* needs are usually present than people want to acknowledge.

A third consideration in clarifying perceptions of the other party's needs focuses on situations in which partners seem unclear as to what they need or what the relationship needs in order for them to deal effectively with a particular conflict. A good way to address this problem is to state some of your needs first, then ask what the conflict partner needs. If they have stated a lot of demands, you can say, "I think we both have made some demands and said what we *want*, but maybe we can talk a bit about what we think we really *need*. Perhaps we have some needs we share."

What has led them to think or behave as they do? Although people have significant power to determine how their experiences affect them, each of us has been influenced by those experiences. If you had gone through what your conflict partner has experienced, your opinion about a particular conflict might resemble her or his opinion. In clarifying your perceptions of the other party, it is important to remember this simple yet crucial understanding.

One way to make sure you are trying to empathize is to ask your conflict partners to tell their stories, to share with you some of their background. If you are in a close relationship with someone, you may already know his or her past. If, however, your conflict partner is someone you do not know well personally, such as a fellow worker, learning about a few key experiences he or she has had might prove quite enlightening.

Another helpful approach is to ask *why* they did a particular thing, or *why* they are seeking certain outcomes of the conflict resolution process. You might even want to say, "I think I might better understand where you're coming from if you'll take me through the events you think have caused our conflict as *you* interpret those events."

Am I understanding what they are saying and meaning? Attempts at resolving conflicts are often hampered by numerous unclarified statements and meanings. As mentioned earlier, people either fail to listen effectively, want to interpret something in a way advantageous to their own position, or let one of their pushed buttons cause them to let the meaning of a statement go unclarified. We cannot be content with simply hearing statements. We must try to clarify their meanings. By doing so, everyone involved in a conflict is able to understand the situation more clearly and to open the door to working on their conflicts more effectively. We can say, "Let me tell you what I heard you say and see if I understand what you mean."

Am I defining them based only on their most negative behavior? A person does something that you feel is wrong, unfair, and very damaging to the relationship. You feel hurt and angry. You can easily focus only on that negative behavior and see that person as wrong and unfair, but are they really a wrong and unfair person because they committed an act that you feel is wrong and unfair? What right and fair things have they done in the relationship? Don't those things also matter? If we allow ourselves to become so focused on the negative behavior of another party that we ignore their positive behavior and their positive potential, we are, in effect, obstructing their more positive potential from being expressed. By reminding ourselves that it is unwise to define someone else only by their negative behavior, we are not condoning that behavior. What we are doing is reaching for their more positive potential. We can still express our hurt and anger over what was done, but we can also affirm their positive capabilities and use that positive foundation as a base on which to build an effective way of dealing with the conflict. If the other party can see how their positive behavior enhances the relationship, there is a better chance that the destructive, negative behavior will lessen.

Am I trapping myself in a fixed-image perception of the other party? One of the more prevalent patterns people use in relationships is what I call fixed-image perceptions. The other party has done something or said something that we allow ourselves to use to define that person. Once that image becomes lodged in our minds, we give the other person or group no chance to be seen as anything other than that fixed image. Similar to trapping another person in the stereotype box, this pattern greatly damages effective conflict resolution. The other person is doomed to be perceived by us in terms of that fixed image regardless of the fact she or he may be sincerely demonstrating more positive behavior.

Fixed-image perceptions also entrap the person who won't let go of the fixed image. The trap is a serious one, for it denies that person the dynamic development of a relationship, the richness of experiencing the growth of a relationship partner, and the benefits of the *process* of effective conflict resolution.

What misperceptions might I have of the other party? Many people never ask this vital question when involved in a conflict. They would rather convince themselves that certain negative perceptions they have of the other party are validation for blaming them for the conflict and trying to make them pay. We need to ask this question in all situations of conflict. There may be no misperceptions operating, but it is enormously more effective to try to find out than plunging ahead with false or misleading assumptions.

For some people, simply asking themselves if they might have some misperceptions of the conflict partner is enough to begin the clarification process. For others, it's not so easy. They may need to explore some additional insights, such as all of the questions and suggestions included in this section on clarifying perceptions of the other party. They might also ask themselves, "What am I basing that perception on? Is there a specific act that leads me to that perception? Does that act represent a pattern, or is it inconsistent with their usual behavior?"

What part does their role play in their behavior and in my behavior toward them? Some people deal with conflict well until they encounter people who are in certain roles. Perhaps it will be a general role such as authority figure, or a more specific role such as management, labor, parent, or in-law. Whatever the role might be, if a person allows a particular role to push buttons or obstruct the use of effective skills, that person needlessly disempowers himself or herself in being able to deal with conflict effectively.

We need to reach for the person behind the role. We also need to concentrate on the fact that, regardless of their role, we are in a partnership with the other party in dealing with a conflict. We are important; they are important. We are powerful; they are powerful. Roles don't really deal with conflicts, *people* do. Roles cannot simply be *assumed* to deal with conflict in a way that promotes an improved relationship. Up front, *tell* someone who is operating *only* from within a role, "We are more than just our roles, and I think we have a better chance of resolving this problem if we deal with each other as *people,* too."

What buttons or vulnerabilities do they have, and how can I avoid exploiting them? In my work I frequently encounter people who describe themselves as good negotiators. They often tell me of a book or article they have read on how to win in negotiation. They then go on to say, "I'm good because I know how to exploit the other party's vulnerabilities. I know how to push all of their buttons."

Many traditional approaches to negotiation do indeed promote this pattern. Assumed, temporary victories may be won by using this combination of the conquest and bargaining approaches, but, as the conflict partnership process repeatedly stresses, the relationship has not been improved (and may even be damaged), and no groundwork has been developed to deal with future conflicts effectively. Pushing the other party's buttons or pouring salt in their wounds ultimately creates additional conflicts and eventually destroys relationships.

CLEANING THE MIRRORS AND LENSES OF OUR MINDS

Clarifying perceptions is an essential skill if we are to deal with conflicts effectively. Just as unclear mirrors and windows can distort reality, so it is that unclarified perceptions about the conflict, about ourselves, and about our conflict partners can distort and obstruct the process of conflict resolution. Let's summarize the major points.

Clarifying perceptions of the conflict involves:

- Perceiving clearly that the conflict is but one part of the relationship, and that you need to deal with each conflict in the context of the overall relationship
- Working *with* your conflict partners to make sure that you know what the conflict is really about rather than assuming that only your own preconceived notions or pet gripes constitute the conflict
- Sorting the conflict components to understand whether needs or desires, values or preferences, goals or methods, and so on are involved, and then focusing on the particular components you believe are the most effective starting points in the conflict resolution process
- Understanding that conflicts over values require you to clarify how important a particular value is in the context of the overall relationship, and then realizing that you

and your conflict partner can agree to disagree on some values while building a positive relationship on other aspects of the relationship

Clarifying perceptions of the self involves:

- Honestly looking at yourself, what you really need, what your goals for the conflict and the relationship really are, and what you have done to contribute negatively to the conflict
- Identifying and clarifying any misperceptions the conflict partner may have of you and how your behavior may have contributed to those misperceptions
- Understanding in what ways you need your conflict partner

Clarifying perceptions of the other party involves:

- Avoiding stereotyping
- Trying to understand your conflict partners: what they need, why they are behaving as they are, and what positive potential they have in the midst of the negative aspects we see in their behavior
- Avoiding defining the other party based only on their negative behavior
- Using well the communication skills of listening, sensing, and asking clarifying questions
- Clarifying how much you are allowing roles to play a part in dealing with the conflict
- Recognizing the buttons and vulnerabilities in yourself and your conflict partners, and avoiding using them as weapons

Focus on Individual and Shared Needs

Building on our previous discussions of needs as conditions we perceive we cannot do without—conditions critical to the well-being of people and relationships—we now focus more specifically on the skills involved in the third step of the conflict partnership approach: focus on individual and shared needs. A brief review of several key points covered thus far will get us on our way.

- Needs form one of the essential foundations of relationships. Unless both the needs of the parties in the relationship and the needs of the relationship itself are dealt with effectively, the relationship cannot realize its full potential.
- We often confuse needs with desires. Understanding the difference between the two is an important component of effective conflict resolution.
- In relationships, the *personal* needs perceived by individuals should allow for consideration of the needs of the *relationship*.

• Conflicts often arise when needs are ignored or obstructed, or appear to be incompatible.

With these understandings in mind, we are equipped to take the next step along the conflict partnership pathway to effective conflict resolution. We will concentrate on developing insights and skills pertaining to four sets of needs present in every relationship: personal needs, the partner's needs, relationship needs, and shared needs.

DEALING WITH PERSONAL NEEDS

Many examples of how dealing ineffectively with personal needs can cause conflict and obstruct conflict resolution were provided in Chapter 3. In exploring those examples, we saw that people sometimes have a difficult time understanding their own needs. Several questions you can ask yourself may help in dealing with your personal needs.

1. *Looking at the current conflict, are any of my needs being ignored or obstructed? If those needs were being met, would there still be a conflict?* These questions can help clarify whether the conflict is actually over needs or over some other aspects of the relationship such as goals, values, preferences, misperceptions, and so on.

2. *If I don't get what I say I'm needing, how will I be damaged?* This question can help differentiate between needs and desires.

3. *What do I need to feel positive in this relationship? Are those needs being met? Does the current conflict have anything to do with those relationship needs? Does this particular need help promote the goals I have for the relationship?* These questions get you thinking about the overall relationship, not only the current conflict, and on how a particular need relating to the current conflict fits into the importance of the overall relationship.

4. *Have I made my conflict partner aware of my needs, and*

have I clarified those needs so that they can be understood? Sometimes the other party might not be aware that you are feeling a particular need, or you may have been unclear in expressing that need. People sometimes blame the other party for not responding to a personal need, but really haven't expressed that need.

5. *What can be done specifically to get those needs met?* Some attempts at conflict resolution falter because people offer no specific action that can help meet a particular need. They merely state the need, complain that it isn't being met, and then fail to move forward in a partnership discussion to identify specific steps to meet the need.

6. *Try to picture what your life, or the relationship, will be like during the next week, month, or year if you do not have what you say you are needing.* This imaging process can help clarify how important a particular need is among other needs you may be feeling, and can help sort various needs to identify which should be dealt with first in dealing with the conflict. With these questions in mind, let's look at two specific conflicts to understand how personal needs can be dealt with effectively.

Jake and Judy are middle-level managers in the Office of Development at the same university. Jake is in charge of fund-raising; Judy is in charge of publications. Both supervise a separate staff of ten people, but the projects they work on often require cooperation between the two staffs.

Recently, the fund-raising department has been rushing to meet this year's funding goal. Jake and his staff have become frustrated because Judy's publication department has been unable to have the essential publications ready quickly enough to send to prospective donors. Jake takes his complaints about Judy to the Vice President for Development. Judy hears about the complaints, and becomes angry with Jake for going behind her back and complaining to the boss. The vice president insists that Jake and Judy sit down and work out their problems. Judy will be the one demonstrating an effective use of the conflict partnership skill of focusing on personal needs.

"How do you expect us to meet the funding goal if you don't have those publications ready on time?" Jake says angrily.

"Jake," Judy replies, "I understand your need to have the publications. But I have some needs, too. I need to have more lead time. There is no way my staff can produce the publications with only one week's notice."

"Look, Judy," Jake complains. "This is supposed to be a professional organization. If your workers aren't competent, maybe you should fire some of them."

"Do you think our publications are of high quality?" Judy asks.

"Well, yeah. They're good. But—"

"Then I wonder if the competence of my staff is really what's at issue here," Judy points out. "What did you hear me saying about what I need?"

"You said you wanted more lead time. But that's unrealistic."

"I said I *needed* more lead time, Jake. Sure, I might *want* a lead time of a month, but I *need* at least two weeks. Not even a super-human staff can get by with less. Can we figure out how we can make sure we have at least two weeks?"

"I want those publications ready when we do our mailings!" Jake insists. "That's your job!"

"Jake, I think you and I both like our jobs, right?"

"This is exactly the job I've always wanted," Jake answers.

"I feel the same," Judy agrees. "So you and I are probably going to be in this work relationship for some years to come. I think we need to put our heads and our schedules together to make this the best relationship we possibly can."

Jake is quiet a moment, then sighs. "You're right, of course. I need that as much as you do. But are you sure you need a two-week lead time?"

"I've figured it out carefully, Jake. We need two weeks. Let me show you a list of the time requirements for each step in our process."

Jake studies the lists, looks out the window pensively, then nods his head. "I see what you mean."

"Got any ideas on how we can make this work?" Judy asks.

"Well, maybe we can get our Donor Search Committee to send in the names of prospective donors *twice* a week rather than just on Fridays."

"Great!" Judy exclaims. "And you and I can go over the lists first thing every Monday and make up a date-due chart."

Judy did an excellent job of clarifying her own primary need to Jake. She was careful to make sure that the two-week lead time was actually *needed*, not just wanted. She made sure they both understood the importance of that particular need within their overall work relationship, and she came prepared to discuss specific steps they could take to meet the need.

Mona is a single parent with a sixteen-year-old daughter named Sandy. Mona works long hours each day just to make ends meet for the family. Sandy carries a full academic load at high school, and works at a part-time job on weekends.

Partly because of their busy schedules, Mona and Sandy do not spend a lot of time with each other. Mona feels troubled by this lack of time with Sandy, and interprets the situation as an indication that her daughter has no interest in being with her mother. The relationship begins to experience stress as Mona is short-tempered, depressed, and self-pitying.

Sandy realizes that they have to do something or life will become even more miserable. Let's say that she has read the conflict partnership steps, and decides to focus on the specific skill of dealing with personal needs.

First, she tries to figure out what her own needs are in her relationship with Mona. She decides that she needs her mother to take more of an interest in the school studies and activities that she personally feels are so important. She also needs to do fun things with her mom.

Second, Sandy looks at the various conflicts they have been having, namely their frequent fights over little things such as the music she listens to, the clothes she wears, the friends she talks to on the telephone, and her mother's annoying habit of leaving her hair-curling iron near the bathroom sink. Sandy perceives those conflicts as being symptoms of the larger relationship problem of not spending enough time with each other, and tells herself she will have to check out that perception with Mona.

Third, Sandy tries to figure out if she has clearly expressed her needs to Mona—if Mona is somehow obstructing those needs or just isn't aware of them.

Sandy then asks herself if there are any incompatible needs involved, and thinks not, except for the possible incompatibility between Mona's need to bring home paychecks, and the time that requires, and the need of mother and daughter to spend time together.

After exploring these questions, Sandy now feels ready to talk to Mona. This morning, Sandy asked Mona if they could have a long, heart-to-heart talk after dinner tonight. When the dishes have been washed and put away, the following talk takes place.

"Mom," Sandy opens, "I think we should talk about what each of us feels we are needing in our relationship and which of those needs aren't being met."

Surprised at Sandy's mature way of handling the situation, Mona hesitates, and then replies, "I . . . I think that's a very good idea."

Sandy goes on, "I've been thinking a lot and believe I know what I'm needing. I need to feel you are interested in what I'm doing at school, and I need for us to do more fun things together."

"You think I'm not interested in your life?" Mona says, a little hurt.

"I didn't say that, Mom. But sometimes I feel we're both so busy, and we fight a lot, and then I guess we don't have any energy left to talk about what's going on in our lives."

"I have to work a lot to get money for us, Sandy. You know that."

"Mom, I'm not blaming you. I just wish we could figure out what's really important to us as a family, and then I'm sure we could find a way to make time for those important things. I'm willing if you are."

"Well, of course I am, honey. But I'm not sure how. And when you say I don't care about your school life. . . ."

"Did I say that, Mom?"

"Well," Mona says in that same hurt tone, "you said you need for me to be more interested in you."

"I said I need to feel you are interested in what I do at school. Maybe we can talk about how you could do that in a way I would *feel* it, Mom. Like, maybe you could come watch one of my basketball games sometime. That would help a lot."

"Really?" Mona frowns. "I didn't realize that was important to you. But I work late on some Thursday nights—"

"I really would appreciate it if you would try to save some Thursday nights just for us. After the game, we could go out for ice cream or something," Sandy suggests.

"Hmmm," Mona grins. "That might be fun."

"We have a game this Thursday with our big rivals. Will you come?"

"Well, I guess I could try. No, I'll do better than that. I'll come for sure!" Mona smiles.

"Thanks, Mom. But I know you have some needs, too, things I'm not responding to as well as I could."

"Well, yes, I do," Mona answers. "I need to have more time with you to talk about some decisions we're going to have to make. The main one right now concerns this house. The rent is killing me, and I feel you really don't appreciate that and wouldn't be willing to look for a cheaper place."

We'll leave Sandy and Mona at this point. Already we have seen that Sandy's clarification of her own needs has helped significantly. They will eventually have to deal with how to meet some of Mona's needs, with how important the conflicts over other matters really are, and how they can deal with their work schedules to allow more time together. But they are well on their way to improving their relationship. If they do move to a less expensive house, it may mean Sandy can work fewer hours at her part-time job and thus leave more time on weekends for the two to do things together. Dealing with the personal needs and the relationship needs provided a foundation on which the two can now deal with their conflicts and take specific steps to build a more mutually beneficial relationship.

DEALING WITH THE CONFLICT PARTNER'S NEEDS

If we are to develop meaningful relationships and deal with conflicts effectively, we must focus on the needs of the people who share in the relationship and the conflict with us. These people, of course, are our conflict partners. We must be just as concerned about their needs as we are our own. Some of *their* needs must be met, too, if the conflict is to be resolved effectively and the relationship improved.

As we discussed under the heading Dealing with Needs, people sometimes have a difficult time identifying and acting on their *own* needs. To understand and respond to another person's needs can often prove even more difficult. In conflict partnership, the partners share in the task of identifying, clarifying, and acting upon both their own needs and the needs of their partner. They try to help each other make sure that the needs of all concerned are understood so that specific action can be taken to address those needs.

Even without realizing we are doing it, we often convince ourselves we know what others need. Frequently, our assumptions are based on what we *want* the other party to be or to have so that either they will meet *our* expectations or we will feel at an advantage in the relationship. That unhealthy pattern is, in effect, replacing their actual needs with our own self-serving desires.

Rather than assuming you know what they need or what they should need, ask your conflict partner two essential questions:

- What do you need our relationship to provide?
- What do you need as an outcome of our dealing with this conflict that will make you feel strengthened (or more enriched) as a person and that will help you feel our relationship has been improved?

Asking these two questions does several important things. First, you are helping both you and your partners focus not just on the conflict at hand, but on the overall relationship, of which the particular conflict is but one part. Second, you are letting your partners know that you are sincerely interested in *their* needs, not just your own. Third, you are helping your partners focus on conflict resolution outcomes that will strengthen or enrich your partners as individuals, not just satisfy some of their desires or wants. Some desires might not really strengthen or enrich a person. It is important to note that the questions mentioned above are not phrased as What do you want?, but as What do you *need*? Fourth, you are creating an atmosphere in which the improvement of the relationship is a priority.

In addition to these two crucial questions we should ask our conflict partners, there are several questions we can ask *ourselves* to help us focus clearly and responsibly on the needs of our relationship and on the needs of our conflict partners and the relationships we have with them.

If I were in their place, what would I need in this relationship or in resolving this conflict? Asking this question helps us emphathize with our conflict partners. Trying to understand the place they are in builds on the conflict partnership skill of clarifying perceptions of the partners, and goes one step farther by imagining what we would need if we were in their place.

If they secure this particular need, even if I have perceived it as being something I feel is unimportant or even somewhat negative to me, will I really be damaged? Asking this question helps us get away from the misleading and unhealthy patterns of both conquest and bargaining—patterns that perceive conflict resolution as a battle to determine who comes out ahead or who is conceding more than the other. Just because the conflict partner gets some needs met does not mean that she or he is gaining some sort of advantage over you, or that you are somehow weakened. On the contrary, the relationship will be strengthened if both partners feel some critical needs are being met by the relationship and by the conflict resolution process.

Will their getting this particular need I perceive them as having promote their positive power, and thus the health of our relationship? This question helps you focus on the positive potential and power of the conflict partner and the relationship, not just on the negative potential and power that situations of conflict so often tempt us to accentuate. In my experience, a particular need that Party A has may appear to be threatening to Party B until Party B realizes that if Party A gets that need met, the positive potential of both Party A and the relationship will be enhanced. Party B then realizes that both parties are better off, as is the relationship.

To demonstrate how the conflict partnership skill of dealing with the conflict partner's needs works, let's look at a conflict involving Holly and Erika, two employees at Durel

Industries who, until a month ago, were also close personal friends.

The event that seemed most responsible for the cooling off of their relationship was Holly's promotion to a higher position at Durel, a position Erika had also sought actively for a long time. The promotion meant that Holly became Erika's immediate supervisor. Erika let the bitterness and disappointment of having "lost out to Holly" (as Erika put it) negatively affect both her work and her personal and work relationship with Holly. To make matters worse, Erika had been dating Carl, another Durel employee, until Carl met Holly. Erika's ego suffered another blow when Carl told her he had fallen in love with Holly.

We will eavesdrop on a conversation at Holly's apartment after she finally convinced Erika to come over for dinner. Their weekly dinners together had been a treat for a year-and-a-half, but Erika had abruptly broken the pattern when both Holly's promotion and Carl's attention to Holly shattered the happy friendship. As Holly and Erika talk, Holly makes use of the "partner's needs" skill, and other conflict partnership skills.

"Erika," Holly begins, "your friendship means too much to me to just let it wither away like it's been doing."

"I've just been preoccupied with other things," Erika replies, falling into the avoidance pattern.

"But you seem so . . . so angry with me. Are you?" Holly asks.

"I'm not angry!" Erika says angrily. "Why would I be angry?"

"That's what I'd like to understand. Would you help me understand?"

"Nothing's wrong," Erika says, still avoiding the issues. "I haven't come to dinner lately because I just . . . want to expand my circle of friends."

"I can understand that," Holly says sincerely. "But I get the feeling that's not all that's going on here."

Erika remains silent.

"What do you feel you need out of our relationship, Erika?" Holly asks.

"What do I *need*?" Erika frowns. "I . . . I don't know. I don't *need* anything." Erika pauses, then says, "I just want things to be like they used to be, that's all."

"In what ways?" Holly asks.

"You know, like they used to be," Erika answers, obviously frustrated.

"Do you mean having weekly dinners? And going to movies? Having the really good talks we used to have? Things like that?"

"I don't know," Erika sighs. "It's just . . . different now."

"Does it have to be different now?" Holly asks. "What's suddenly made everything so different?"

Erika fidgets with her hands, then glares at Holly. "If you don't know, then you're not as smart as everyone thinks! You're the supervisor now! You're supposed to be the smart one!"

Holly holds Erika's eyes and says, "I don't think we have to let the decisions other people make at the office get in the way of our friendship. You could be just as good a supervisor as I hope I will be, but for some reason Durel decided I would be the one to be put in this particular position. I hope you get the next promotion, because you deserve it. But that's office stuff, Erika. What does that have to do with our friendship?"

Erika stares at the floor thinking, then sighs heavily. "It's just that I really wanted that promotion. I've worked hard for it. But you're right. That shouldn't have anything to do with our friendship. You asked me what I need in our relationship. I need to know that you're there for me when I get depressed and have disappointments. I need to be able to talk, and to have some fun together. You're the closest thing to a sister I have."

"I feel the same way. I need those things, too, Erika. Do you think I haven't been there for you this past month? If I haven't, I need for you to help me understand what I could have done better."

"You tried, Holly," Erika says gently. "Maybe it's not the promotion. I know those things happen, I know it's not your fault. Maybe it's just that a lot of bad stuff happened at the same time, and I just couldn't . . . you know."

"Are you talking about Carl?" Holly asks.

Erika almost tries to avoid the painful subject of Carl, but because Holly has created an atmosphere in which she is obviously concerned about Erika's needs, Erika feels more comfortable in going ahead and dealing with the subject she knows has to be discussed eventually.

"Yes," Erika finally says. "It really bothered me that Carl dropped me for you. I feel like you just let it happen without talking to me. You're talking about needs; well, I needed you to let me know you and Carl were becoming close. I mean, sure, I knew Carl and I weren't really best for each other, and we weren't seeing each other much anymore, but then you and Carl started dating, and it just seemed you were stabbing me in the back."

"I didn't mean for that to hurt you. I thought everything was over between you two. We never talked about his problems much . . . ever. Maybe I was insensitive to your feelings, Erika, and I really regret it if I was. What did you need for me to do? If we can figure that out, then maybe we won't let things get out of hand in the future."

Erika replies with feeling, "I needed you to come to me and say, 'Carl and I are beginning to develop a close relationship and I want to make sure everything is over between you two.' Something like that."

"I think you're right," Holly admits. "That would have been a good thing to do. Best friends need to do that sort of thing. I'm sorry I just assumed things were okay."

"Let's not ever just assume we know what the other

person's needs are, okay?" Erika says earnestly. "If the situation had been reversed and Carl had ended with you and become close to me, maybe *you* wouldn't need me to go to you and ask if you and Carl were finished, but *I* need that kind of friendship, Holly. I really do."

Holly created a very positive partnership atmosphere and continued to build on that atmosphere. She clarified her perceptions of what Erika needed, both in the friendship and in the particular conflict involving Carl. She also helped Erika clarify her own perceptions of what the conflict was really about, that it was not the promotion as much as it was Holly's failure to realize that Erika needed Holly to come and talk when Carl was becoming important in Holly's life. By employing the conflict partnership skills discussed thus far, and especially by focusing on what Erika needed in the relationship and what she needed in the situation with Carl, Holly was able to work with Erika to deal with their conflicts effectively and to clarify and strengthen the relationship.

DEALING WITH THE NEEDS OF
THE RELATIONSHIP

Many of the skills involved in dealing with the needs of the relationship have already been discussed and demonstrated. The important points to remember follow.

While focusing on the needs of the self and of the conflict partner in specific situations of conflict, we must also diligently pay attention to the needs of the overall relationship. As we saw with Holly and Erika, Erika was focusing primarily on what she needed and wanted in the promotion situation and in the Carl situation. She wanted the promotion, and she wanted, and needed, not to feel dropped by Carl so that he could start a relationship with her best friend. By focusing on the needs of the Holly-Erika *personal* relationship (and by using other skills we have discussed), Holly was able to invite Erika into the conflict partnership process so that together they could identify ways in which they might improve their relationship. In a very real sense, the particular conflicts were dealt with effectively by dealing with the needs of the relationship.

Sometimes particular personal wants (or even needs) one of the parties in conflict is feeling may not seem as critical as she or he first assumes when the needs of the overall relationship are considered. In other words, some wants or perceived needs may be personally gratifying in certain situations, but may not really strengthen the relationship for the future.

For example, in one case I encountered, a boss felt a need to have her administrative assistant get to work thirty minutes early each day to prepare an agenda for the boss's meetings and tasks for that day. The assistant had to travel a long distance in rush-hour traffic to get to work, and with travel time and responsibilities at home, the assistant found it very difficult to get to the office thirty minutes early. When the assistant repeatedly arrived at work at the regular starting time of 9:00 A.M., instead of 8:30 A.M., a conflict emerged.

The personal wants or perceived needs of the boss in this particular situation hampered the overall relationship, as the assistant felt unfairly burdened by the weight of unrealistic expectations. Some of the needs of the overall work *relationship* included (1) a mutually respectful atmosphere, (2) a well-planned agenda for each day, and (3) enough quality time to plan the daily agendas. The way the boss was handling the daily agenda need was considering only her own convenience and desires at the expense of the relationship needs. By focusing on the relationship needs, the two people could have devised a better process; namely, a regular fifteen-minute meeting at 9:00 each day to set the agenda together.

Sometimes there are situations in which some lesser personal needs may have to be toned down or postponed because they may harm the overall relationship. Although this realization is sometimes quite difficult to accept, it is an important one in effective conflict resolution. A recent labor-management conflict I was asked to help facilitate serves as an example.

Using the traditional bargaining approach, the labor representatives and the management representatives each came to the negotiating table with about nine demands. Each group felt they deserved their respective demands. Two weeks of impasse resulted. I was called in at that point, and I met with each group separately and asked them to focus not on the demands they had made but on several questions, two of which were: What are the things you need most? and What do you think the workplace relationship needs so that you can avoid the recurring battles you have been having over the years?

The result of dealing with the first question produced a list of six primary needs labor felt they had to have, and five primary needs management felt they had to have. I suggested that they try to perceive and refer to these items as needs, not demands. After then going through their lists and asking them the question, If you don't get this particular item, will you be greatly hampered?, the lists were reduced to four needs labor felt were essential, and three needs management felt were essential.

Dealing with the second question proved difficult at first, primarily because they had never been asked the question. Once they got into the process, however, each group identified some relationship needs. The two lists were very similar. I then asked them to discuss if any of the individual needs they had listed earlier might obstruct some of the relationship needs they had just identified. To their surprise, labor found that two of their personal needs did seem to obstruct the relationship needs, and management found one of their personal needs that seemed to obstruct the relationship needs.

The next step was to get the parties together again now that they were beginning to use conflict partnership. I asked them to share their respective lists of the relationship needs, and when they saw how similar they were, one of the labor representatives said to management, "This is really encouraging. We had no idea you saw these things as being important." One of the management representatives replied, "There's no way either of us could have realized these common goals by looking at the demands we've both been throwing at each other. Maybe we should take these *relationship* needs and try to build some agreements on them, not the demands."

For the next two hours I sat and watched the two groups work cooperatively. As the third-party facilitator, I wasn't needed except to intervene occasionally to make sure perceptions of what was being said and proposed were clarified. By the end of the day, focusing on the importance of building a relationship that would provide labor and management with a better way of dealing with future differences produced agreements that met the primary needs of each party. Several of the other perceived "must have" needs were no longer conflict-producing because both groups realized those items would obstruct the more important relationship needs and could be dealt with later.

DEALING WITH SHARED NEEDS

We now come to perhaps the most critical single component of the conflict partnership process: shared needs. Picture a relationship as a weaving composed of many threads. In that weaving the threads must entwine to provide the strength and durability to keep the weaving from unraveling. In a relationship, those places of connection, those places of strength and durability are shared needs.

Shared needs are the connecting points holding together a relationship, the essential points forming a weaving strong enough to allow the uniqueness of each partner to contribute value. Each partner has individual needs, but the partners also have needs they share. It is based on those shared needs that we begin the journey along a pathway to true partnership.

What Is a Shared Need?

There are several ways to recognize, develop, and build upon shared needs, as the following examples illustrate.

You will remember that I asked several questions of the labor and management representatives in the example discussed earlier. As you saw, I asked them about their primary individual needs, and then about relationship needs. But I also asked them what needs they shared. At first they resisted acknowledging that they shared *any* needs with the other party. But when I phrased the question as, "At what points do you think your needs and their needs intersect; *how do you need each other in order for you and your relationship to be strengthened and improved?*", they were able to identify some shared needs.

They shared the need for workplace harmony and efficiency, and the need to avoid protracted labor/management disputes. They shared the need for individual respect and dignity. They shared the need for clearly defined and realistic expectations, policies, and production plans. They shared the need for better communication on differences of opinion before those differences were allowed to get to the conflictual stage they had reached so many times. Building on these shared relationship needs, the two parties were able to move forward effectively.

In families, shared needs abound, yet often only personal needs are voiced and accentuated. The parents may argue vociferously and perpetually about disagreements each feels are major. Their children see the battles, take the same combative attitudes into their friendships, and then the parents wonder why their children get into fights or have to be reprimanded at school. Life at home is tense, frustrating, and unhappy.

All of the members of the family have a major shared need: for the parents to be positive role models for their children. By focusing on that *shared* need as a major priority, the parents might be able to see that some of their personal disagreements pale in comparison. They may still disagree with each other on many matters, but the shared need of carrying their parenting responsibilities well can be the impetus to trying to improve their own relationship, whether it means attending a conflict resolution workshop, seeing a counselor, joining a parental support group, or learning and practicing less violent ways of dealing with their conflicts.

Going back to Holly and Erika, we see several shared needs operating. Both Holly and Erika needed to have Erika return to the excellent workplace performance she exhibited consistently before the promotion occurred and Carl began dating Holly. Even though they may have had different reasons for the shared need (Holly because, as supervisor, she needed Erika's fine work as part of the team, and Erika because she needed to keep her job), they still *shared* that need.

Holly and Erika also shared the need to restore the positive qualities to their very meaningful relationship, and a need for better communication and for understanding what had happened in the Carl situation. Perhaps most important of all, they had a shared need to clarify and affirm the difference between their workplace relationship and their personal relationship. If they continued to allow every negative event at work to damage their friendship, it would soon be in serious trouble.

Needs: Building Blocks for Effective Conflict Resolution

Needs are the foundation of existence and the building blocks of effective conflict resolution. Many people and groups locked in conflict focus their energy on making demands they want the other party to meet, or on assumptions they make about the other party, or on the perceived desires and interests incorrectly assumed to be the heart and soul of oneself and of the other party.

Only when the energy of conflict resolution focuses on the four sets of needs operating in every relationship—personal needs, the partner's needs, relationship needs, and the critical area of shared needs—will the conflict resolution process be effective and the relationship improved.

Build Shared Positive Power

Every relationship involves power. Because people, groups, and societies so often limit the way they perceive and use power—as a means of controlling or manipulating someone else—*power* is frequently seen as a dirty word. The adage power corrupts shows just how negatively power is often perceived.

But power in and of itself does not corrupt. *People choose* how they use power and whether they allow it to corrupt. We can use power negatively or positively. Conflict partnership employs positive power to deal with conflicts effectively and to improve relationships, and thus is not a passive escape from confrontation that simply urges parties in conflict to be nice to each other. Rather, conflict partnership is an active, creative, persevering, *powerful* process.

But what is power, this word, this concept we use so frequently to mean so many different things? The dictionary gives several definitions, including, "the ability or capacity to exercise control"; "authority"; "strength or force capable of being exerted"; "might." As dictionaries often do, these definitions seem to focus on the most frequently used and applied perceptions of power, perceptions that accentuate some sort of control over other people or groups.

I would like to suggest a different definition of power. *Power consists of the attitudes, perceptions, beliefs, and behaviors that give people and groups the ability to act or perform effectively.*

We do indeed have a choice as to the type of power we use and the type of effectiveness we want to promote. We can adopt and act on attitudes, perceptions, beliefs, and behaviors that produce either negative or positive results. Thus, the type of power we use greatly influences the quality of relationships and the lasting effectiveness of conflict resolution.

In discussing power, we will focus first on the differences between what I term negative power and positive power. We will then explore the three sets of power operating in all relationships and conflicts: self power, the partner's power, and shared power. Throughout these discussions, the major task will be to discover how the conflict partnership process uses the positive power of one's self, of the partner, and of the vital component I term *shared power*. First, a discussion of negative power.

NEGATIVE POWER

Negative power has four major characteristics. First, it attempts to disempower the other party in an attempt to increase one's own advantage. Second, it focuses on specific attempts to gain advantage over the other party and ignores or deemphasizes the negative effects those specific attempts have on the overall relationship. Third, it focuses on a "power over" rather than a "power with" relationship. Fourth, it uses what I call seesaw power.

Seesaw power is one of the most damaging aspects of negative power. In the playground game of seesaw, when one person is up, the other is down. If the person who is down wants to go up, the other person must somehow be made to go down. When people use seesaw power in relationships, it means that one party believes their power is in part derived from making the other party weak or at least lessening its power. In other words, my power is in part dependent on how much power you have.

As will be discussed throughout the remainder of this chapter, the conflict partnership process focuses on the value and importance of *both* partners having positive power, not on trying to weaken the other party. But for now, let's look at two examples of how negative power operates.

Bev works as the administrative assistant to the dean of a department at a university. She is the glue that holds the department together. Frank, one of the professors, has been managing a grant for the current year, and has done a poor job of keeping the budget straight. The dean asks Bev to compose and write a letter to Frank telling him of his budgetary mismanagement and cautioning him that he will have the grant taken away if he does not get the budget in order. Bev writes as nice a letter as possible, tells Frank the dean asked her to write it, and invites Frank to talk to her if he wants to discuss the matter.

Frank is incensed that a mere administrative assistant would write a reprimand letter to a professor. He goes to the dean and criticizes Bev severely. The dean defends Bev and tells Frank to straighten out the budget.

Frank then turns his negative power on Bev. He belittles her in front of other professors and her own staff, calling her a radical feminist for having supported the affirmative hiring of female professors, and begins dumping an impossible amount of work on Bev's desk, knowing that no one could complete it all and thus causing Bev to miss some deadlines and be vulnerable to his criticisms of incompetence.

Frank was foolishly attempting to gain some sort of advantage over Bev by making her appear weak. As often happens when negative power is used, Frank's approach backfired. It created enormous tension in the office and inspired all of the other professors to come to Bev's defense. Frank actually *lost* power and respect in the department rather than gaining power.

POSITIVE POWER

Let's take the previous scenario and show how Frank would have behaved if he had been using positive power. After going through the scenario, we will then discuss specifically some of the characteristics of positive power. Frank, upon receiving the letter, goes to talk to Bev, using the positive power of the conflict partnership approach.

"Bev? May I have a minute?" Frank asks.

Bev is extremely busy, juggling ringing phones, typing, and trying to resuscitate Frank's wounded budget. "Uh . . . can you give me about fifteen minutes to get a couple of things finished?" Bev asks.

"Sure," Frank responds. "Give me a ring when you're ready and maybe we can go into the lounge."

In twenty minutes Frank and Bev are in the lounge. Frank says, "I got your letter about the grant budget. I'm surprised the dean had you write it for him."

"Me, too," Bev answers. "I think he was on his way to catch a plane."

"Well," Frank continues, "the letter bothered me, but I'm not sure why. At first I was upset that it came from you and not the dean. Does that make sense to you?"

"Well, I'm not sure," Bev replies. "You mean because I'm an administrative assistant and you're a professor?"

"Maybe that's part of it," Frank says, trying to understand his own reasons. "But I guess you couldn't just tell the dean you wouldn't write it."

"Was the letter clear enough?" Bev asks.

"Oh yes," Frank chuckles. "It was painfully clear. I hadn't realized the budget was in such bad shape, if it really is that bad. I don't want to lose the grant, so I think I need the two of us to go over parts of it more carefully to see how bad it really is. When would you have some time?"

"Gee, I don't know," Bev shakes her head. "This is a hectic week."

"Well," Frank suggests, "maybe I could get the dean to pay you time-and-a-half overtime if you could stay an extra hour tomorrow evening after work, or some other day this week."

The new Frank is demonstrating positive power. He is not trying to tear Bev down in an attempt to make himself appear more powerful; he is trying to nurture the positive power in himself and in Bev. The old Frank's use of negative power created a horrible relationship with Bev and numerous other conflicts. The new Frank's use of positive power results in a mutually beneficial relationship with Bev and a healthy outcome to what could have been a messy conflict.

Let's now look more specifically at what constitutes positive power.

Fundamental Components of Positive Power

Positive power seeks to promote the constructive capabilities of all parties involved in a conflict. Both Frank and Bev helped energize the other's positive capabilities.

Positive power energizes a "power with" process rather than a "power over" pattern. Frank and Bev ended up working together, both using their positive power.

Positive power avoids seesaw power, the misguided perception that weakening the conflict partner will somehow strengthen one's own power. When the old Frank tried to weaken and belittle Bev, he did not really gain anything. Using the seesaw pattern almost always brings out the negative power in the other party, obstructs an effective and lasting resolution of the conflict, and ends up weakening the positive power of all parties. When Frank employed positive power—when he helped nurture the positive power in Bev— he was able to deal effectively with the problem.

When people are using positive power, they work to help their relationship or conflict partners become positively powerful, too. Successful relationships and effective conflict resolution require that all parties involved be positively powerful. The parties need each other to be working powerfully and positively if the conflict is to be resolved and the relationship improved.

Now that we have identified what positive power is, and how important it is to the conflict partnership process, we need to understand how positive power operates in the three sets of power inherent in all relationships and conflicts: self power, the partner's power, and shared power.

DEVELOPING POSITIVE SELF POWER

Positive self power reflects internal strength and an internal harmony among the various components of the self. Of the many components of positive self power, the following are among the most important in dealing with conflict.

Positive self power involves having a clear self-image. Positive self power involves being clear and honest with ourselves. As we discussed under the heading Clarifying Perceptions of the Self, many conflicts are caused or escalate because of unclarified self-perceptions.

Developing positive self power through a clear self-image means that we base our perceptions of ourselves not on what others expect of us or want us to be, but on what we believe to be our own needs, capabilities, priorities, and goals. Earlier, we saw that Jon Smythe was not developing his own self power because he was allowing the image and expectations others had of him as Clarence and Marian Smythe's son to determine how he saw himself and how he acted.

Developing positive self power through a clear self-image also means that we base our perceptions of ourselves not just on how we are treated by others, but on how we believe we and others should be treated. This component of self power can be complex. Let's go back to Bev and Frank to help clarify.

When Frank was using negative power on Bev, she could have easily felt so intimidated by Frank's dominant position as professor that she might have actually started believing she was a pushy and incompetent person. She might also have seen herself primarily as a victim, and might have expended a lot of energy in complaining and letting her victimization hamper her work. However, if Bev is to develop her self power, she needs to focus on what she believes to be the most effective relationship a professor and an administrative assistant should have, and then work to make that effective relationship become a reality. In her own behavior, she can model that type of relationship and, quite likely, help Frank see the merits of such a relationship.

Positive self power involves having a clear understanding of our values and a consistency between our values and our behavior. Self power involves having a clear understanding of our values and then living those values in our daily lives. When people aren't clear about what their values are, or when they say they believe something and then violate that belief in their behavior, their relationship partners become confused and lose respect for them.

Positive self power involves being in charge of yourself. This is one of the most important components of self power in situations of conflict. When you allow the negative behavior of your conflict partner to determine your own behavior, you are not in charge of yourself. A brief scenario will help demonstrate this critical self-empowerment skill.

Sue and Ann are co-directors of a project aimed at cleaning up a toxic waste site in their community. Sue wants to initiate legal action against the company dumping the waste; Ann wants to avoid offending the company because it provides a lot of jobs for people in the community, including her brother. We will look at two conversations between Sue and Ann, the first showing how Sue is not in charge of herself and how she lets Ann's negative behavior determine her own, and the second showing how Sue *is* in charge of herself and therefore showing self power.

"You're just too combative, Sue," Ann says. "You're just wanting to prove you're some kind of radical at the expense of the community!"

One of Sue's buttons is usually activated when people yell at her or call her names. She feels her blood beginning to boil, and says, "And *you* are just caving in to the corporation! This toxic waste is serious, Ann!"

"The *jobs*, Sue!" Ann yells. "Think about all the jobs! Just because *you* don't have any family members working for the company doesn't mean—"

Sue has always prided herself on caring about the community, and when she is accused of not caring just because she doesn't have a family member working at the company, she loses it. "How dare you! I thought you were my friend! I think I'll just bring a lawsuit on my own!"

Sue allowed Ann's negative power approach to determine her own behavior. She gave up her own self power and let Ann take charge of her behavior. Now let's see how Sue could have used positive self power by being in charge of herself.

"You're just too combative, Sue," Ann says. "You're just trying to prove you're a radical at the expense of the community!"

"That's not what I'm doing, Ann," Sue replies. "You and I *both* care about this community. I think we both share the goal of getting this toxic waste cleaned up, right?"

"Well . . . yes. But your methods are counterproductive!" Ann says, still angry. "The jobs, Sue! Think about all the lost jobs if you get the company mad at us! The company might move, and it would be *your* fault!"

"I care about the jobs, too. I think we can figure out a way to get the waste cleaned up without jeopardizing jobs. I think a lawsuit will help, but let's discuss some other options, too. Got any ideas?"

Ann wants to stay angry, but Sue is reaching for Ann's positive power, and Ann begins to realize the conflict might be resolved effectively if she, too, tries some positive power. "Well," Ann says, "maybe there are other options. I just don't want us to jump into a lawsuit." (Notice how Ann used the "we" instead of the I-versus-you of the previous scenario. Sue's use of conflict partnership invited Ann to use it, too.)

"Maybe we could set up some meetings with the company," Sue suggests. "If they see we are united as a community group, maybe they will realize their need to maintain good community relations and respond to our needs. Could your brother help arrange the talks?"

"Hmmm. That's a possibility," Ann responds, now using her positive power to work with Sue's positive power.

By staying in charge of herself and using positive self power even in the face of Ann's negative power, Sue was able to bring out the partnership potential in Ann.

Positive self power involves learning and applying effective relationship and conflict resolution skills. People have self power when they develop and use effective skills. Instead of assuming that all we have to do in dealing with a conflict is to let our emotions take over, or treat the other party negatively when they treat us negatively, we should persevere in actively using the conflict partnership skills. As Sue demonstrated, positive self power stands a very good chance of inviting conflict partners to get involved in the conflict partnership process as they see its effectiveness in meeting some shared needs and in energizing their own positive power.

THE POSITIVE POWER OF THE CONFLICT PARTNER

A second type of power operating in every relationship and every conflict is the partner's power. In the example in which Frank and Sue were using positive power, we saw how they not only used positive self power but helped energize the positive power of their partner.

Several important points need to be emphasized in regard to how we can affirm and help activate the positive power of our conflict partners.

Keep reaching for the partner's positive potential and power. In situations of conflict people often tend to focus on the negative aspects and power of the other party. Whatever the other party did to contribute to the conflict tends to get the most attention. There is a strong temptation to forget that those people also have positive potential and have probably made some positive contributions to the relationship.

Sue kept reaching for Ann's positive power, and she eventually energized it. She affirmed Ann's concern for the community, she affirmed the goal they shared of cleaning up the waste, she asked for Ann's constructive suggestions, and she avoided focusing on Ann's negative power and behavior even though Ann was displaying it repeatedly.

Keep reaching for the partner's positive power. You might not always find it, but chances are good you will eventually. If you don't reach for it, if you accept the negative power as the only potential he or she has, you can be sure you won't see any positive power in the partner's behavior.

Don't define the other party only by their negative power and behavior. This important skill in helping activate the partner's positive power has already been mentioned. It is a logical extension of the first point, and deserves emphasis. If the other party uses negative power to deal with the conflict, as Frank and Ann did in the first conversations we viewed, it is quite tempting to define the other party according to that negative power and behavior. They can become convenient stereotypes for the "box" mentality, which categorizes people as roles (e.g., irrational person, bully, enemy, or sole culprit in the conflict). Once they are labeled and defined, it is easy to justify treating them with negative power.

Conflict partnership provides skills and a process through which we can avoid defining people only by their negative power and behavior. Conflict resolution works best when the positive power of all parties is sought, developed, and activated. Seeing people as having potential only for the negative behavior they may be expressing can destroy effective conflict resolution.

Realize and act on the principle that you need the other party to be positively powerful and to use that positive power. The severely damaging seesaw power approach creates the illusion that you are more powerful when you can make the other party less powerful. Conflict partnership says loud and clear that such thinking is grossly misleading and harmful, that you need the other party to be powerful in a positive-power context.

Staying with the examples used in this chapter, it is apparent that Frank needs Bev to possess and use positive power if their conflict is to be dealt with effectively and their relationship improved. Frank also needs to straighten out the grant budget. Bev works closely with the budget, and therefore also needs it to be straightened out. The two definitely have a shared need. If they are unable to resolve their conflict over the letter Bev wrote Frank, or if Bev is so upset and angry she cannot or will not contribute her positive power to the relationship and to the budget, Frank is in deep trouble.

Thus, Frank's needs, Bev's needs, their shared needs, and the needs of the relationship may all hinge on whether or not they use positive power. If Frank wants the conflict resolved, he needs Bev's positive power and his own positive power. *He* should keep reaching for Bev's positive power, *she* should avoid defining him only on his negative outbursts and try to reach for *his* positive power, and they should both realize and act on the fact that they need each other as positively powerful partners in dealing with their relationship and their conflicts.

Help create a process that leaves options open for the partner to make use of positive power. Sue did a good job of employing this skill once she adopted the conflict partnership approach. She remained in charge of herself and used her own positive power to clarify their shared goal, to affirm Ann's commitment to the community, *and* to ask Ann questions that encouraged her to shift from her negative-power approach to one of positive power and partnership.

SHARED POSITIVE POWER

Shared *needs* can be referred to as critical building blocks on which conflict partnership constructs its process, but it is shared *positive power* that actually constructs the process and moves it toward effective conflict resolution. With positive self power and the positive power of the partner actively working, the remaining link in the interconnected process of positive power is formed when the conflict partners combine their power. This shared positive power, "our" power, is stronger than the individual power of each of the partners.

Frank and Bev developed shared positive power when they realized they needed each other and then combined their power to fix the ailing budget. Neither of them could have accomplished the task or resolved the conflict just by using their respective individual power.

Sue and Ann were getting nowhere until Sue kept persevering in her effort to help Ann make use of her positive power. The next step came when they used their shared positive power and worked together toward an effective resolution of their conflict.

Shared positive power employs all of the conflict partnership skills discussed thus far. Shared positive power flows from a partnership atmosphere; from clarified perceptions of the self, the partner, the conflict, and the relationship; from the recognition of individual and shared needs; and from the individual positive power of each of the partners. Shared positive power is the energy that makes a relationship effective and conflict resolution successful and lasting. Shared positive power also accomplishes the remaining steps in the conflict partnership process. It is to the fifth step, looking to the future and learning from the past, that we now turn.

Look to the Future,
Then Learn from
the Past

E very relationship and every conflict has a past, present,
and future, and resolving conflicts effectively requires
that we deal with all three. The conflict partnership process
encourages us to use positive power to focus on what I call
the present-future, and to learn from the past.

The past provides an experiential landscape for the present
and the future, but the past is *not* the soil in which the present
and future are irrevocably rooted. The present brings past
memories onto new ground and tills that fresh soil with improved tools, always mindful that the future will reap what
the present has sown. The present and the future are insepara-
ble, and the future develops in the womb of the present. They
are all linked: past, present, and future. Blending the three
into a dynamic reach for improvement is the essence of being.

We will begin by dealing with how the past can impede
conflict resolution. Then we will explore how we can learn
from the past. Finally, we will look at the present-future and
explore how focusing on this time frame helps us to deal with
present conflicts and improve the future relationship.

HOW THE PAST CAN IMPEDE
CONFLICT RESOLUTION

Here are a few of the more prevalent ways we allow the past to impede effective conflict resolution.

People sometimes allow the past to hold present and future possibilities prisoner by thinking that because they did not deal well with a conflict in the past, they cannot deal effectively with a current conflict. In this pattern, people think that because they were unable to deal with problems in the past, or because they have in the past defined their relationship as a struggle for dominance and advantage over the other party, it is futile to believe that they can ever act differently or even try to apply improved relationship and conflict resolution skills.

This negative use of the past is, in effect, a self-deprecating and self-*dis*empowering pattern. It implies that people are incapable of growing and improving. Of course, those who use this pattern usually say it is the *other* party who is incapable of improving, but such a stance hinders the development of positive power and positive influence in both parties. However, when one party moves beyond this negative use of the past and takes the lead in demonstrating improved relationship and conflict resolution behavior, the other party usually begins to feel more hopeful that improved behavior *can* be implemented.

People sometimes see only the past negative behavior of their conflict partner, refusing to see the positive potential, even if their partner's present behavior is encouraging. This particular pattern seems to be one of our favorite ways of using the past to obstruct both the improvement of relationships and the actualization of the positive potential of conflict resolution. Examples abound. Perpetually harping on one or two incidents of a conflict partner's especially negative behavior in the past when dealing with a current conflict, regardless of her or his stated willingness to avoid repeating that behavior, is one example. Another is evident when people and groups are perpetually held accountable for past mistakes or inadequacies, even though they have tried to make amends and have not repeated those mistakes.

Another example involves perceiving people as they were at a past age and never allowing them the possibility and right to grow up, to change and improve. Sons and daughters who have reached maturity but are still seen by a parent as "my little boy or girl" in need of protection are being perceived as the role they once were, not as the human beings they now are and can be.

People sometimes blame themselves for what they were or did at some time in the past and continue to punish their own lives and their relationships in a subconscious attempt at penance. Perhaps no misuse of the past is more agonizing and complex than allowing a past mistake to cover with guilt and shame one's own self-image in the present and future. People involved in such a pattern often become obsessed with a past mistake and ignore how they can improve in the present. They may even strike out at any person or event that reminds them of that past mistake.

People sometimes are unwilling to let go of a particular demand or behavior they expressed in the past, even though that demand or behavior is no longer relevant or helpful in the present. I'm sure we have all heard people say, "I've done things that way all my life and I'm not going to change now!", or, "If I go back on that demand now, it will make me look weak." There are usually several hidden reasons underlying this use of the past to justify a continuation of damaging or ineffective behavior in the present.

One of these reasons is that people do not want to admit that a past behavior pattern or demand was damaging or ineffective. They see that as an admission of failure. Another is that some people feel they have little insight or confidence in designing alternatives to ineffective or harmful patterns. Still another is that certain narrow, vested self-interests are *perceived* as being served by a continuation of the past behavior or demands. Finally, people sometimes hold onto old behavior patterns or demands because they fear the unknown of trying new patterns or making effective, shared-need, positive-power proposals rather than demands.

Impeding conflict resolution by holding onto past patterns is evident, for example, when a parent invests a great deal of energy and money in a daughter's education toward becoming a doctor or teacher and then cannot accept the daughter's decision that teaching or medicine is not the most fulfilling profession for her. The parent stubbornly tries to force her not to change directions, or charges the daughter with being a failure.

Another example is a business that, for twenty years, has kept a particular organizational pattern, and now, when that policy is proving unpopular and counterproductive among the work force, refuses to change because that is the way they have always done things or because it would take too much time and expense to change.

People assume that because something has always been done a certain way, it somehow means it's the best way. This obstructing use of the past might be called the wisdom-of-the-ages syndrome. Just because a particular behavior pattern, or business policy, or family habit has been around for some time does not automatically mean it is best. It may have been appropriate for the past, but is it appropriate for today and tomorrow?

Involved in this pattern is that complex and resilient phenomenon we call tradition. Tradition certainly has its place, but in conflict resolution we need to rely on effective *skills*, not just tradition. Sometimes traditional ways of conducting a relationship or dealing with conflict have, in part, *contributed* both to the conflict and to an inability to resolve it.

People sometimes romanticize or glorify the past to such a degree that present behavior or relationships can never compare favorably with that past behavior or that past relationship. Pleasant memories do not make demands or require attention to needs. They do not prove bothersome, stubborn, or intransigent. They do not have budget deficits, confused policies, or unfavorable public opinion. They don't even call us in the middle of the night seeking help on a matter we feel totally incompetent to address. Pleasant memories just float in a lovely morning sky, reminding us of better times as we struggle through the storms and stresses of our present lives.

In other words, we not only use the past unwisely by carrying its *negative* behavior into the present and future, we sometimes use the past unwisely by creating glorified interpretations of the past that cause us to see the present and future as undervalued comparisons to the good old days. Pleasant memories of a past time, event, behavior, or relationship are wonderful and cherished gifts, *but we must beware of using them as nostalgic hindrances to resolving conflicts effectively and making the present and future the best we possibly can.*

LEARNING FROM THE PAST

We are all products of the past, as are our relationships and our conflicts. The past may be brief or long, but it still has an influence on our present situation. Even though the past does indeed matter, we deny our own power and the power of development and change if we allow ourselves to be defined by the past, to be trapped in perceptions that use past patterns to limit present and future possibilities.

We are in charge of whether the past is used to help or

obstruct our efforts at conflict resolution. We do not have to let the past hold present and future possibilities prisoner. With improved relationship patterns based on the conflict partnership skills, something that may not have been possible in the past may indeed be possible now and tomorrow. In dealing with the past, there are three major steps we need to take to make our conflict resolution efforts effective.

1. We need to try to focus on what we can do now and tomorrow, no matter what has occurred in the past. Even though we should always try this step first, some conflicts are so embedded in past events, or in perceptions of what happened in the past, that one or both of the conflict partners may not be willing to deal with the present and future until the past has been confronted. But we should still *try* to focus on the present and future first.
2. We need to understand the part that past events have played in creating a particular conflict.
3. We need to develop and use skills that can help us learn from the past so that the way we deal with our differences and our relationship in the future will be improved.

Try to Focus First on the Present and Future

Even though in some conflicts the past will have to be dealt with before moving on to what can be done in the present and future, it is important that we initially affirm and reach for the positive power the conflict partners have to create an improvement over past patterns. We do that by emphasizing the present and future before dealing with the past. Let's first look at how a failure to employ this first step obstructed effective conflict resolution in a dispute I was asked to help resolve several years ago. We will then explore how focusing first on the present and future could have helped the two parties in conflict resolve their problem without having to bring me in as a third-party facilitator.

Dot and Rae were not especially close friends, but worked together in their jobs as members of the marketing staff at a computer company. The company had recently developed a new educational software program for use in schools and was eager to develop a good marketing plan. One day at lunch, Dot, Rae, and several other employees were informally discussing the new software program. Dot, who had been with the company for several years, but who had received only token promotions, casually remarked that she thought the best way to market the program would be to invite a group of teachers and students to a workshop at which the software program would be explained by the company and practiced by the teachers and students. Positive recommendations from the educators and students would then be solicited and used in a marketing campaign.

About a month later, the head of the marketing department asked the staff for ideas about how best to market the new software. Dot was on vacation, and so was unable to submit her idea. Rae, who had been with the company for only a year, submitted the idea Dot had casually mentioned during the lunch a month ago. Rae did not mention that the idea came from Dot. When Dot returned from vacation, she found that the idea had been accepted as the marketing plan and that Rae had been put in charge of it. Dot was assigned to work with Rae on the project as the chief assistant.

Dot felt both hurt and angry. She had long felt her contributions to the company had gone unrecognized, and this latest incident intensified that feeling. She felt Rae had been unethical in stealing her idea, but being a person who tended to avoid any type of confrontation, Dot let the anger fester inside her. Her work relations with Rae became so antagonistic that Rae finally went to Dot's office to find out what was wrong. After Rae asked what was wrong, Dot began by using an opening definitely *not* advocated by conflict partnership.

"Rae," Dot said, "you took my idea and claimed it was your own. You knew it was my idea. I suggested it at lunch.

I think you're very unethical! I'm tired of never getting credit for the things I come up with."

Rae frowned, a bit perplexed. "I didn't do anything unethical. When we were all asked to submit ideas, I remembered some of us tossing some ideas around during the past month, but—"

"You're just avoiding the fact that you stole my idea," Dot countered. "I think I deserve an apology and for you to tell everybody it was *my* idea."

"I think you're being a bit petty, Dot. I didn't knowingly steal that idea."

Dot angrily went to her window and stared out. Then she turned to Rae and said, "You can't just do stuff like this and dismiss it as petty. I'm asking to be taken off this project. I don't want to work with you. Now please leave."

"But you're needed on this project, Dot. We can't meet the deadline if you—"

"Please leave," Dot repeated, and kept staring out the window.

During the next two weeks the development of the marketing plan for the innovative software program ground to a halt. The entire marketing division became embroiled in frustration and conflict as the president of the company realized that the new program, a cornerstone of the company's future, was in jeopardy, and threatened to make personnel changes if the marketing plan wasn't ready by the deadline. A manager of one of the other departments in the company had attended a workshop I had given earlier that year and suggested to the president that I be called in as a consultant.

After interviewing a number of employees, I learned that the main problem seemed to revolve around Dot and Rae. I met with each of them separately, and then got them together for a discussion. We eventually worked things out, but my role as facilitator is not the point of this example. The point is that, had Dot and Rae focused first on the present-future (taking steps to develop the marketing plan) so that the deadline could be met, they could have then sorted out the past misunderstanding much more effectively. At the end of our first meeting, I asked them to think about the skill of focusing first on the present-future and come back the next day and tell me how they could apply that skill.

Dot's initial approach to dealing with the conflict focused solely on Rae's wrongdoings of the past, and Rae allowed herself to get caught up in defending her past actions. When they came back the next day, I urged them to talk to each other about what they had thought about the previous evening, and exerpts from the conversation went like this.

"Rae," Dot began, "I was just so angry about not getting credit for my idea that I couldn't think about working on the project."

"Dot, what could you have done differently?" I asked.

"Well, I guess I could have realized we had a deadline to meet, that both our jobs more or less depended on meeting the deadline on this really important project . . . and I guess we could have gotten things rolling before we argued about what happened in the past."

"Rae?" I asked. "How does that sound to you?"

"That makes sense. I didn't know how to make things good enough between us so we could go ahead and work on this project. I felt I had to defend myself about something a month ago, something I really didn't remember very clearly."

"What could you have done differently?" I asked Rae.

Well," she said to me, "I could have told Dot—"

"Go ahead and tell Dot," I said. "*You* two will be working together. I'm just here to encourage you to talk with each other and work things out."

"Okay," Rae smiled. "Dot, I could have said we would talk about our past misunderstanding, even with the president if that's what you want, but that we had a deadline to meet and maybe we could get some work done on the marketing plan before we dealt with the past.''

Dot and Rae wisely realized that instead of immediately getting trapped in a battle over the past, they could have used the conflict partnership skill of focusing first on the present and future. By doing so, they would have been able to meet two needs they shared—to keep their jobs and to promote a new software program they both believed in. Dot's deep concern about her perception that Rae had stolen the marketing idea would have to be dealt with, but by focusing first on the present-future, they would have been able to create an atmosphere and process in which the past could then be dealt with constructively. The story has a happy ending. Dot and Rae worked diligently to develop an excellent marketing plan, and then went together to see the president to explain the origin of the idea and how Rae had not intended to steal the idea from Dot.

As mentioned earlier, sometimes parties in conflict unwisely and unnecessarily choose to perceive certain past events or perceived wrongdoings as so serious that they simply do not allow themselves to deal with present and future possibilities until they have dealt with the past. I am not saying that this is always a mistake, but I am saying it *usually* is, and that it does not *have* to be the approach people use. We should always *try* to focus on the present and future first, accomplish a couple of positive steps, and then use that positive atmosphere and process to deal with the past more constructively.

Once we begin dealing with the past, it is important to do it effectively. We can acknowledge the past and learn from it without making it the primary focus in addressing our conflicts. Several skills can be of great help. Let's arrange these skills under the next two steps in this section on learning from the past: understanding the part the past plays in a particular conflict, and learning from the past.

Understanding the Part Played by the Past

1. Trace the relationship back to a point before the conflict began to emerge. What positive things gave your relationship strength and meaning?

This helps you and your partner understand that the past may have played a positive part in your relationship, not just a negative role. You may then be able to deal with the past not as the enemy or culprit, but as a part of the relationship from which you can learn.

2. Try to identify and understand what specific acts or events played a part in creating the current conflict. Then take only one of those specific acts or events and see how each of you perceives what happened and why it happened. How do you perceive your own behavior and reasons for that behavior, and how does your partner perceive her or his behavior and reasons?

This important task helps to keep you from looking at the conflict as an "it," as something so general, huge, and elusive that you have no place to begin working on resolving the conflict. It also encourages you to clarify perceptions of the past, a critical skill in conflict resolution. Some conflicts are actually rooted in misperceived or unclarified perceptions of past events or actions. This step also makes you try to understand the partner's *reasons* behind his or her behavior, not just focus on the negative *effects* of that behavior.

3. Ask yourself and your conflict partner what each of you needs to have done about that past event in order to move beyond it and deal with what you can do now and in the future to improve your relationship.

Sometimes all that is needed is for a partner to acknowledge that he or she could have done a past event better. Other people seem to need a direct apology, although I would like to caution people not to put too much emphasis on wanting an apology. Apologies might make us feel better, and might even make the partner feel better, but insisting on apologies can frequently turn into a needless ego battle. If there is something that can be done about the past event, we should work cooperatively with our partner to try to do it.

As an illustration of how these three steps can be used in helping parties understand the part the past plays in a conflict, we turn to another actual case. Cliff and Rosie manage competitor toy companies in a very small town in which I had given a workshop. There is just enough business for each company to stay afloat. If one of the companies suddenly found a way to entice some of the customers away from the other company, that other company would likely go out of business.

Rosie and Cliff serve together on the Chamber of Commerce, attend the same business conventions, have children in the same school, and attend the same church. Because of these shared experiences, they perceive themselves as friends, although not close friends.

As business people, they have competed vigorously during the five years they have been in business. Rosie had more money to put into her new business than did Cliff, and so was able to build a better store, do more advertising, and capture a larger share of the market. Cliff has been playing catch-up ever since.

Problems started two years ago when Cliff began an ad campaign that alleged Rosie was selling toys that were unsafe. He offered no proof, but the allegations caused many customers to switch to Cliff. Rosie countered with an ad campaign focusing on Cliff's undesirability as an owner of a family-oriented store because he had been arrested for drunk driving seven years prior. Incensed, Cliff then hired some people from out of town to picket in front of Rosie's store with signs such as Boycott Dangerous Toys, Cliff Cares. Does Rosie Care?, and other pithy slogans. Rosie got so angry she pushed one of the picketers, and then tried to take Cliff to court.

The other members of the Chamber of Commerce were aghast that their peaceful community was being subjected to such shenanigans, and demanded that Cliff and Rosie bury the hatchet. In the meantime, Rosie attended a workshop on conflict partnership. She realized that she and Cliff had shared needs as members of the town and the Chamber of Commerce, as parents, and as role models for young people interested in business careers. She studied the conflict partnership skills and decided to try especially hard to understand the part played by the past in her conflict with Cliff. She used the three steps previously discussed.

"Cliff," Rosie began, "I'm willing to let bygones be bygones and start dealing with each other more positively. I think we—"

"That's easy for you to say," Cliff interrupted. "You still have sixty-five percent of the market. When you dragged my one-time-only arrest out into public, and when you tried to take me to court, I made up my mind to beat you any way I could. And now you want to forget all that and—"

"I didn't mean we can forget the past, Cliff," Rosie clarified. "I meant that we don't have to let the past keep us from doing better now."

"I'm really mad, Rosie! You deeply offended me."

"I regret that, Cliff, I really do. And I feel you offended me. We can sit here and argue who offended whom the most, or we can both acknowledge we let things get out of hand and take some positive steps from this point on."

Cliff remained silent, still smoldering about the past.

"We've had a pretty good relationship for a lot of years," Rosie went on. "Back before all this fighting started, remember how we worked well on the PTA together, how we talked together and both decided to close our stores to honor Martin Luther King's birthday? We have some *good* past memories, too. Remember those things?"

"Yeah," Cliff answered. "I guess we did okay before all this . . . this . . ."

"What happened to get us on this negative track, Cliff? Can you remember when things started getting nasty?"

"Well, I guess it was the ad campaigns two years ago," Cliff remembered.

"I agree. Maybe we should look at why we ran those kind of ads. What were your reasons for that ad claiming *my* toys were unsafe? You know we mostly sell the same toys."

Cliff studied his hands for a few seconds, then sighed. "I had to get an edge, Rosie. You had all that start-up money; I had very little. You were way ahead of me. I had to get more customers. I was desperate. You ever been desperate before?"

Rosie thought for a minute. "Yes . . . I guess I have. Desperation can make us do unwise things. I still think your ad was unfair, but I guess I can see you did it more out of desperation than meanness."

"Speaking of meanness," Cliff jumped in, "that drunken driving ad you put out was really a low blow. Why did you do something like that?"

"I guess I was so hurt and angry I wanted to get back at you," Rosie sighed. "I felt bad the minute the ad went public, but I guess my anger won out over my wisdom."

"So you did feel bad about it, huh?" Cliff replied, feeling a little better since he knew Rosie had at least realized he might feel hurt by the ad. "I guess my desperation and your anger took charge of us, huh?"

"I'm afraid you're right," Rosie agreed. "I'm wondering what we can do about those past things now? Is there something we can do to put those unwise things we did to rest?"

"Well, I think we've made a start just by explaining to each other why we did them," Cliff reasoned. "Maybe we could take out another ad this week; do it together, saying we let our competitive urges go too far."

"That's a great idea!" Rosie said enthusiastically. "We could even have a statement saying that the kids thinking about going into business professions can learn from our mistakes, that competition should be kept clean and honest."

Rosie did so well in using the three skills involved in

understanding the part played by the past that she encouraged Cliff to get involved in the process, too. In this case, they had to deal with the past before they could improve the relationship, and they did it well.

How to Learn from the Past: Three Helpful Skills

1. Look at a past event or behavior and take some of the conflict partnership skills and ask, "If we had used that skill, what different and better steps could we have taken?" These skills can help you identify effective relationship and conflict resolution skills that might have been used in the past.

For example, you may find that clarifying perceptions really wasn't done at a critical point, and that the resulting misperceptions influenced behavior and helped cause the conflict. Or perhaps you and your partner never identified any shared needs, or never realized that you were using negative power against each other when you could have developed your shared positive power. By focusing on how some of these skills could have been used at key points in the development of the conflict, you can learn from the past rather than fighting the same past battles in the same old way.

2. Remind each other of times and events in the past when you and your partner enjoyed a solid partnership.

Because a particular negative event in the past contributed to the conflict we are now facing, we sometimes let that negative event color the *entire* past. That makes it tempting to see the past as all negative, and to forget that there have also been positive past events. By reminding each other of those positive past events, we sometimes find that we can then approach a discussion of the past more constructively.

This second step in learning from the past also shows us that we have some solid relationship ground on which to build a resolution to the current conflict. Citing an example we have used before, two people have spent three years building a strong marriage. For the past month, one of the spouses has come home from work every day and directed a steady stream of complaints, extreme criticism, and confusing, almost violent anger at the relationship partner. There is no way the one receiving the attacks will choose to stay in the relationship if he or she focuses only on the behavior of the last month. However, when this recent negative behavior is seen in the context of the previous three positive years, perhaps overreaction can be avoided and the cause of the recent damaging behavior can be clarified and dealt with constructively.

3. In the midst of a troubling present conflict, remind each other of specific past conflicts you were ready to give up on, yet managed to deal with adequately enough to keep the relationship alive and well.

Tying this step in with the other two, you can say to your conflict partner, "I realize we are having a hard time with this particular conflict, but remember when we had one [mention a past conflict] just as tough last month [or whenever]? We got through that one okay, and now that we have even *better* skills to use, I think we can work together to deal effectively with *this* conflict."

Let's look at a specific conflict and see how the three skills just discussed can be applied. This conflict involves Fred and Miguel, co-owners of a small printing company. When they went into business together two years ago, Fred put up most of the money and Miguel supplied most of the printing know-how.

After their first year in business, Fred and Miguel got into a rather heated conflict over whether to print 20,000 leaflets for a group promoting fund-raising for the Contras, the U.S.-backed rebels trying to overthrow the Nicaraguan government. Miguel, a native Nicaraguan whose family still lived there, was opposed to the Contras and argued that the printing company should not print leaflets supporting the rebels. Fred argued that the issue was strictly a business deal, and that he would print leaflets for any group, regardless of their politics, just so long as they paid for the job. The pro-Contra group got fed up with the delays caused by the bickering between Fred and Miguel, and hired a competitor company in town to print their leaflets. Fred blamed Miguel for the loss of income, and their relationship became strained.

Soon after the leaflet incident, Miguel had to return to Nicaragua to visit his ailing mother, and was gone for a month. Fred's son had a serious accident while Miguel was away, and, having inadequate medical insurance, Fred had a huge medical bill to pay. He borrowed $7,000 from the company, totally depleting the company bank account. When Miguel returned, he was incensed that Fred had unilaterally put the company in severe financial trouble by borrowing so much money. The two business partners almost came to blows as they argued vehemently. In the first conversation we visit, notice how they allow the past to impede conflict resolution.

"You have made us bankrupt!" Miguel thunders. "You had no right to take *our* money!"

"We would have had more money if you hadn't caused us to lose that leaflet account!" Fred yelled back. "Besides, I put more money into this business at the beginning than you did!"

"One of my brothers was killed by the Contras!" Miguel cried. "And you wanted to help that group get more money for the people who killed my brother!"

"That kind of thinking shows just what a lousy business-man you are!" Fred growled. "I never should have gone into business with you!"

If one of the two men, in this case Miguel, had used the skill of learning from the past, along with other conflict partnership skills, here's how the conversation might have gone.

"Fred!" Miguel says in horror. "We're broke! Did you really have to use all of the seven thousand dollars?"

"My kid needed surgery!" Fred says indignantly. "Of

course I had to use it! We wouldn't *be* broke if you hadn't lost that leaflet account for us!"

Miguel is tempted to use the same old patterns, but remains in charge of himself and says, "Look, Fred, we will probably always disagree on that leaflet incident. Business partners disagree sometimes, but we've still been able to work together well enough since then to do quality work and bring in a decent profit. And we dealt with some other conflicts okay, like the conflict over the secretary, and the one about the new printing press. We've shown we *can* work through our differences."

"Don't change the subject!" Fred says, still angry. "That fool leaflet mistake really cost us!"

"Okay," Miguel says. "I guess we need to deal with the leaflet thing again, but let's learn something from it this time, not just fight over it again. I can understand your position. You saw it as purely a business decision, right?"

"Well, of course," Fred answers, "because that's what it was!"

"Do you understand why I opposed the leaflet contract?" Miguel asks.

"I'm not sure I *care* why," Fred grumps. "It cost us a lot of money."

"Well, if we're going to stay in business together, I think it's important that we both try to understand each other's reasons for why we do things. My brother's murder was as important a value to me as your son's surgery was to you. If we can see it that way, maybe we can understand why I opposed the leaflets and why you took the seven thousand."

Fred thought for a minute, then sighed, "Yeah, I guess you have a point. I never looked at it that way."

"Looking back on how we dealt with that leaflet incident, I wonder if we could have spared ourselves a lot of pain and fighting if we had handled that conflict differently."

"Probably," Fred answered. "But what could we have done?"

"Well, we could have focused on how much our company needs each of us, and how we need each other. I need your management skills and you need my printing skills. Focusing on those things would have helped *me* realize that sometimes I have to respect a particular personal value you have if we're to keep our company working well, even if that particular value isn't as important to me as it is to you, or vice versa. We *are* the company, Fred, so respecting each other is respecting the company."

"Hmmm," Fred says thoughtfully. "That makes sense."

"I wonder what we could have *done* about that leaflet problem?" Miguel asks. "I mean, what *action* would have been better?"

"I'm not sure," Fred responds. "Maybe I could have realized the situation in Nicaragua was such an important issue to you. I would have agreed not to accept the job instead of just fighting about it for a year. But to be honest, that seems like I'm the only one making concessions."

"But maybe," Miguel reasons wisely, "maybe we shouldn't look at it as a concession. That makes it seem like somebody is giving up something rather than what it really is: you doing something for the good of our relationship as business partners and, therefore, for the good of the company. I could have done better, too. I could have gone out and really worked hard to get a few additional contracts to make up for the income we didn't get from the leaflet job."

Fred lets it all sink in, and then says thoughtfully, "This is really something. Going back over the leaflet incident and seeing how we could have done it better makes me feel a lot stronger about our relationship and the company. Of course, we still have the seven thousand dollars to worry about."

"Well, let's deal with it like we've now learned we could have dealt with the leaflet problem. I should respect that you felt you needed to get the money quickly, and saw the company funds as the only way. Now we have to focus on how to replenish the bank account, and on how we can keep something like this from happening again."

"I agree," Fred says. "Maybe we can sell the old printing press. I can put some personal money into the company account, and then we can devote the next month to finding some new clients. What do you think?"

"Good idea," Miguel agrees. "And I think we should seriously consider some kind of company medical plan. Maybe that's long overdue."

As the scenario shows, Miguel initiated a process that eventually invited Fred to participate in learning from the past. Many of the other conflict partnership skills were also used, resulting in an effective resolution of their conflicts and an improved relationship.

FOCUS ON THE PRESENT-FUTURE

Using the term *present-future* is my attempt to emphasize how the present and future are inseparably linked. Every action in the present extends into the future, because the immediate future is but seconds away from the present. Thus, in dealing with conflicts, we need to try as best we can to make sure the conflict resolution decisions and agreements we make in the present are wise and strong enough to stand up to future challenges.

The point has already been made that people involved in a conflict should first try to focus on positive steps they can take in the present-future, even though it is tempting to focus only on *past* behavior and events. There are other aspects of focusing on the present-future that also deserve attention.

The Power of Forgiveness

Forgiving past behavior can provide a strong foundation on which to build positive steps in the present-future. Forgiveness does not imply approval of past negative behavior. Rather, forgiveness accomplishes several important things. Forgiveness

- acknowledges the fact that we all sometimes fall short of the best we can do, that we are all still growing and improving.
- communicates to conflict partners that they are not being defined or judged solely on some past negative behavior
- reaches for the positive power of the conflict partner to learn from the past and make positive contributions in spite of past behavior that has helped create and perpetuate damaging conflicts
- helps create an atmosphere that encourages both conflict partners to move beyond the past and focus on the present-future
- increases the positive power of the person doing the forgiving.

Focusing on the Present-Future Encourages Process

Conflict resolution is not an event, it is a *process*. Focusing on the present-future helps us to understand and act on this important realization. The process of a relationship involves the past, present, and future, and the process of effective conflict resolution involves learning from the past and using shared positive power to take steps of improvement in the present and future.

When people employ the conflict partnership skills to resolve a conflict, they eventually agree on certain steps they can take to learn from and to resolve the conflict, to move beyond the conflict, and to improve their relationship so that they can deal with future differences more effectively. Those steps that they agree to take extend into the future, and, therefore, must be able to stand up under the challenges of the future.

How to make conflict resolution decisions and agreements that can survive and grow in the future will be discussed in Step 8, Makes Mutual-Benefit Agreements. But for now, let's be content to emphasize that effective conflict resolution is a process that extends into the future, not just an event in the here and now in which people stop only the pain and confusion of a particular conflict. Thus, when dealing with a conflict, it is helpful to focus on and talk about not just the present, but the present-future.

Imaging an Improved Relationship in the Present-Future

Another way to focus on the present-future is to engage your conflict partner in an imaging exercise through which you try to get both a mental picture and a feeling of what the relationship will be like if you deal with the current conflict effectively.

One partner might say to the other, "I think we're getting bogged down in thinking that because of this conflict and the way we've been acting, the immediate future of our relationship doesn't look too good. Let's try something. Let's try to picture and feel what it will be like if we resolve this conflict effectively, and if we use some of the conflict partnership skills to deal with the differences we will have in the future." Some people find imaging more helpful than do others, of course, but at least it is another way to try to use focusing on the present-future to help us resolve conflicts.

All of the conflict partnership skills discussed thus far prepare us to take the next critical step in resolving conflicts effectively and sustainably: generating options.

Generate Options

Our ability to discover new possibilities within relationships and within conflict resolution is often impaired by the "packaged" truths and limited vision we hold onto in times of stress, insecurity, and conflict. Generating options can often break through the preconceived limitations we bring with us into the conflict resolution process.

Generating options makes use of all of the conflict partnership skills we have discussed thus far, and provides choices from which specific steps to resolve conflicts and improve relationships can be agreed upon.

THE PREPARATION PHASE

Throughout our discussions, much emphasis has been placed on using the power of the partnership *process*. Mention has been made of how important it is for people in relationships and in conflicts to use their *shared* positive power rather than basing their behavior only on the perceived individual power each has. Emphasizing how the parties should work *together*, however, should not cause us to ignore an important prior step: each party should prepare individually before ever entering into dialogue with a conflict partner.

Preparing oneself in the skill of generating options when dealing with a conflict can involve several tasks.

Trace the conflict back to a time before it reached its current level of difficulty and ask yourself what options you may have left unexplored as the conflict increased step by step. This process can remind you that alternatives were probably present in the past *and* that you need to put more energy into generating options in the present–future.

Spend some time envisioning new possibilities. Put aside the choices you may have already identified and let your mind consider a wide range of options. In doing so, you will be less likely to let yourself stubbornly hold onto narrow choices.

Come prepared with several specific options you have determined meet some shared needs, require shared power to be implemented, and can probably become specific steps toward dealing with the conflict and improving the relationship. Even if you are unsure about the feasibility of the options, don't let that concern you too much at this point. You and your partner will have the opportunity to weed out any options that may prove inappropriate.

Remind yourself that the options you are identifying are but possible starting points for the process of generating options you and your partner will do together. Conflict partnership means that the parties in conflict work together to build a process of conflict resolution and relationship improvement. The options *you* prepare, and those prepared by your partner, will need to be put into the partnership process. Some may be agreed upon as they are, some may be altered, and some may be dropped.

Whatever the outcome of a particular option, that outcome needs to be determined within the partnership process.

The four suggestions just stated can help you prepare for the important conflict partnership step of generating options. Let's look at a specific conflict to see how these suggestions can be applied.

Ellen is a twenty-seven-year-old social worker who has just been assigned to a newly built youth center in a neighborhood beset with youth gangs, drugs, and intense social alienation. Phil, a social worker with fifteen years of experience in a smaller town containing less severe problems than Ellen's city, has been hired as the youth center's director. At the first staff meeting a month ago, Phil said forcefully, "Kids today are losing basic American values. We have to get them back on track. We have to restore the value of the family. We have to keep harping on the evils of drugs. That will be the focus of the youth center."

Ellen disagreed just as forcefully, saying that the programs of the center should be developed in collaboration with the youth, not imposed on them by what to them is just another group of untrustworthy authority figures. Ellen and Phil let their differences escalate into a full-blown conflict— so much so that the city's director of social services told them to work out their differences immediately or the center's potential effectiveness would be undermined.

After attending one of my conflict partnership workshops, Ellen decided to focus on the preparation aspect of the generating options step. First, Ellen looked back on the past month of her conflict with Phil to see if she had ignored any helpful options. She decided she could have asked Phil to tell some stories of his experiences with youth so that she could understand his reasoning better. Then she could have related some of *her* experiences to help him understand her rationale.

Second, Ellen tried to put the options she had devised aside, and brainstormed some new options. She even talked with a few friends to see if they had any creative ideas. She discovered that a couple of quite creative and hopeful possibilities emerged.

Third, Ellen envisioned what the center would be like if some of Phil's options were made policy, and what the center would be like if some of her options were accepted. In doing so, she felt she had stretched her mind beyond just the two or three pet options she had initially devised.

Fourth, Ellen went through the expanded set of options to see which ones were based on needs the youth, Phil, the center, and she herself all shared—needs they all seemed to feel were important. Then she looked at those options to see which ones could best use the shared positive power of all parties concerned.

Fifth, Ellen went for a long walk in the park. She encouraged herself to keep remembering that her options were just starting points, that the process she and Phil would participate in together was the critical part of generating effective options.

We will return to Ellen and Phil throughout this chapter, but we already see that Ellen did a good job of using the preparation stage in the conflict partnership step of generating options. Other suggestions for effectively generating options are also important. One of those suggestions involves moving beyond preconceived answers.

BEWARE PRECONCEIVED ANSWERS

Even if a person uses all of the conflict partnership skills to identify healthy options, that person still must realize that what might seem a solid option to her or him might not be accepted as a viable option by the other party. In other words, we need to try to find an effective balance between coming up with viable options on our own and working *with* our conflict partners to identify and implement steps we can all agree are positive.

Some situations of conflict contain such deeply held differences of opinion, needs, and values that an option acceptable to one party is wholly unacceptable to another party. If the relationship is to continue as something more positive than a constant battle over recurring conflicts, the relationship partners need to move beyond seemingly incompatible individual options and not let arguments over them become the central issue of the conflict resolution process. Several suggestions can be offered on how we might move beyond these preconceived answers and seemingly incompatible options that each party may feel are the only choices.

Moving Beyond Preconceived Answers

1. *Look more deeply to see if there might be some commonalities hidden within seemingly incompatible options.*

Far too often we shut off our minds once we hear something we don't like, once a particular button is pushed, once an idea the other party suggests contradicts one of our own pet ideas, or once an expected negative perception of the other party seems confirmed by one of their suggestions or statements.

In Ellen and Phil's conflict, one of Ellen's preconceived answers was to hold a street dance to announce the new center to the neighborhood. She knew the youth liked to dance, and *she* liked to dance, so she felt strongly about the street dance option. When she brought it up during the conflict resolution meeting with Phil, he said he thought, in general, that dances were okay, but that he believed Ellen just wanted to be liked by the youth, that she was acting immaturely, and that holding a dance on the dark streets would simply invite a gang battle, particularly because the police would insist on a high-profile presence, which would further incite the gangs.

Ellen was tempted to let her "acting immaturely" button be pushed, but she remembered the conflict partnership skills and remained in charge of herself. She was also tempted to hold onto the street dance option because she had invested a lot of time in planning how it could be managed, and because it was one of her pet options, but she wisely *tried to focus on any possible commonalities* she saw in her position and Phil's, and realized that they both seemed to think dances were potentially effective. She asked Phil if he did indeed think holding dances was positive. He affirmed that he did, and so she let go of her preconceived idea of having the dance in the street, and they agreed to hold a dance inside the center.

Another example of this important step in moving beyond preconceived answers can be found in a situation in which two community committees are in conflict over a general grant awarded to their parent organization. The Child Welfare Committee has decided that the only option it will accept is to use the grant for daycare centers in the downtown area of the community, where most of the community works. The Downtown Beautification Committee has decided the only option it will accept is to use the grant to develop a lovely park, where office workers can spend their lunch breaks. If the two committees define conflict resolution as a battle over these two preconceived answers, they will get nowhere. However, if they look more deeply into the two seemingly incompatible options, they may find a shared value: improving the quality of workday life for the work force of the community they share. Using this shared value as a springboard to generating other options, they may discover an option that provides mutual benefits, such as using the grant to establish a daycare center within the proposed park. If additional funds are needed, the two committees working together would probably stand an excellent chance of raising the required money, in that they would be meeting the needs of the community *and* creating a greater partnership atmosphere for future community endeavors.

2. *If no commonalities appear within the seemingly incompatible options, clarify where the disagreements are and then set aside*

those options and work together to generate other options around other parts of the relationship or conflict.

Taking this action is not *avoiding* the conflict; rather, it is wisely acknowledging that an impasse has been reached on only one part of the relationship or conflict. If the parties use one of the skills in Step 2 (Clarify Perceptions) of the conflict partnership process and look at the components of the conflict, they might see that there are some other components in which steps can be taken to find some agreement and mutual benefit.

Going back to Ellen and Phil, one of Ellen's other major options was for the center staff to convene a conflict resolution meeting involving the leaders of the three neighborhood gangs. Phil again disagreed forcefully, condescendingly pointing out that the center should not reinforce the youths' self-perception as primarily gang members. His option was to purposely choose *non*–gang members to attend the meeting.

Even though Ellen realized she and Phil had hit upon incompatible options, she couldn't make herself let go of her own option. She was angry at Phil for his condescending attitude, and let that take charge of her. She and Phil argued the gang-versus-nongang issue for two hours, and got so angry they finally had to end their increasingly bitter meeting and meet the next day, thereby wasting valuable time.

If Ellen had been using conflict partnership, she might have said, "Well, Phil, it's obvious we don't see eye to eye on this option, so maybe we should set it aside for now and deal with some options we can cooperate on first. This one issue isn't going to determine whether the center sinks or swims." By setting the incompatible issue aside for the time being, Ellen and Phil might have been able to work cooperatively on other options, thereby gaining more trust and respect for each other and the conflict resolution process. They would also have started building a pathway to effective conflict resolution.

3. *Try not to* lead *with those preconceived answers you suspect might be unacceptable to the other party.*

I have been a third-party facilitator in many situations in which one party has learned from the process of generating options *together* that the preconceived answer she or he had thought was ideal was actually much less beneficial than one of the options generated during the process. If that party had *led* with his or her own rigidly stated answer, the other party would probably have countered in like manner, and additional spin-off conflicts might easily have been created. It never hurts to generate options together. You can still introduce your own preconceived suggestions, but when you do, it will be in an improved atmosphere if you first worked with the other party to generate other possibilities.

Phil had learned that Ellen was strongly opposed to turning the center into just another school in which students were forced to listen to lectures and read books. Phil resented the fact that the much younger and less experienced Ellen would dare presume to tell him, the director, what the center should do or not do. Therefore, Phil let that resentment take hold of him, and he purposely led off the meeting by stating that the area of the center that Ellen had suggested would best serve as a coffee house where youth could discuss and listen to music, should become a library instead, where antidrug lectures and classic books would be presented.

Predictably, Ellen responded strongly against this "school" idea Phil knew she hated. Once again, they became locked into the conquest pattern, creating further obstacles to effective conflict resolution. If Phil had practiced conflict partnership, he would have realized that leading off with such a threatening suggestion would only make Ellen defend one of her preconceived answers fiercely. Whatever personal satisfaction Phil hoped to gain from his unwise approach was miniscule in comparison to the damage it did to realizing the goal he, Ellen, and the center shared: getting the center moving effectively.

IMAGING OPTIONS

A third major component of generating options is what can be termed *imaging*—a powerful and creative phenomenon. We do it all the time as children when we create alternative worlds in our minds. Once we become adults, we seem more intent on absorbing the existing order and trying to make it work to our advantage. Adults need to retain and energize that wonderful and crucial childlikeness so apparent in the process of imaging. Imaging an improved life is one of the most mature and needed skills we can develop. It is of great assistance in generating options.

As an example of imaging options, let's choose one of your relationships in which you are experiencing some conflicts. Get some quiet time away from other people and away from interruptions and focus on the best qualities of that relationship, on the attitudes and behavior that, when operating, make the relationship a benefit to both you and your relationship partner. In your mind, for the next week, go day by day through the interactions you and your partner will probably experience, and create images of these interactions as they would be experienced using the positive attitudes and behavior, the best qualities, you identified earlier.

Now look at a particular conflict you are experiencing in the relationship. Imagine yourself in the future, after the conflict has been dealt with effectively. Image the way you want to feel, the way you want your partner to feel, and the way you hope the relationship will be after dealing with the conflict. Try to be specific. For example, your imaged future relationship may include a nonthreatening, constructive, clarifying dialogue on a particularly bothersome difference in values. Or it may include an agreement for each of you to try to stop doing a particular thing that always seems to cause conflict.

Once you have (1) focused on the more positive potential in the relationship, and (2) imaged some particular outcomes of mutual benefit, you are ready to generate some options capable of serving as steps toward the creation of those future positive feelings and outcomes.

LEARNING YOUR CONFLICT PARTNER'S OPTIONS

Even though we should prepare ourselves by generating options in our own minds, it is often helpful to learn about the other party's options *before* we expound on our own. Of course, they may be reluctant to discuss options, or they may not have thought of any, but a positive partnership process is nurtured when we at least offer the other party an opportunity to suggest some of their options before we launch into our own. When you start the conflict resolution step of generating options, ask for *their* options first. This is especially important if the other party is feeling disempowered. It also helps us avoid the temptation of becoming trapped in our own preconceived answers.

As the other party offers options, we need to be concentrating on and listening for any shared needs, shared power, commonalities with our own options, and mutual benefits being expressed within their options. Far too often we concentrate instead on feelings of personal threat, on contradictions to our own ideas, and on how to convincingly state our own options once the other party stops talking.

Once they have stated some options, it is helpful to pick up on one of their suggestions in which shared needs, shared power, commonalities, and so on are most present and, if possible, to blend some of their ideas with one of our own options.

Let's return again to Ellen and Phil, our two social workers, to see a good example of learning your conflict partner's options. Although this was not mentioned before, there was another social worker assigned to the center staff. Her name was Kris, and she was extremely quiet. She had quietly sided with Ellen on some issues, and with Phil on others. She was an important part of the center and thus an important player in resolving the conflicts relating to the center.

Ellen really didn't know Kris very well. Based on the few things Kris had said, Ellen *assumed* she knew what Kris's suggested options might be on a key part of the youth center conflict—what hours to keep the center open—but she needed to be certain what Kris's options were. Ellen also wanted to get Kris more involved in the discussion. Therefore, before offering her own options on the center's hours, Ellen asked Kris for her options.

Kris responded, "I don't know. I do think we should choose hours that are safe but are also free enough for the youth to feel they can come here when they have no place else to go."

Ellen quickly explored her own option—to keep the center open from 7:00 A.M. until 11:00 P.M.—to see what shared needs, goals, or opinions there might be between Kris's suggestion and her own. She realized that she shared Kris's concern that the youth have a place to go when nowhere else was available. That meant that staying open until 11:00 P.M. might be an option Kris could support.

Then Ellen turned to Phil. "What are your suggestions, Phil?"

"I like what Kris said about safety," he replied. "We can't have the center becoming a place where young toughs bring their violence off the streets into here."

Ellen heard Phil's emphasis on safety, something Kris had also emphasized, and asked herself how important that was to her and what that would mean to her idea for an 11:00 P.M. closing time. She decided that 11 P.M. might be too late, and realized that her original option would probably have to be revised to consider an earlier closing time.

Ellen could have blurted out her 11:00 P.M. suggestion, but by learning the options of the other two people involved in the conflict, she was able to let go of her own preconceived option because she heard some good ideas and because she wanted to work cooperatively with Kris and Phil.

FREE-FLOW OPTIONING

One of the most positive steps in the optioning process is what I call free-flow optioning, a cooperative effort in which parties in conflict creatively suggest and imagine a wide range of possibilities. As a professional conflict resolution facilitator, I frequently find free-flow optioning to be quite helpful in encouraging parties in conflict to realize that there well may be other possibilities, even in the midst of seemingly intractible impasse.

I am sure many of you have participated in the familiar group process known as brainstorming. In free-flow optioning you not only brainstorm ideas but also image some of their possible effects. The process is as follows.

1. All parties are encouraged to set aside temporarily the previously suggested ideas and to make new suggestions.

2. As the new ideas are suggested, someone has the responsibility to record all suggestions, ideally in a place where all parties can see the growing list.

3. Although it is tempting to discuss each new idea as it is suggested, the creative flow of optioning is usually enhanced if at least four or five new ideas are listed before exploring the feasibility and pros and cons of any of them. If the list is short, waiting to discuss each one until there are no more suggestions is a manageable strategy. However, care must be taken not to let the list become so long before discussing some of the ideas that the parties lose sight of the need to begin narrowing the list down to the most mutually agreed upon possibilities.

4. Rather than discussing each idea separately, I usually find it more effective to look at the list for any common

threads among the various suggestions. Making a new list titled Common Threads can emphasize the fact that there are indeed some mutual concerns and needs among the parties.

5. Once the list is narrowed down to those suggestions involving common threads, the next step in the free-flow optioning process is to image the possible outcomes of each of the common thread options. Those options whose imaged outcomes meet shared needs, promote shared positive power, and seem to improve the relationship for the present-future become first priorities; those whose imaged outcomes cause one or more of the parties to feel uncomfortable or disadvantaged become lower priorities.

Free-flow optioning contributes several important ingredients to the conflict resolution process. First, hope can be created where there once seemed only impasse. Second, all parties can feel more empowered as they are given a chance to make suggestions. Third, tense moments can be relieved by focusing on a creative process rather than on the continuation of rehashing the same old arguments. Fourth, emphasis on commonalities, shared needs and power, and improving the relationship can be emphasized once again. Fifth, the imaging process can focus attention on the present-future rather than on the past. Sixth, the process leads the parties to the discovery of doables, the subject of the next section, Step 7: Develop "Doables."

One final comment on free-flow optioning addresses the interesting topic of humor. Some people have a difficult time accepting the notion that there is a role for humor in conflict resolution. To the contrary, I have been in numerous situations in which humor has contributed significantly to humanizing a conflict and to relieving almost unbearable tension. Quite often in the free-flow optioning process, humorous suggestions will emerge. Although most of them do not represent real possibilities for action, humorous suggestions can serve as a breath of fresh air in an otherwise tense environment.

IDENTIFYING KEY OPTIONS

The time comes when the most possible options (key options) must be identified. There are several ingredients constituting a key option. A key option

- meets one or more shared needs.
- meets one or more individual needs that are not incompatible with another party's individual needs.
- requires mutual positive power to be implemented, either shared positive power (the optimum condition) and/or individual positive power.
- has the potential of improving future relationship patterns and is itself a doable ("doables" are discussed in the next chapter), or it has one or more doables within it.
- can at least be accepted or, even better, enthusiastically supported by all parties.

Let's make one final visit to Ellen, Phil, and Kris. They eventually came up with some key options, primarily because they covered just about every item in the conflict partnership list of what constitutes a key option.

They realized that 10:00 P.M. would be the best time for closing the center each night because that time best met the shared needs of all three social workers, the youth, and the neighborhood.

Phil's option of setting up a library for lectures and reading classics was *not* a key option because it was incompatible with the needs felt by the youth and incompatible with Ellen's ideas.

Ellen and Kris strongly supported a coffee house being set up inside the center, but Phil was not so sure. He was still a little miffed that the library option had to be discarded, so he dragged his feet on the coffee house. But Phil's participation was needed if the coffee house was to be successful. In other words, his positive power was needed, as was the positive power of Ellen and Kris. Ellen kept reaching for Phil's positive power by asking him for suggestions on how the coffee house should be structured and run. Many of Phil's ideas were accepted, and he began to feel a part of the idea. The coffee house became a key option once it required and used the shared positive power of all parties involved in the conflict.

All of the options—the dance, the 10:00 P.M. closing, the coffee house—were the type of options that stood a good chance of making the center effective *and* improving the relationship among Ellen, Phil, and Kris. The way they generated the options, the way they identified them as *key* options, and the fact that those options met shared needs and required shared positive power to be implemented all improved the working relationship of the social workers for the present-future.

VIABLE OPTIONS AND PAST EXPERIENCE

This section on generating options ends with a vitally important component. Many people allow themselves to dismiss a potentially viable option because the ineffective relationship and conflict resolution patterns they used in the past didn't allow that option to work.

I urge conflict partners to realize that when the conflict partnership process is employed, each person individually, and the parties in conflict together, have now empowered themselves with effective skills they may not have had in the past. A particular option that could never have worked using the old patterns may now be possible using the conflict partnership process.

Demi and Rich learned this important lesson in the twelfth year of their marriage. After ten years of solid relationship, they began to experience a growing number of conflicts when Demi suspected Rich of having an affair with Charlene, a co-worker at his office. Demi accused Rich of betraying her trust, and Rich vehemently denied having the affair, saying that Charlene was a dear friend and that he had a right to enjoy the friendship of both men *and* women.

As the tension and mistrust increased, things they would never have fought about before became conflicts. Small disagreements became intense battles. Where to go out to dinner; whether or not their young son could take ballet, or their young daughter could join a first-grade soccer team; what type of car to buy; and what friends to see socially all became damaging conflicts. Soon, Demi began sleeping in the guest room. Only when their children begged them to stop fighting did they realize they had to try to come up with better ways to resolve their conflicts.

They came up with two main options. One, they would go to a marriage counselor, and two, they would try a trial separation. They went to the marriage counselor for a year, but the experience proved ineffective as Demi refused to consider that she might have been wrong about the affair, and Rich refused to forgive Demi for accusing him unfairly. The sessions turned into shouting matches, punctuated by long periods of tearful withdrawal and the introduction of many ghost conflicts.

After the option of seeing a marriage counselor failed, they tried the second option and went through a six-month separation. That option proved ineffective as well, as Demi, still convinced that Rich was having an affair with Charlene, hired a private investigator to follow him, and Rich kept demanding that the children live with him during the separation even though he had moved into a small apartment far from their school and friends.

In the sixth month of the separation, Demi attended one of my workshops. She came up to me afterward and said that she felt some of the conflict partnership skills might help her save her marriage. She then asked if I would work with Rich and her if she could get him to agree. I said I would, and she called Rich. He told her the idea was ridiculous because they had already tried that option and it had failed. Demi tried to explain that I was not a marriage counselor but a conflict resolution facilitator, and that there was a process called conflict partnership that she felt confident would work. She suggested Rich call me.

When Rich finally called, I described some of the conflict partnership skills, and then said to him, "Just because some of your options didn't work in the past, maybe if you use more effective skills, those options might work now." Rich finally agreed for the three of us to meet.

First, I met with each of them individually, asking many of the questions you have been reading as part of the conflict partnership process. I tried to help each of them clarify perceptions, focus on individual and shared needs, discover what their individual and shared positive power could be, focus on the present-future and learn from the past, and generate options that could meet shared needs and activate shared positive power. We went through the entire process. When I felt both Demi and Rich were empowered with an effective process, I asked them to meet with me together, and they agreed.

They agreed to meet because they realized that even though the option of meeting with a third party had not worked in the past, they now had improved skills and a potentially effective process that could now make that option viable. Using the conflict partnership skills, Demi and Rich did almost all of the work themselves. My interventions were few.

The two clarified Rich's relationship with Charlene, Rich even suggesting the option that Demi and Charlene have a talk. Demi realized that if Rich was willing to suggest such an option, maybe she had overreacted to her suspicions. Together they clarified that the reason the separation had been disastrous was Rich's unrealistic demand that the children live with him.

They strongly identified the individual and shared need of being with each other because they still loved each other, and the shared needs of being good parents and providing a complete family for their children. They went back over what they could have done to deal more effectively with their conflicts as they arose, identified key conflict partnership skills they could have used, and even redid a couple of the conflicts using the skills. They were able to move beyond the past because they were now *learning* from it. They used their positive power to come up with some excellent options, several of which became viable doables.

All of this took place three years ago. Demi and Rich now have three children, and are doing quite well. They have had additional conflicts, but they have used those conflicts to further clarify and improve their relationship and to grow as individuals and as partners.

As we have seen in each of the real-life stories in this chapter, people involved in conflicts often find it difficult to see beyond certain narrow resolution possibilities. Many of these narrow options are preconceived in one's own mind as ways of getting one's own desires satisfied. Generating new options can empower all parties as they break mental logjams, discover heretofore unseen possibilities, realize areas of shared needs and goals, and move ever closer to taking those steps that can resolve particular conflicts and improve the relationship.

As Demi and Rich demonstrated, as options are generated, their possibility should not be evaluated on the incapabilities within past relationship patterns. The conflict partnership process of relationship building and conflict resolution contributes to the establishment of improved relationship patterns. Thus, options that might not have been possible in the past might be possible within the improved relationship patterns.

Some options should not and cannot be implemented. Those options that *can* become steps toward effective conflict resolution and relationship improvement are called doables in the conflict partnership process. Developing doables thus becomes the next step in the process, and is the subject of the next chapter.

Develop "Doables":
the Stepping-stones
to Action

A s has been emphasized throughout this book, all of the conflict partnership skills can contribute significantly both to building stronger long-term relationships and to dealing effectively with conflicts. As components of the conflict resolution process, the previous six steps move us toward the crucial task of implementing those specific actions parties in conflict can take to improve their relationship and resolve conflicts within the relationship.

We all know that every journey begins with a single step. We also know that life itself is made up of individual moments, various decisions, and particular experiences that have both a singular identity and purpose in themselves *and* a connection to the entire life process. Yet, in situations of conflict we often seem to act as though we have forgotten the importance of and need for building the resolution process on stepping-stones. We frequently try to jump straight to the macro solution, the outcome that we have predetermined is the only circumstance indicating that conflict resolution has really worked.

The stepping-stones along the pathway to resolving conflicts are what I term doables. Doables are specific acts that stand a good chance of success, meet some individual and shared needs, and depend on positive power, usually shared power, to be implemented. As we act on the doables, we lay the stepping-stones and begin to build a pathway leading to an improved relationship and the effective management of the conflicts that are parts of our relationship. Perhaps a story can further emphasize the critical importance of this stepping-stone concept.

Three people are standing in a meadow looking at a mountain range twenty miles away. A young climber has suffered an accident on the other side of the mountain and will die if not rescued in three days. There is no helicopter or other rescue equipment available, and the only tool the three people have is an ax. They realize that they must cross the mountain range on foot. From their vantage point in the meadow, they see what appears to be a gap in the range, and they decide that this is the ideal place to cross the mountains. They focus on the predetermined place of crossing and set out on their rescue mission.

As they move resolutely forward, keeping their eyes on the gap, signs begin to appear indicating that the gap may hold less promise than appeared to be the case from the meadow. They see a trail worn by mountain goats leading off in another direction, but they pick up the pace and keep focusing on the gap they have already decided is the best place to cross the mountains.

After a day and a half of walking, they finally reach the predetermined point of crossing only to discover that the gap is actually a yawning gorge 100 meters deep. They want to leap the gorge, but it is fifteen meters across. They curse fate and go back down the mountain to find another way to cross. The retreat takes another day, leaving them without enough time to take an alternate route to reach the young climber on the other side of the mountain before he dies.

Two lessons emerge from our story: (1) the frequent ineffectiveness of predetermined plans or grand designs and (2) the limitations we create by prematurely believing that leaping from point A to point B in a single bound is the best way to reach the ultimate goal point B represents.

Standing in the meadow, the potential rescuers were not in a very good position to determine the best place to cross the mountain range. Yet in their rush to feel assured that they had a plan, they stubbornly fixed their attention on the seemingly perfect crossing place, the gap. Had they focused instead on a few progressive steps and learned from what those steps were revealing to them, they might have found a pathway developing out of those initial steps. For example, if they had agreed to take a certain direction for the first mile, and that they would read the signs along the way, they could have decided to follow the goat tracks as their next step. In doing so, they would have discovered the safe crossing used by animals. But no, their grand plan became their rigid solution.

When they reached the gorge, another problem occurred. They again focused only on the quick-fix solution of leaping the gorge, a task they could not realistically accomplish. They did not consider taking several smaller, yet critical steps, such as using their ax to fell trees and perhaps construct a crude bridge across the relatively narrow gorge.

In dealing with conflict, we often fail to build the conflict resolution process on stepping-stones, or doables. Thinking we know what the desired outcome should be, we delude ourselves into believing we can always leap straight for that outcome. Rarely is such an instant solution possible. The parties in conflict may not have enough trust in each other to take such a single, gigantic leap, or they may not feel secure enough in their conflict resolution capabilities. If they focus instead on developing doables, they may be able to prove to themselves and to each other that they can indeed work together. They might also come to feel more energized and confident about moving on to the more difficult components of the conflict, components that must eventually be resolved.

Furthermore, working on and accomplishing some do-ables can sometimes help the conflict partners see more clearly where they need to go. I have seen numerous cases in which conflict partners revised their preconceived definitions of both the conflict itself and the expected solutions because of lessons learned and perceptions clarified through working on do-ables.

WHAT IS A DOABLE?

A doable is an action that embodies the following:

1. It stands a good chance of being accomplished.
2. It does not favor one party at the expense of other parties.
3. It usually requires the participation of all parties involved in the conflict in order to be implemented successfully.
4. It meets one or more shared needs.
5. It meets one or more individual needs that are not incompatible with another party's individual needs.
6. It uses the positive power of the conflict partners, ideally involving shared positive power, in which the partners need each other to make the process work.
7. It helps build trust, momentum, and confidence in working together.
8. It adds another stepping-stone along the pathway to improving the overall relationship and reaching mutual-benefit outcomes of particular conflicts within the relationship.

Getting to the point at which doables can be identified and acted upon can involve all of the conflict partnership skills discussed thus far, but several of the skills are especially crucial to developing and implementing doables. Understanding the various components of a conflict can help clarify those parts around which doables can be developed. Focusing on shared needs provides doables with their building blocks, and shared positive power gives doables the energy and strength that make them work. Generating options can reveal possible doables, and identifying key options from among those generated can reveal that some of the key options can indeed become doables.

Thus, developing doables becomes the culmination of the other conflict partnership skills, the next-to-last step in the process. We will devote most of our discussion on Step 7 to providing examples of doables taken from actual conflicts and pointing out things to be careful of in developing doables.

EXAMPLES OF DOABLES

Let's develop in greater depth an example mentioned earlier. Although it is a specialized example, try to focus on the skills being employed.

Example 1

Ron and Eve have been married five years. When they met, Eve was working as an assistant manager at a grocery store and Ron worked on the assembly line at a defense plant making a small device that eventually became a component in a nuclear weapon. Six months ago, Eve met several friends who were active in the peace movement. She grew more and more concerned about the need for nuclear disarmament, and three months ago quit her job and began volunteering twelve hours a day as a peace activist. Her peace movement colleagues had a difficult time accepting the fact that she was married to a man who worked in an armaments factory. Eve became more tense at home, Ron reacted defensively, and the relationship began to suffer.

Eve finally decided to discuss the increasingly conflictual situation with Ron. We will eavesdrop on their conversation. (Please note the numbers in the left margin. They mark points at which the conflict partnership skills are being used. We will pause along the way to comment on these skills.)

1   EVE: You know that speech I was supposed to give at the peace march tomorrow? Well, now they don't want me to appear on the program. And do you know why? Because they fear it will weaken the cause if a woman whose husband makes nuclear weapons appears on the program!

RON: So now it's *my* fault your peace friends are so narrow-minded. I wish they would just realize that in the real world we need defensive weapons to *keep* the peace!

EVE: But nuclear weapons are *offensive* weapons, too. And if we keep relying on violence as our major way of dealing with conflict, we'll eventually destroy the entire human race, and furthermore . . .

2   [Eve pauses, realizing that they are not dealing with the conflict very well. She decides to start with a better opening, indicated by number 1.]

EVE: I'm sorry, Ron. I didn't mean to start arguing about the nuclear arms race. We can't solve that between the two of us. I want to keep our relationship strong even though we disagree on some things. I love you, Ron, and I think if we focus on what we can do to make our relationship even more meaningful, we will be able to deal with our differences on the peace/war issue.

RON: I love you, too, Eve. So . . . how should we deal with this conflict?

3   EVE: Well, I guess I need to clarify some things. How do you feel about my having become so involved in the peace movement?

RON: If that's what you believe, then you have to do it. I

am concerned about finances, though. I'm not sure my salary alone is enough to keep us going.

EVE: I realize that's a problem, and I'm willing to talk about that. But I need to know if you're still happy in our relationship now that things have . . . well, I guess *changed* is the word I'm looking for. You know, now that I'm a peace activist.

RON: [worried] Changed? You mean you are thinking about a divorce?

4   EVE: What did you hear me say, Ron? Did I mention divorce?

RON: Well . . . no, I guess you didn't. You said "now that I am a peace activist." [pause] And yes, I am still happy in our relationship. It means everything to me.

Let's pause for a minute and look at how some conflict partnership skills are being used. The parenthetical numbers in the text below refer to the margin numbers indicating where the particular conflict partnership skill is being employed.

Eve did not begin with a good opening (1). She created an atmosphere in which it was easy for Ron to assume he was being blamed for the conflict. Predictably, Ron became defensive.

Eve wisely tried more of a partnership opening (2) by focusing on their *relationship*, not just on one of their differences of opinion. She also pointed out that determining who was "right" on the peace/war issue was not a doable. Her opening set a "we" atmosphere and emphasized that their shared positive power could help them work together on shared needs and goals.

Eve then began clarifying perceptions. She clarified her own perceptions of how Ron felt about her working as a peace activist (3), and she helped Ron clarify his perceptions of what she had just said, specifically that she had not mentioned divorce (4).

We pick up the conversation where Eve and Ron left off, with Ron just having clarified that he is still happy in the relationship and that it means everything to him.

> EVE: That makes me feel good. I guess I'm just having a hard time with what you do at your job. I'm not sure
> 5   I understand why you're working at the plant. Are you working there as a way of serving one of your values, like peace through military strength?
>
> RON: [sigh] I'm not sure I really believe that way, Eve. When you get going on your peace argument, I guess I get defensive and argue the other point of view. But the truth is I'm working at the plant because it's a job I know how to do. I could be making some other product and still be happy, so long as I could get a decent salary and contribute to our family. Our family is more important than what work I do.
>
> 6   EVE: That helps clarify things for me. I've been trying to understand my own feelings about whether or not I can live with myself when my husband is making weapons. And I've decided that although your work troubles me greatly, I love you enough to try to work together to find a way we can resolve things.
>
> RON: Well, I'm willing to try, too. But what can we do?

Eve clarified some vital perceptions (5 and 6). She helped them both clarify why Ron was working at the defense plant (5). As it turned out, Ron realized he was working there primarily because it was a job he could do. Eve had to know that. If he saw the job as a way of expressing some core value, such as peace through military strength, the conflict would have been much more serious.

Eve helps Ron see how strongly she opposes nuclear weapons, and then makes a critical clarifying and empowering statement: "I've decided that although your work troubles me greatly, I love you enough to try to work together

Eve has just asked Ron which options look feasible in an attempt to help them identify key options, some of which might become doables.

RON: You tell me.

9   EVE: Well, I feel the peace movement is a major value to me. If I quit, I think I would feel I violated my values. I really don't think that's a viable option, Ron. But your suggestion that I go back to work to earn some money makes sense. Maybe I could get a part-time job.

RON: I think that would be good. I could spend some time helping you find a good job.

10 EVE: Let's do it. Any of the other options sound good?

RON: Well, I do think it would be good to meet some of your friends. Let's have a dinner party next week. Think anybody will come?

EVE: I know of several who would come.

11 RON: Good. You know, your being willing to go back to work makes me think of another option. I guess I would consider changing jobs. I'm kind of scared about that, though. I mean, I've never really been in love with the plant, you know. It's boring work. But I'm not sure I can find something else. I'm willing to look into it, but . . .

12 EVE: My organization has a list of nonmilitary jobs that require some of your skills. They've helped other people find good jobs. Want me to look over the list and make some inquiries since I've got more time than you do? I can do it tomorrow.

RON: Sure. But let's make certain the pay is just as good as I'm getting now.

13 EVE: Okay. So let's see what we've decided. I'm going to invite some of the peace people over for dinner next week, and I'm going to look over the nonmilitary job list and make some inquiries.

RON: I'll make some calls, too, and get my résumé updated.

to find a way we can resolve things." In that statement she affirms their shared power and the value of their relationship to her, and then energizes the partnership process of working together by emphasizing that they can find a way to resolve their conflict. Ron then asks, "What can we do?", paving the way for generating options.

7   EVE: Maybe we can throw some ideas around. Once we get some options, then we can discuss how feasible they are. Got any ideas?

RON: Well, you might consider quitting the peace movement for awhile and going back to work at the grocery store.

EVE: One option I've thought of is that I could help you find another job that would use your skills. Any other options?

RON: I guess we could talk more about our beliefs on the whole military thing. We've sort of avoided that topic on purpose. It would be good for us to learn from each other.

EVE: I have another option. I'd like for you to meet some of my peace movement friends. They need to see the type of person you are so that they won't define you solely on your job.

RON: [grinning] And maybe you could join the navy and see the world. They pay well these days, you know.

8   EVE: [chuckling] I'd be hanging over the rail every minute. But these are some options we can work with. Which ones look feasible?

Eve and Ron generate options superbly (7). They do some free-flow optioning without arguing each suggestion, Eve makes sure she learns at least one of Ron's options before she states hers, and they exchange some healthy humor (8). Now they are ready to identify some key options on their way to developing doables.

And I'll ask around about some part-time jobs for you. John Daley's wife just got a good part-time job at a place still looking for good people. Let's do these things and set aside tomorrow evening to see what we've found out and where we go from here.

EVE: Great.

Eve makes sure that she and Ron are both clear that the peace movement is so important to her values that quitting really isn't a viable option (9). But she still looks for some shared needs and goals within Ron's option, and she realizes that additional income for the family is something they both need and a goal they share. Building on the part of Ron's option that suggested she return to work, she then develops a doable.

That doable—Eve's getting a part-time job—is agreed upon (10). It is a good doable because it meets the shared need of additional income, and it becomes an even better doable when Ron adds his positive power by volunteering to help Eve find a good job.

The conflict partnership process built on shared power also energizes Ron to come up with a new option—his looking for another job. Eve turns that option into a possible doable when she makes it a shared power effort by volunteering to get names of nondefense jobs from her peace organization's files (12).

At the end of the dialogue, Eve and Ron clarify the steps they have agreed upon (13). All of the doables are solid. They show how a potentially damaging conflict can be turned into a positive growing experience by using the conflict partnership skills, and how effective doables can be developed.

Example 2

A large national organization, Citizens Action on the Environment (CAE), is hurriedly producing an advertising brochure to recruit new members and raise funds. CAE's director assigns the task to Fiona, the head of the Membership Department, but does not give her specific guidelines for the brochure. Fiona starts working on it, but needs information for the brochure from the Fund-raising Department and Program Department.

When Fiona quickly produces the rough draft, the other two departments start complaining about being given less space in the brochure than they deserve. They blame Fiona. Fund-raising says it will do its section by itself and wants it included in the brochure without any editing by Fiona. She argues that Fund-raising's section is too long and *must* be edited.

The conflict intensifies, and the publication of the brochure is precariously close to missing the important deadline. Jeff, the head of Fund-raising, really doesn't like Fiona very much, and certainly does not want to get into a long conflict resolution attempt with her. He goes to the director for support, and the director tells Jeff to work things out with Fiona.

Can you see any possible doables in this conflict? I hope your answer to that question is, "Even if I think I do see some possible doables, Fiona and Jeff will probably need to go through a lot of the conflict partnership process before *they* will be able to develop and implement any doables."

Let's assume that Fiona employs conflict partnership. She will need to open with something like, "Jeff, we're in this thing together, so, for the sake of CAE, *our* organization we care so much about, let's see if we can work together to make this brochure a really good one."

Then Fiona and Jeff need to clarify some perceptions. Jeff needs to understand that the director more or less threw the brochure task in Fiona's lap at the last minute without any guidelines, and that Fiona is not out to get Jeff. Fiona needs to clarify to herself that Jeff is simply trying to raise funds effectively, and that his personal dislike for her should not tempt her into letting him push any of her buttons or make her dismiss a good option he might generate just because it is his. Jeff needs to clarify the same perception to himself about Fiona.

Fiona also needs to deal with the past effectively, reminding Jeff that they have worked extremely well on previous projects and, therefore, have the potential to work well together on the brochure. She also needs to point out that just because they have also had some past conflicts they did not resolve well, they *can* use improved skills to resolve the brochure conflict.

Then Fiona can get a discussion going on their individual and shared needs. Jeff needs to raise funds; Fiona needs to get new members and to complete the job the director assigned her. Those individual needs can then be combined into the shared need of producing a brochure capable of improving the organization they both care about. Jeff's need to raise funds and Fiona's need to get new members are both essential to the shared need of improving the organization.

They will need shared positive power to make all of this happen. There is no way an effective brochure can be produced if they try to use their individual negative power to dominate or conquer each other. Fiona can activate that shared positive power by initiating the process of generating options that require both of them to contribute positively to making some of them become doables.

Fiona uses conflict partnership well, and two critical doables are developed. They agree to go together to see Anwen, the best writer in CAE, and ask her to edit the brochure. Fiona and Jeff volunteer to do some of Anwen's other work because she is giving of her time to do the editing. That takes care of the immediate problem.

The long-term problem, however, involves (1) the negative relationship patterns Fiona and Jeff have allowed to dominate their recent interaction, and (2) the conflictual production patterns the director has allowed to develop, as evidenced by the way he threw the brochure assignment in Fiona's lap without any guidelines. The doable Fiona and Jeff develop to deal with these long-term problems is a good one because it is built on shared needs and activates shared positive power. The doable? They set a meeting (to be held after the publication of the brochure) of all department heads and the director to devise a greatly improved system for assigning and completing interdepartmental tasks.

Example 3

An inner-city community was in terrible disarray. Gangs roamed the dark streets at night; the hospital had moved to the distant suburbs, leaving the community with no health-care facility; ambulance drivers refused to transport patients for fear of being dragged from the ambulance and beaten; the youth had no place but the dark streets to spend their idle time; and those who could afford to move out of the community were doing so as quickly as possible.

At the time, I was working as a community development organizer and was asked to go to the beleaguered community to see if I could work with the citizens to help improve the situation. As I listened to a wide range of community members express their own needs and the priority needs of the community, several goals kept reappearing: a people's clinic, a youth center, training for police in racial conflicts, and several other important needs. But there was no way the various conflicting factions would work together on such major cooperative ventures. They had no trust of one another and no history of working together for the good of the community. We had to begin building some stepping-stones through which trust and cooperative effort for the good of all could be learned and experienced. In other words, we needed some doables.

The initial doable became street lights! With all of the

major needs staring us in the face, you might ask, why in the world would a community organizer settle for such a minor step as street lights? The reason is that putting street lights on the ten streets where violence occurred almost nightly accomplished several important building blocks for improved relations in the community, an essential prerequisite for the attainment of some of the major needs of the community. Let's go back to the eight criteria that constitute a doable, and see how the street lights accomplished all eight.

1. Getting street lights was *feasible* in the existing situation.
2. *No one faction gained an advantage* because all members of the community would benefit from safer streets, including even the gangs who had complained about so many of their members being injured in fights at the most dangerous streets.
3. *The participation of all factions was required* if the doable were to work. I had worked out an agreement with the city to construct the lights *only* if *all* factions formally signed the request form.
4 AND 5. As in number 2, street lights met *shared needs*.
6. *Shared positive power* was required because all factions needed one another to make it work.
7. *Trust and confidence in one another developed* (the entire community eventually came out to paint the street lights in a variety of colorful designs, and a street dance was held to launch the cooperative venture), and all factions realized that they could indeed work together on a shared need and a mutual benefit.
8. *With the initial doable accomplished, other doables followed*, eventually leading to the immediate creation of dialogue groups throughout the community, a federal grant for the improved training of law enforcement personnel, the completion of a youth center within two years, the opening of a people's clinic in three years, and the voluntary disbandment of three of the four youth gangs as the youth center increasingly earned the respect of the youth.

TAKING CARE IN CHOOSING DOABLES

Doables are so important to effective conflict resolution that it is tempting to see every tiny step parties in conflict can agree on as a doable. Such is not the case, and here are a few of the considerations we need to be mindful of in making sure we choose actions that can serve as viable stepping-stones leading to mutually beneficial ends.

Make sure that the doable is not just a temporary quick-fix Bandaid. Two recently divorced parents wanted to avoid a wounding court battle over custody rights to their five-year-old daughter and three-year-old son. Feeling they had failed in their relationship and fearful of what a trial would do to their children (not to mention what it might do to their standing in their closely knit community), the parents decided to settle the matter without going to court. That decision would have been a good one if they had dealt with their conflict effectively, but when they got together one evening, they came up with a Bandaid rather than a doable. They decided to alternate custody of the children every three weeks.

After about three months, both parents and both children were miserable. The mother came to my office and asked if I would work with them to resolve the situation. When we reached the point of discussing doables, both parents said, "But our temporary step *was* a doable!"

But it was not a doable. It was a quick-fix attempt that had little chance of doing much other than confusing the children and putting off making necessary decisions. Sure, both parents accepted the plan, but that was the only criterion of the eight which constitute a doable that was really met. When I discussed all of this with the parents, they eventually admitted that the only reason they had agreed to such a disruptive plan was to feel as though they had at least done *something*, and that neither of them would have to lose.

Make sure that the doable is not a delaying tactic favoring only one of the parties. The Bogat Corporation has discriminated against minorities and women for decades in its hiring practices, purposely avoiding placing job ads in minority publications and even refusing to hire women managers. Under pressure from both its employees and the community, Bogat's directors decide to make a few minor reforms to create the illusion that the racist system is being changed. The directors put additional job ads in publications, including in bold print the phrase, "an equal employment corporation." But the readership of these publications is ninety percent white. No attempt is made to put job ads in publications primarily targeted to minorities. Another reform was to construct new washrooms in those sectors of their plant to which minorities were traditionally assigned.

These and other similar reforms did nothing to deal with the real core of the conflict: that disadvantaged minorities were not actively sought for employment, and that well-qualified minority employees were consistently passed over when promotions to management positions were offered. Yet, when I was called in to help with the conflict and discussed the conflict partnership approach, Bogat's directors told me they had indeed developed some doables.

I pointed out that doables are developed by the parties in conflict working *together*, not by one party in the conflict simply decreeing a reform. I also got the directors involved in a discussion to see if they could find any significant shared needs or any shared positive power within the reforms they were calling doables. Needless to say, they could not find any shared needs or shared positive power within what they had incorrectly perceived as doables.

The Bogat reforms are a good example of false doables. They really weren't even significant reforms. They were what I term *right-angle reforms*; that is, making changes that travel in a direction akin to drawing a rectangle so that, in essence, you end up where you started.

Thus, Bogat's reforms do not represent effective doables, even if some of the disadvantaged factions might like the minor changes. The reforms are not stepping-stones to an improved relationship in which (1) shared positive power is enhanced, (2) the needs of the minorities are met, and (3) the shared needs of improving the functioning of the overall corporation are addressed. Rather than serving as doables, the reforms are probably just attempts by the corporation to alleviate some of the pressures being directed against its policies.

Doables are not ends in themselves. They are steps that can move conflict partners closer to mutually healthy decisions on major issues. In a recent case I know of, two department heads in a corporation were told by the director to decide how to allocate an extra $30,000 suddenly discovered in the budget during the final week of the fiscal year. She told the department heads that the money must be allocated within the current tax year, and that it must go for only one project, not divided between the two departments. Each of the department heads had his own pet project for which the money seemed ideally suited. Each stubbornly held out for his own project until there were only a few hours left to make the decision. The director became angry and ordered them to decide within the hour.

Fearful of losing their jobs and refusing to give in to the conflict opponent, the two department heads decided to flip a coin, the winner getting his pet project funded. They flipped, one department got the $30,000, and the loser made life miserable for the winner throughout the ensuing year. As the job performance of both men became less and less productive, the director called them in and finally discovered how they had reached their decision on the $30,000. Both men were fired the next day.

A conflict is not completely resolved just because a temporary agreement is reached. The relationship between the two department heads was made worse, not improved, by the temporary solution. The common goal they shared, that of making the corporation more productive, was obstructed. The flip of a coin was certainly not an example of mutual positive power. In other words, what seemed to be a way out of the dilemma actually turned out to lead into an even bigger mess. This shows that a doable is not just any agreement that seems to be the last resort.

A much more healthy conflict resolution process would have been for the two department heads to realize that they had reached an impasse on the two pet projects, that neither was willing to support the other's most cherished plan for the extra money. A good doable would have been the creation of a project combining some of the goals of each of the pet projects, or if that proved impossible, the creation of a totally new project. It did not have to be an either/or situation focusing only on the two projects.

In bringing this section on doables to a close, we should reemphasize that doables are the critical stepping-stones capable of building trust and mutual confidence in working together, that doables are built on individual and shared needs, and that shared positive power is critical in making doables effective. Doables can form a pathway to capabilities previously thought impossible, and can help conflict partners deal with major issues effectively. When coupled with the other conflict partnership skills, doables play a major role in resolving conflicts and improving relationships.

Doables either lead to the final conflict partnership step, which I call developing mutual benefit agreements, or are significant enough to be mutual benefit agreements in themselves. Developing these agreements is the task to which we now turn.

Make Mutual-Benefit Agreements

The seven conflict partnership steps we have discussed have built a structure of relationship improvement and effective conflict resolution that is now strong enough to support the goal to which we have been steadily progressing: the development of mutual-benefit agreements capable of resolving specific conflicts within improved relationship patterns. These agreements become the next step along the conflict partnership pathway.

Conflict resolution agreements must be realistic and effective enough to survive, and perhaps even to develop further, as the challenges of the future confront them. By employing the conflict partnership steps discussed thus far, we can make present decisions and agreements that stand a good chance of remaining effective in the future.

Effective and lasting mutual-benefit agreements must be built on clarified perceptions of the conflict, the partners involved in the conflict, and the specific steps each partner has agreed to take to improve the relationship. Solid mutual-benefit proposals must also be built on individual and shared needs. If people know that some of their own needs are being met by a particular step the conflict partners have agreed to take, and, especially, if some shared needs are being met, there is a strong chance the agreement will hold up in the future.

For agreements to be effective and lasting, they need to be based on individual and shared positive power. Positive power becomes the energy of the improved relationship. There are other elements of mutual-benefit agreements that are also important. Let's explore some of the more critical of these elements.

MUTUAL-BENEFIT AGREEMENTS
REPLACE DEMANDS

Effective conflict resolution and healthy relationships cannot thrive in the atmosphere created by demands. Demands tend to lock relationship parties into patterns characterized by negative power, a struggle for dominance, threats used as weapons, and the assumption that conflict resolution is simply the trading of portions of demands.

Because most conflicts involving the traditional bargaining approach begin with the parties making unrealistic demands that they know will not be accepted by the other party, there are only two possible outcomes, both of which leave much to be desired. The parties can refuse to alter their demands, thereby reaching an impasse, or the parties can back down and lessen the extremity of their demands, thereby losing face and establishing a precedent in which power is perceived as the ability to retain greater portions of demands.

In the conflict partnership process, the parties in conflict move beyond the ineffective pattern of seeing each other in terms of the demands each has made. Instead of demands, the parties focus on developing agreements that can meet some of each party's needs, accomplish some shared goals, and establish a precedent in which power is defined as positive

mutual action through which disagreements can be dealt with constructively.

MUTUAL-BENEFIT AGREEMENTS ARE BUILT ON DOABLES

Mutual-benefit agreements are the culmination of the conflict partnership process and one of the two ultimate goals (the other goal being the improvement of the relationship for the future). Mutual-benefit agreements include some of the major issues involved in the conflict and in the relationship.

However, mutual-benefit agreements on major issues usually become possible only after the conflict partners have developed some doables on matters involving less volatile components of the conflict. In other words, parties in conflict are often unable to deal with the most difficult components of a conflict until smaller steps (doables) are taken, steps through which trust can be improved and experience in working together can be internalized and affirmed. Larger, more comprehensive mutual-benefit agreements on major issues can then be developed more effectively.

Going back to our stepping-stone concept, another way of describing the relationship between doables and mutual-benefit agreements is as follows: *One of the ultimate goals of conflict resolution is for the parties in conflict to develop and implement mutual-benefit agreements, and doables are the stepping-stones we use to find our way to that ultimate goal. The work of conflict resolution is not finished just because some doables have been accomplished. In many cases, the more difficult issues still await attention and decision; they await mutual-benefit agreements.*

To illustrate, let's go back to the section on doables, to the community-organizing effort I helped to coordinate. The community had some quite obvious major issues and goals that would eventually need to become mutual-benefit agreements. The development of a peoples' clinic and a youth center were two of those potential agreements. It would have been impossible to reach these eventual mutual-benefit agreements without first building trust, confidence, and momentum through working together to accomplish a doable, in this case, street lights.

Having pointed out the difference between doables and mutual-benefit agreements, it is instructive to note that some doables are significant enough and comprehensive enough to become mutual-benefit agreements. However, to stress the main point one more time, before conflict partners can settle on mutual-benefit agreements involving major issues, they usually need to accomplish some smaller doables first. To wrap up this discussion on the relationship between doables and mutual-benefit agreements, let's take a brief look at a specific conflict in great need of both doables and mutual-benefit agreements.

At a university where I was a professor, a student named Patrick consistently made low grades. Suddenly, he got a high mark on an exam in a class taught by a colleague of mine named John. Being a rather suspicious fellow, John assumed Patrick had cheated, and sent him to the dean to be disciplined. Patrick emotionally professed his innocence, but neither John nor the dean believed him. Patrick got revenge by disrupting John's class in every way imaginable throughout the next month. The dean finally asked me to help John and Patrick work out their conflict.

Think for a moment about some doables and mutual-benefit agreements you see as being possible in this conflict. Now that you have thought of some possibilities, let's see what actually happened. I met with Patrick and John individually, and tried to get them to clarify their own perceptions, look at some individual and shared needs, find some shared positive power, and come up with some options for dealing with the problem. Then I asked them which options seemed like possible doables.

Both Patrick and John played it safe and, independent of

each other, said that the first doable would simply be getting together, with me present, to discuss the matter constructively. Getting together was a minor doable, but a doable nonetheless. It was a stepping-stone on the pathway to coming up with some mutual-benefit agreements.

Once they got together, other doables led to other mutual-benefit agreements. One doable was to admit to each other that they had both acted rather irresponsibly—John having immediately assumed Pat had cheated, and Pat disrupting class for revenge. The mutual-benefit agreement growing out of that doable was for Pat to take a few minutes right then and there to discuss one of the exam questions so that John could see he really did know the material, and for Pat to agree not to disrupt the class anymore.

Another doable was for John and Pat to go together to the dean after our meeting and ask him to remove the notes he had taken on Pat's "cheating" from Pat's file. That doable prompted them to come up with another mutual-benefit agreement: the three of them agreed to discuss why Pat had done so much better on this one exam. The purpose was to get Pat to identify better study habits that he could use to prepare for future exams.

With these few doables and agreements accomplished, John and Pat were ready for the major mutual-benefit agreement: how to deal with the grade for the exam. John had a policy of never giving makeup exams, but because of the healthy conflict resolution process they had developed, and because the doables let them see they could work together on at least *some* steps, they agreed Pat would take another exam on the same four chapters but would answer different questions. (Pat, by the way, made an A on the makeup exam.)

To reemphasize a point previously made, mutual-benefit proposals usually deal with the most difficult issues and combine steps of improvement into a comprehensive agreement. I have seen situations in which mutual-benefit proposals were finally developed as much as a year after the first doables were accomplished. It took that long for the parties to accept the fact that they had moved beyond negative patterns of the past, that they were beginning to feel at least a little mutual trust, and that working together with a conflict partner did not have to end up weakening either party.

The lesson to be gained from such experiences is that even though mutual-benefit agreements may appear impossible at first because of impasse on seemingly intractable issues, these issues can become more manageable and eventually be addressed if the conflict partnership process is followed.

BEING A CARETAKER OF THE PARTNER'S WELFARE

One of the critical elements of mutual-benefit agreements is that all conflict partners serve as caretakers for the welfare of the self, of the other partner, and of the relationship. If the future is to hold the possibility of an improved relationship in which the same old conflict mismanagement patterns no longer permeate relations, each partner needs to evaluate agreements based on mutual benefits. In other words, I must be concerned about whether or not a particular proposal is meeting some of *your* needs as well as some of my needs. Not to do so will inevitably lead to additional damaging conflicts, and will set in motion an unhealthy view of how conflict resolution should be accomplished.

MUTUAL-BENEFIT AGREEMENTS NEED TO CONSIDER GIVENS

As we develop mutual-benefit agreements, it is important to realize that in almost every conflict there are certain components (situations, needs, values, goals, and so on) that are of such critical importance to one or both of the parties that they cannot be altered or compromised. I call these components *givens*. (However, sometimes parties involved in a conflict cannot identify givens objectively until they have gone through other steps and skills in the conflict resolution process.)

Before suggesting some examples of givens, it is imperative that we caution ourselves to resist the temptation of incorrectly identifying everything we want in dealing with a conflict as a given. To do so is usually an attempt to secure our *demands*, however unrealistic, by claiming that a particular desire is not open to discussion or to the possibility of alternative options. Because the conflict partnership process aims for a mutually beneficial resolution of a conflict and for an improvement in a relationship, *it is important to take special care not to use the idea of givens as a manipulative tool.* To do so will harm the relationship and obstruct healthy conflict resolution. Givens are usually few in number and consist of fundamental components we need to accept as fact.

The following are examples of givens.

Example 1

Two close friends hold diametrically opposed views on a controversial issue. The given is that neither will change her values and beliefs on that particular issue. The task for conflict resolution and relationship building, therefore, is for the friends to agree to disagree on the issue, yet continue to gain mutual benefit from the rest of their relationship. If, however, the issue is of paramount value to one or both of the friends, so important that they do not want to associate with someone who holds the opposing view on that issue, the two friends end their friendship. I would suggest, of course, that they not let a single issue define an entire relationship or a person, and that they consider the mutual growth potentially awaiting them *because* they disagree on that one issue. Most conflicts can be used positively. But each friendship must make the decision about how important a particular issue is in the overall relationship.

Example 2

A supervisor named Chad is constantly loaded down with work. He demands that the company hire an administrative assistant just for him. His demand creates a conflict with the president of the company and other supervisors, none of whom has a private administrative assistant. The company's financial records clearly show that the company is barely making ends meet as it is, so there is no money available to add an administrative assistant to the staff.

The given in this case is that there is no way an administrative assistant can be provided to Chad. If he wants to help resolve the conflict, he needs to accept that given, let go of his unrealistic demand, and then work with the other supervisors to address the real problem his request for an assistant is trying to address: that none of the supervisors has anywhere near the workload Chad has, yet each of them has a full-time secretary, as does Chad. That means that Chad's secretary is overworked, while some of the other secretaries are underworked.

By clarifying what the conflict is really about rather than making demands, Chad may lay the groundwork for a doable and a mutual-benefit agreement. The doable might be to have the head of the secretarial pool keep records for two weeks on which secretaries seem to have a lot of free time. After the two-week period, a mutual-benefit agreement might emerge; namely, that some of Chad's overflow secretarial needs be assigned on a piece-work basis to the secretaries who have free time.

Through these brief examples we can see that understanding givens is an important step both in clarifying perceptions of a conflict and in focusing energy on those components of the conflict we *do* have the power to affect.

CLARIFYING SPECIFIC RESPONSIBILITIES

Sometimes I hear of parties in conflict who have gone through the conflict partnership process admirably, developed several excellent mutual-benefit agreements, and then quickly charged out into the night, either excited about their success or simply relieved that their fear of someone losing had not materialized. During the next several days or weeks, confusion as to what each party had actually agreed to begins to erode the effectiveness of their agreements. Why? Because the parties had not taken the time and care to make sure that they understood the specifics of their mutual agreements before ending their discussion on the conflict.

The simple step of going over what each party has agreed to do can help clarify individual responsibilities. Frequently, some confusion still exists, and while the parties are still in the conflict resolution session it is wise to make sure that each party has indeed agreed to certain actions and understands those actions. Trying to pick up the pieces of confusing misperceptions down the road is difficult and need not arise if the specific responsibilities and agreements are clarified.

THE MUTUAL-BENEFIT AGREEMENT:
AN END AND A BEGINNING

After a particular conflict has been dealt with and mutual-benefit agreements are implemented, individuals and groups will continue to express their own uniqueness. This means that differences among relationship partners will continue, and new conflicts will sometimes emerge. But because the relationship partners have learned and experienced the conflict partnership skills, they have increased their ability to use the differences and new conflicts as opportunities for clarifying and, it is hoped, enriching the relationship.

Thus, mutual-benefit agreements do not really *end* the conflict partnership process. On the contrary, the agreements and the process employed to reach those mutual-benefit agreements actually *begin* an improved process for enriching relationships and dealing with differences. The conflict partnership pathway that the relationship partners blaze and travel on ends only if and when the relationship itself ends; and even then, the pathway can continue in other relationships.

KEEPING THE CONFLICT PARTNERSHIP PROCESS ALIVE

Some of you may be thinking, "Sure, maybe now that I've read this book I can use conflict partnership to resolve a particular conflict. But I can see myself forgetting these skills in a few months and slipping right back into my old patterns."

Keeping the conflict partnership process alive in your relationships and in the way you deal with conflicts might not be as difficult a goal as it seems. I would like to offer several suggestions to help you accomplish that goal.

First, keep reminding yourself that the conflict partnership skills are not just for conflict resolution. They are also relationship-building skills that you can use whether a conflict is present or not. By making the skills a daily part of your relationships, you will be internalizing them so that when a conflict erupts, conflict partnership will be your *natural* response.

Second, look through the eight steps and see which ones you most frequently ignore or violate. Work on those particular skills first. In your next encounter with a relationship partner or a situation of conflict, practice the skills you have identified as those you need to concentrate on. Conflict partnership is indeed a process composed of these eight steps, but I am sure you do some of the steps well already. Try not to look at the process as a complicated model, which it is *not*. Choose a few of the steps and work on them until they become a part of you, then go on to the other steps.

I know some people who have taken this second suggestion to heart so diligently that they outlined, on three-by-five notecards, the three or four conflict partnership steps they wanted to work on, including a brief outline of the major skills within those steps. In idle moments on commuter trains going to work, or in the quietness of their homes, they review their understanding of the steps to keep them fresh. You might not choose to do the notecard exercise, but it shows how people can devise ways of keeping the skills alive in their thinking and in their behavior.

Third, keep reminding yourself that whenever you use the skills, you are empowering yourself, your relationships, and your conflict partners. The power you are increasing is positive power, a power that will enrich your relationships, your family life, and your work life. Reminding yourself that you are increasing your positive power can encourage you to view the skills as practical, self-improvement tools, and then to keep practicing them.

Fourth, use Step 2 in the conflict partnership process, clarifying perceptions, as soon as the first signs of a conflict appear. Many people hesitate when they sense or see the first stages of a conflict emerging, probably because they hope the conflict will simply go away. Clarifying perceptions is a vital skill that is fairly easy to set in motion. Go back over the headings in Chapter 6 (or your three-by-five notecards) to refresh your memory; then clarify, with your conflict partner, the perceptions of what the conflict is about. I have seen many conflicts that would have escalated into mutually damaging situations had not perceptions been clarified at an early stage.

Fifth, share what you have learned from this book with your friends, your spouse, your children, your work colleagues, teachers, ministers, politicians, and so on. Help empower them so that they can help empower others. By becoming a teacher of the conflict partnership skills, you not only spread the knowledge but also help to develop a partner who can help *you* effectively resolve the next conflict you are in with that partner.

One of the suggestions I make at my workshops is for people to go home and put on a miniworkshop for the rest of the family, or to go to the office and ask the boss if the company can arrange an in-service staff development workshop on conflict partnership. The letters I receive from the people who have followed through on this suggestion are overwhelmingly positive. Again, you not only spread the word to others you also keep the skills alive in yourself.

Afterword

Conclusions to books can easily insult both the author and the reader by choosing random portions of the material to leave the reader with, or by trying to summarize that which cannot be so simplistically summarized. Therefore, I will not offer a conclusion to this book. Instead, I have chosen to include two appendices. Appendix A shows how we can use conflict partnership to deal effectively with several frequent problem areas in relationships and conflicts. Appendix B presents two real-life conflict scenarios showing a step-by-step use of all the conflict partnership skills.

So, rather than leaving you with a conclusion, I leave you with a challenge. If you have found conflict partnership to be an empowering and helpful process, make it a part of your life; make it a *way* of life. My experience has taught me that if you do, mutual and lasting benefits will come to you and your relationships, whether they be with friends, family members, workplace colleagues, or in the larger contexts of your organizations, communities, or society as a whole. With confidence in your abilities, I wish you well in this important challenge.

Afterword

Handling Frequent Problem Areas

DEALING WITH ANGER

Anger is an emotion with which we are all familiar. We express anger in different ways, and we certainly know that what makes one person angry might not make someone else angry. Even though we have all experienced anger numerous times, and will again, I am not sure we fully understand what anger really is.

Anger as Energy

Dictionaries define *anger* with words such as extreme hostility, indignation, wrath, and rage. I am sure we have all felt those emotions, but to me, anger is mostly energy. We have the power to channel that energy in numerous ways. We can channel the energy of anger into rage, or assault, or internal stress, or a host of other damaging behavior patterns. Sometimes we aren't even sure why we express anger in certain ways. We simply feel angry, and let it erupt. It's almost as though anger captures us and takes command of our next act. But if anger is actually energy needing to be expressed, then we can also channel that energy into more positive expressions.

Being in Charge of One's Own Anger

Part of our self power comes from being in charge of how we express anger. Rather than choosing to feel guilty about feeling anger and suppressing it, rather than allowing our anger to consume us and take command of our behavior, we do have the power to take charge of anger's energy and make it serve a constructive purpose. We often give away that power: "They made me angry, so it's their fault I attacked them!" "Well, they got angry at me so I got angry at them!" Such statements are quite disempowering to the self, besides being unreasonable. The fact of the matter is that "they" may have done something that made it very easy for me to *choose* to feel angry and express myself in a damaging way, but in the final analysis, *I chose to feel angry and express myself in a certain way.*

Being in Charge of How We Receive Anger

Imagine two parties standing toe-to-toe with clenched fists. One party chooses to use the energy in anger to throw a punch at the other party who is being perceived as the adversary. The other party must choose how to receive that anger. Some people choose to react with the pattern of meeting violence with violence, fist with tighter fist, negative anger-energy with negative anger-energy. But imagine what can be if the energy held in the anger and fear is transformed into a shared power for mutual development, into an open hand reaching for the positive potential in the other party.

Picture a dance of anger, a conflict partnership dance of anger. One dancer throws a fist at the other; the other receives the angry blow with an open hand and transforms the fist thrown in anger into another open hand and offers it back to the other dancer. This is the power of being in charge of how we receive anger. It is saying that I refuse to allow my own behavior to be captured and controlled by the anger of someone else, that I am in charge of how I react to another person's anger, and that I refuse to let their negative behavior become more powerful than my own positive behavior. Our conflict partners may not always choose to receive our open hand with an open hand of their own, but we can be certain that if we hurl fist against fist, either the larger fist demolishes the smaller one, or both fists shatter and rain fragments of waste on what could have been. *Hear the other party's anger; then, rather than acting defensively, focus on what is within the anger that both parties can do something about to resolve the conflict.*

How We Can Express Anger Constructively

As noted earlier, conflict partnership is not a passive approach to conflict resolution that advocates a robotlike calmness at all times. Many conflicts do indeed involve feelings of anger, and that anger may need to be expressed. A person who never expresses anger in very anger-filled conflicts will often experience an increase in tension and other internal damage, which in turn can obstruct the effective use of conflict resolution skills. Thus, the key is *how* we express anger in those moments when not to do so may have even more damaging effects than expressing anger.

If you establish and maintain a partnership atmosphere, if you employ the conflict partnership skills, you can create a process in which expressing anger has a good chance of resulting in something helpful to the conflict resolution process. This is true even if you do *not* express your anger in the most constructive way. However, we all need to try our best to express anger constructively. Expressing anger constructively involves several keys.

- *Share responsibility for your anger; don't put the cause for your anger completely on the other party.* You can say, "I am feeling angry about this situation and I feel what you did contributes to that anger."
- *Try not to personalize your anger by attacking the other person or group; focus instead on the behavior that angers you.* By saying that the other party is a person or group that makes you angry, you are, in effect, saying that their *character* is an anger-producing character. People are usually more willing to see how a particular *behavior* they have committed can be improved than they are to see how their overall character can be improved. In other words, you do not really help empower people to improve their behavior by attacking their personhood.
- *Understand your expression of anger not only as a therapeutic release of feelings but as a way of communicating how deeply the conflict and a certain behavior or situation affects you.* The other party needs to be clear on the depths of your feelings.

To summarize these suggestions on how someone might express anger constructively, here is a statement I have found to be effective: "I'm really angry about this situation! I'm angry about what you did and I don't understand why you did it! I could keep it locked inside, I guess, but I want you to know how deeply I feel about this. But just because I'm angry doesn't mean I don't want us to work together to resolve this thing. I *want* us to work together. And I want *you* to have enough confidence in our ability to work it out so that you'll express *your* anger, too, whenever you feel it. Within our anger, let's find some things we can *do* to resolve things."

WHEN ONE PARTY THINKS THERE IS NO CONFLICT

Another frequent problem area in need of attention arises when one party in a conflict does not acknowledge that there *is* a conflict. There are several possible steps we can take to deal with this problem.

Are you sure the conflict is not an internal conflict, a problem you are feeling inside yourself that may not really involve the other party? After you are fairly certain it is not just an internal conflict, you then need to take additional steps.

Consider *why* the other party is not acknowledging the conflict. Try to look first at your *own* behavior. Perhaps you have not adequately expressed how deeply you feel about the conflict. Perhaps you have not clarified what you think the conflict is about in terms the other party can understand. Perhaps you have not established a conflict resolution atmosphere in which the other party can feel secure enough to deal with the conflict or even admit there is a conflict.

If any of these conditions seem to prevail, look over the conflict partnership skills to see what you can do to improve your own behavior in dealing with the conflict. You then need to focus on the other party more carefully.

- Are certain extremely sensitive matters involved— matters that the other party cannot face right now? If so, perhaps you can focus on some doables involving less sensitive areas and make a pathway that will help the other party feel more secure in dealing with the sensitive matters.
- Are there perceptions that need clarification—perceptions that will help the other party see that there is indeed a conflict?
- Is the other party seeing the conflict as an I-versus-you situation and wanting to avoid the battle that will result? How, then, can you help develop a "we" partnership atmosphere so that the other party will not feel as though it is her/his power fighting against your power?
- How can the other party be helped to see that the two of you can use shared power? I have found that dealing with this question can often help the other party realize

that it is okay to acknowledge the conflict because now there is a power ("our" power) stronger than either party's individual power to help deal with the situation.

Even though you have thought about these questions, you are left with the task of confronting the other party. I have found that a good opening with people who are not acknowledging that there is a conflict is to say, "I'm feeling there's a conflict in our relationship. I'd like to describe what I think it is." If you then use the appropriate conflict partnership skills in describing the problem, you will clarify just why it is you feel there is a conflict.

Even if you do use this opening or a similar one you devise, the other party may say, "Hey, that's *your* problem!" A good reaction to that comment is, "Well, I'm sure *I'm* involved in the problem, and it's affecting our relationship, so I think both of us need to be involved in trying to work it out."

WHEN YOU FEEL UNSURE ABOUT CONFRONTING SOMEONE

Many people see confrontation as a task full of enormous strain and some degree of fear. I have learned that two of the major reasons are that those people feel (1) confrontation means conflict, and conflict is bad, and (2) they feel they have no effective confrontation skills.

Let's look at a workplace situation to get insight into how conflict partnership can help people get up the courage to confront someone, and to do it effectively. Curt, a manager of a department, feels tension with an employee named Ned. The tension has been brewing for weeks as Ned increasingly shows lazy work habits, a lack of enthusiasm for tasks assigned, and an overall combative attitude when dealing with colleagues. Curt has not confronted Ned because Ned really hasn't made any errors in his work or violated any company policies. Ned doesn't know anything is wrong. Still, Curt feels he is in conflict with Ned.

Why has Curt not confronted Ned? Perhaps Curt is unsure how to deal with Ned's behavior, in that no policies have been violated. If Ned *had* violated a policy, it would make it easier for Curt to confront him. Or perhaps Curt is one of those people we mentioned who hates to confront people, either for the reasons discussed earlier, or because he fears Ned will get angry (and Curt does not deal well with anger) or because he's worried that Ned will say, "What's the problem?", and Curt really hasn't figured out how to describe the problem.

In spite of these misgivings, Curt knows he must confront Ned because (1) Curt is letting the tension eat away at him, and (2) the atmosphere in the department is suffering because Ned's behavior is causing tension with other employees. How can Curt get up the courage to confront Ned, and then how can he confront Ned effectively?

Getting Up the Courage for Confrontation and Confronting Effectively

Courage is a matter of self power. It is also a matter of "power with," not "power over." Curt can get up the courage to confront Ned by doing the following:

- Realizing that confrontation and conflict can have positive results; namely, Curt can relieve his tension, Ned can be made aware of the difficulties his behavior is causing for himself and for the work of the department, Curt can find out *why* Ned is behaving as he is, and the other employees can see that Curt is exercising his responsibilities as manager. All of these are positive results.
- Curt can do further preparation by going over the conflict partnership skills and focusing on those he feels are most pertinent to the situation involving Ned.
- Curt can also make sure he knows what his goals are in confronting Ned, how he will open the discussion, and

what specifically he will suggest as possible ways the situation can be improved. In other words, Curt can gain courage by being prepared.

Curt does these things and feels a bit more courage and a bit more empowerment. He now feels ready to confront Ned. Let's look at how he applies conflict partnership in doing so.

Curt asks Ned to meet him in a vacant office to discuss some work-related matters. Curt purposely avoids meeting in his office so that Ned will not feel intimidated.

Curt begins by asking Ned, "How do you feel work has been going these past few weeks?" (Curt is clarifying a perception; that is, finding out whether or not Ned feels there is a problem.)

"Okay, I guess," Ned replies. "Why? Is something wrong?"

"Well, I'm feeling a bit concerned about a couple of things," Curt says. "I'm not comfortable with the overall atmosphere in the department, and I want to see if you have picked up on any possible causes."

"Well," Ned says, "I feel some of the others are a little cold toward me sometimes, but other than that, I don't see anything wrong."

"I've noticed that coldness, too," Curt responds. "I guess we all know that most things work out better for everybody when folks get along with one another. Why do you think some of them are cold toward you?"

"Beats me. Just a difference in personalities, I guess."

"Does it bother you?" Curt asks.

"Well . . . yeah. I guess it does. It doesn't make me too eager to come to work every day," Ned says with a trace of bitterness in his voice.

"Has anything specific happened to cause the tension?"

Ned pauses, then says, "Maybe they don't like working with a laid-back guy like myself. They're all so *eager*. Last month I missed a deadline because I was just burned out with the same old jobs I've been stuck with. Walt and Phil got on my case about missing the deadline, and I decided just to ignore them for a few weeks."

Let's leave the conversation for a minute and evaluate Curt's approach thus far. He is trying not to assume that Ned sees the situation the same way he does, and keeps asking Ned questions to clarify perceptions of what is really going on. In answering the questions, Ned is revealing some very helpful information and insights. Let's go back to the conversation.

"Ned," Curt says. "My major concern is to help the department work as effectively as it can. I believe the difficulty involving you, Walt, Phil, and some others is getting in the way of our doing as well as we can. I'd like to get some ideas from you about what you think can be done to make things better for everybody."

Ned thinks for a minute, and then says, "I'm not sure there's really a problem. We don't have to *like* each other to work together."

"I agree," Curt says. "I don't care if you like each other or not, but I'm saying the *work* is suffering."

"Maybe it's *their* problem, or *your* problem," Ned says defensively.

"It's *our* problem, Ned. We're all in this together. You mentioned something about 'the same old jobs you're stuck with.' Can you explain that a little more?"

"I've been stuck with the mailing list update for the past four months. Everybody hates that job, and it's supposed to be rotated every two months."

"I didn't realize it hadn't been rotated," Curt replies. "Is that the main thing bothering you?"

"Yeah, it really is," Ned answers decisively. "It's just not fair."

"Let's do something about it, then," Curt says. "I'll call

a meeting and set out some task assignments for the next six months making sure jobs are indeed rotated. And I'm sure you can do some things to make life better around here, too."

"I guess I probably can do something, but *what*?"

"Think about it a little while," Curt suggests.

Ned thinks for a few minutes, and then says, "Well, maybe something with Walt and Phil. There was a time we got along okay."

"How about having lunch with them and clearing the air?" Curt suggests.

"Man . . . I don't know. It might get tense."

"Did you and I do okay just now?" Curt asks.

"Well . . . yeah, I guess we did," Ned says, pleasantly surprised.

"Well, let's take a minute to look at why we did okay, and then maybe you can try the same things when you talk with Walt and Phil."

We can see that although Curt was uncomfortable about confronting Ned, he did it effectively by employing some key conflict partnership skills. Here's what he did.

He set a *partnership atmosphere* of "we": members of the work force seeking how to make the workplace better for everyone.

He *clarified perceptions* of why Ned was not getting along with Walt and Phil, and perceptions of what the real conflict was about (not simply the desire of some colleagues to see Ned change his laid-back personality, but that the work of the department was suffering and ultimately making life more difficult for everyone).

Curt kept trying to *develop and use positive power* (Ned's power by urging him to make suggestions, Curt's power by agreeing that he would remove one of the causes of Ned's lack of enthusiasm by monitoring the job rotation policy, and shared power by working together on doables).

Curt kept urging Ned to help *generate options*, and therefore several *doables* emerged.

WHEN THE OTHER PARTY SEEMS NOT TO WANT A RESOLUTION

I sometimes hear the comment, "But how can conflict partnership work if the other party does not *want* to resolve a conflict?" Although it is true that there are some people who seem to thrive on keeping a conflict going, there are steps we can take to work toward a resolution.

Look at the atmosphere you are promoting. Before automatically assuming that the other party does not want to resolve the conflict, try to make sure that *you* are not contributing to an atmosphere that discourages the other party's participation. If you are making unrealistic demands; if you are using the conquest, avoidance, or some other ineffective approach; or if you are failing to reach for the other party's positive power, *you* may be contributing to the other party's reluctance to resolve the conflict.

See if you and the other party are dealing with the same conflict. If, after looking at your own behavior, you are fairly certain you are at least trying to set a partnership atmosphere, you then need to focus on making sure that you and the other party are clear about what the conflict really is. I have seen many situations in which each of the parties involved in a conflict is defining the conflict differently. When this situation exists, it is not surprising that the parties may feel the other person or group is not wanting to resolve the conflict. Why? Because, in dealing with something other than what *you* are dealing with, the other party seems to be ignoring *your* definition of the conflict. Using the suggestions for clarifying perceptions of the conflict in Step 2, you can help clarify whether or not you and the other party are indeed defining the conflict similarly. If you are not, you need to sort out that problem before you can move forward toward effective conflict resolution.

Make sure that you are focusing on a realistic and specific component of the conflict. People sometimes keep a conflict going because they can't get a handle on anything specific and realistic to resolve. Try to look at the components of the conflict and focus on one that is most likely to yield a doable. If the other party seems especially reluctant to work on resolving the conflict, try to start with something the other party defines as important, even if that component is not your first choice. Doing so can help encourage participation.

Questions to ask the other party. Let's assume you are trying to set a partnership atmosphere, that you have made sure that you and the other party are dealing with the same conflict, and that you have identified a specific component as a starting point in the conflict resolution process. Still, the other party seems intent on keeping the conflict going. Asking some of the key questions that follow can help move the process along.

You can come right out and ask the other party, "Do you want to resolve this conflict?" Frequent answers include "Of course I do," "*I* do, but do *you*?," "It's your problem, not mine," "I want to resolve it, but I don't know what we can do," "Don't make such a big deal out of it," and "I'm not sure what we're fighting about." Whatever answer the other party gives, you are gaining some valuable information. You can then use the specific conflict partnership skills most pertinent to what is being revealed in the response the other party has given. Furthermore, asking this question can help other parties who really do need to be involved in resolving the conflict realize that their behavior may be leaving the impression that they do not want to resolve the conflict.

Another helpful question is, "Do you think you'll be better off if we resolve this conflict?" In other words, "What are some of the things you need that resolving this conflict can help you get?" As we have said repeatedly, some people have become accustomed to thinking that conflict resolution usually produces a winner and a loser. They don't want to lose, so they convince themselves that they'll be better off if they just keep the conflict going until the other party gives up or the conflict just fades away. Asking this question can help the other party consider the possibility that some of their needs may be met if the conflict is resolved.

Many people keep conflicts going because they feel there are no skills capable of resolving conflicts effectively. To this you can say, "I know of some skills we can both use that may help. Want me to describe some of them?" You can then describe whatever conflict partnership skills you feel are most applicable to the particular conflict and parties.

Some people really may not want to resolve the conflict. Even after you have tried all of the suggestions previously discussed, there may be some people who refuse to become involved in a conflict resolution process. Their reasons may be so complex that you will never be able to figure them out. You are then left with two basic choices.

1. You can look at the overall relationship and decide whether the conflict at hand is serious enough to end the relationship, provided it is a relationship that you have a choice about ending or continuing. Life is too short to stay in relationships that continually damage one or both parties. Neither party benefits from relationships in which one party refuses to deal effectively with major conflicts.

Before making the choice to end a relationship, however, I would strongly urge you to exhaust all of the conflict partnership skills. As I have said, it is amazing how invitational conflict partnership can be, how often seemingly intransigent people can be encouraged to participate once they see and experience the actual application of the skills. You might also seek help from a third party. Relationships of worth are precious opportunities and should not be dismissed prematurely.

2. If the particular conflict the other party refuses to re-

solve is not vital to the continuation of an otherwise healthy relationship, you may need to accept the fact that the conflict may always remain, and then concentrate on making the other parts of the relationship as positive as possible.

DEALING WITH PEOPLE WHO ONLY WANT THINGS THEIR WAY

We all like to have things go our way (at least *some* of the time) when involved in a conflict. There are conflict partners, however, who seem to want things to go their way *all* of the time. How do we deal with such situations?

The most important task is to work hard to energize the very foundation of the conflict partnership process: that parties involved in a conflict are partners, not simply adversaries, and that all parties will benefit if the conflict is resolved in a way that improves the relationship. We need to help our conflict partners see that a relationship in which one party always seeks to get her or his own way is cheating everyone out of the richness that relationships can provide. Let's look at some specific things you might do when you are in a relationship with a person who always tries to get his or her way.

Make sure that you do not allow their behavior to take charge of you. In other words, be careful not to think that because they are trying to get *their* way, you have to be just as obstinate in trying to get *your* way. Try to get them to generate other options with you. People who are focusing on their way often become even more intransigent if they think the other party is doing the same thing. You might even say, "Let's try to think of some other options since we both seem stuck on our own pet ideas."

Explore why they behave this way. Based on the many cases I have dealt with in which one or more of the parties must have its way, I have found that there are several recurring reasons for this.

Reason 1: The other party might be defining conflict resolution as an I-versus-you struggle for victory. Try extra hard to (1) set a partnership atmosphere, (2) state clearly that you have a view of conflict resolution as a process in which you need each other, (3) focus on shared needs and shared power, and (4) generate specific options and doables that will clearly improve the relationship for both of you. These tactics can help the other party see that there is a more constructive way to view conflict resolution, and that simply getting his or her own way may not be as productive as working together to find a way that improves the relationship for both parties.

Reason 2: The other party might be caught up in the seesaw pattern of power, thinking that if they don't control the decision, that if you get power by having some of your ideas considered seriously, they will be weakened. To deal with this possibility you can focus diligently on developing "our" power. One way is to ask them for other options early in the discussion, to give a few of your own, and then to explore key options together. Another way is to remind them of examples of effective shared power the two of you have exhibited in the past. I urge people to talk about "our" power and how it is stronger than any one person's individual power.

Reason 3: The other party might have allowed themselves to focus on their own control over the situation rather than on the needs of the situation. Get them to say what they think the situation really needs, and then try to build doables on those needs rather than allowing yourself to become obsessed with countering their attempt to get their own way.

Don't delude yourself into thinking that by always giving in to the other party's desires, and thereby ending the conflict, that the relationship is improved. The immediate conflict may go away, but you will likely continue to feel unfulfilled, the other party will be encouraged to keep trying to get his or her own way in future conflicts, the relationship will *not* be improved, and neither of you has learned how to resolve conflicts. To repeat, effective conflict resolution is not deciding who gets their way. Using conflict partnership can help you find a resolution that is "getting *our* way," even with people who seem locked in a pattern of "either your way or mine."

DEALING WITH CONFLICTS
INVOLVING INJUSTICES

Conflicts involving injustices test our conflict resolution skills perhaps more than any other type of conflict. I believe we must stand up decisively for the just treatment of people and groups, yet we must somehow do it in a way that leaves open the possibility of working *with* the person we think is committing the injustice. There are several ways to deal effectively with conflicts involving injustices.

Make sure that you understand the difference between behavior that is an injustice and merely behavior you do not like. In our earlier discussion on the difference between values and preferences in conflict situations, the point was made that people sometimes elevate preferences to the level of values so as to give their desired outcomes more justification. The same pattern is sometimes used when people label as unjust a particular behavior or conflict resolution suggestion that is actually something they do wish to see implemented. If you treat as an injustice a particular behavior or suggestion you simply dislike, your conflict partner will likely become offended and respond with a combativeness that obstructs effective conflict resolution. Although there is no fail-safe way of distinguishing between an injustice and something you simply dislike, perhaps a definition of an injustice, followed by an example, will help to clarify the difference.

An injustice involves a violation of certain values or principles you believe to be important. For example, Maria, an immigrant, holds as a value the equal and nonviolent treatment of all people, regardless of race, culture, sex, and socioeconomic status. She works for two years at a company, achieves high performance, and yet is passed over for a promotion that is given to a less qualified white male. Maria complains to her boss, he dismisses her complaint without serious attention, and a conflict ensues. Maria sees the conflict as one involving injustice. She goes back to the boss, tells him why she thinks an injustice is involved, and then uses the skills evident in the material that follows. Eventually, Maria secures the promotion *and* gains the respect of her colleagues, including the boss.

Carmela, Maria's friend, who came with Maria from their home country, works for the same company. Her work performance has been mediocre at best, yet when she is also denied a promotion, she immediately feels discrimination and injustice have been committed, and uses anger unconstructively in confronting the boss. The boss reacts angrily, and Carmela's workplace existence becomes miserable.

Do you believe that both conflicts involved injustice? I would contend that Maria's conflict did, Carmela's did not. By unwisely elevating her disappointment at being denied the promotion to the level of an injustice, Carmela worsened the conflict and damaged her work relationships.

After clarifying the difference between an injustice and a dislike, and feeling confident that the conflict does indeed involve an injustice, you then need to communicate to the other party involved that you believe an injustice has occurred. This step may sound glaringly obvious, but I am constantly amazed at how many people simply assume that *everyone* perceives that an injustice is involved in a particular conflict because *they* feel an injustice is involved. I have seen numerous situations in which the person or group supposedly guilty of committing the injustice has no idea the other party feels that an injustice has been done. Unless the offending party clearly understands that a certain behavior is being perceived as an injustice, he or she will not fully appreciate the seriousness of the conflict. Without that appreciation, the offending party may dismiss the offended party's intense response as overreaction and, in many cases, also overreact.

Focus on the behavior, not just on the person. I would be greatly surprised if most of your relationships were with people who are *always* unjust. During the course of a relationship, most people who commit an unjust act that causes a conflict also commit acts that are fair. As was mentioned earlier, to focus on that person as being an unjust person can obstruct the real conflict: that the person's behavior in a particular situation was unjust. Yet, we frequently hear people saying, "You aren't fair!" rather than the more constructive statement, "I feel what you did wasn't fair."

The difference between those two statements may seem small, but to the person accused of being an unfair person, the difference is important. If someone is an unfair person, if that is their character, then what hope is there that they can exhibit fair behavior? They are led to respond, "Well, if you think I'm an unfair person, then I guess we have nothing to talk about," and the conflict does not get resolved. It is much better to say, "I think what you did was unfair, and I want to understand why you did it. Were you aware I might feel unjustly treated? Would you feel unjustly treated if someone did that to you?"

Forthrightly stand up for justice, clearly state where you think injustice is being done, but do it in a way that reaches for the just behavior, the positive potential, in the other party. You can make a good start on this important step by focusing on the behavior, not the person's character. But there is more to be done.

- Discuss with your conflict partner what alternative behavior could have been used. You might ask them to tell you how they would have liked to have been treated if they had been in your shoes.
- Point out examples of times they *have* been fair in the relationship. This helps them focus on their positive potential.
- Focus on options and doables that can involve both of you in constructive action to meet individual and shared needs and to improve the relationship; don't lock your mind on just the unfair behavior.
- If you feel that receiving an apology for the unjust behavior is essential, I strongly advise that you wait until the other steps have been accomplished.

DEALING WITH SEEMINGLY
UNRESOLVABLE CONFLICTS

It is my belief that no conflict is unresolvable. Some of you might debate such an assertion, but let me explain what I mean. The reason some conflicts go unresolved is not because they are irresolvable; rather, they go unresolved because one or both of the parties involved in the conflict either goes about conflict resolution ineffectively or does not want to resolve the conflict. But the conflict itself is resolvable.

How *resolvable* is defined, of course, becomes rather important in understanding the assertion that no conflict is irresolvable. In my perception of resolvable, there are several levels, as you may remember from earlier in the book.

The top level is reached when conflict partners come to a

resolution that meets some individual and shared needs, results in mutual benefits, and improves the relationship for the future. The conflict partnership process focuses on the top level as its goal.

The middle level is reached when conflict partners come to some mutually acceptable agreements that settle a particular conflict for the time being, but do little to improve the relationship for the future. The traditional negotiation, mediation, and arbitration patterns tend to reach this middle level of conflict resolution.

The lower level of conflict resolution occurs when one party so *defeats* the other that the relationship is ruined or when parties dissolve the relationship in hatred.

Although there are important qualitative differences in these three levels, all involve some degree of resolution. My experience has shown me that many people stop at the lower or middle level, assuming that there is no possibility of reaching the top level. Employing the conflict partnership process can open up the possibility of reaching that top level of conflict resolution.

As has been pointed out, some conflicts are much more difficult than others, especially conflicts involving seemingly incompatible needs, deeply held values, injustices, and/or the use of seesaw power and other types of negative power. Discussing how one deals with these and other seemingly irresolvable conflicts does not require a new array of skills. The skills encompassed in the eight conflict partnership steps provide us with the tools to deal with even the most difficult conflicts. The key task is to focus more diligently on the particular conflict partnership skill or skills most pertinent to whatever seemingly irresolvable conflict is facing us. Thus, I would urge you to review the sections of this book that deal specifically with value conflicts, need conflicts, injustices, developing positive power, and whatever additional areas pertain to the especially difficult conflict you are addressing. The entire conflict partnership process still applies, of course, but particular parts of the process may need special attention in certain extremely difficult conflicts.

WHEN TO SEEK A THIRD-PARTY FACILITATOR

Although the conflict partnership process provides skills capable of resolving conflicts and building strong relationships, there are situations in which a third-party facilitator, a person not directly involved in the conflict, may be needed. Some situations of conflict involve issues, emotions, personalities, and/or past histories which create such sensitive circumstances that it becomes extremely difficult for the parties to resolve their conflict without outside help. Let's look, therefore, at some of the signs that can help in answering the question, When should the assistance of a third-party facilitator be sought?

First, it is important for people and groups involved in conflict to exhaust every possibility of resolving the problem without the aid of a third-party facilitator. If all of the conflict partnership skills discussed in this book are employed, there is a strong chance that most conflicts can be resolved without the aid of an outside facilitator. But it often takes perseverance. Too many people give up too quickly and assume that they must bring in a third-party facilitator. When the premature use of a facilitator occurs, the parties in conflict are often disempowered, a dependency on the facilitator develops, and the parties are deprived of gaining the skills and confidence essential to dealing effectively with conflicts on their own.

Second, if a third-party facilitator is needed, it is important that the parties in conflict realize that seeking the assistance of an outside facilitator does not necessarily mean that the parties are inadequate. As I have said, there are some situations of conflict in which a facilitator's help can result in a more effective resolution than the parties could develop on their own.

Third, let's examine a few of the situations that I have learned usually need the assistance of a third-party facilitator.

• When few, if any, of the conflict partnership skills have been employed

After reading this book, I hope you will want to make use of the conflict partnership process. However, there are many situations involving your friends, co-workers, and groups in which the skills will either be unknown to the parties in conflict or simply ignored. Perhaps you can either share the conflict partnership skills with the parties, or you might even want to serve as a third-party facilitator yourself. My experience has taught me that if the skills are used, perceptions can be clarified, individual and shared needs can be met, shared positive power can energize effective resolution, options can be generated, doables and mutual-benefit agreements can be reached, and the relationship can be improved for the future.

It is also important to note once again that it is not necessary for *all* of the parties involved in a conflict to start out using conflict partnership. As mentioned earlier, if only *one* of the parties uses the skills, the process usually has an invitational effect on the other party or parties, gently coaxing them into a process that they soon come to realize is mutually beneficial and relationship-building.

• When needs are truly incompatible

We must be careful on this one. Fewer needs are incompatible than we often assume. Try to focus on shared needs first. If, however, there are some individual needs involved that are indeed incompatible, a third-party facilitator may be able to help the parties find other areas of their relationship that they can work on and even help the parties to identify some way of dealing with the incompatible needs. Some examples of incompatible needs might include (1) large enough salaries for workers to meet the needs of their families, and a company nearly going bankrupt needing to have enough revenue to stay afloat and (2) a spouse's need to develop his or her own personhood and work skills through additional education, and the other spouse needing to be on the road in her or his job, thus leaving no one to care for the children at home.

• When the parties in conflict continue to insist on unrealistic demands the other party or parties cannot possibly meet

As discussed in Chapter 2, making demands does not lead to effective conflict resolution. Yet the ineffective traditional negotiation pattern most people and groups employ usually begins with each party making demands. When the parties rigidly stick to their demands, usually demanding things the other party either has inadequate power to accomplish or refuses to accomplish, a third-party facilitator can help significantly in assisting the parties to move beyond demands in order to focus on needs, doables, and mutual-benefit agreements.

• When the history of the parties involved in a relationship has such an emotional and mutually wounding past that the parties seem unwilling or unable to move beyond refighting past battles, to learn from the past, or to take new steps for the present and future

In such situations a third-party facilitator can work individually with the parties to help them realize that unless they want the conflict-laden past to dictate the present and future, they need to concentrate on developing doables and mutual-benefit agreements that can serve both individual and shared needs for the present and future, thereby improving the relationship and providing a more secure future.

• When cultural differences are allowed to create quite different approaches to conflict resolution and to obstruct clear communication and understanding

In the numerous intercultural conflicts I have facilitated, I have found that the parties often feel relieved to have an outside facilitator from another cultural background assist the conflict resolution process. What the facilitator can bring is a *process* not defined by either of the cultural traditions involved in the conflict, a process that can respect cultural differences yet provide skills both cultures can learn to trust and employ.

* When the conflict involves the unjust treatment of one party by the other, yet the offending party either refuses to acknowledge or does not see that an injustice is being done

These types of conflicts are among the most severe and complex. People, groups, and entire societies can define injustice differently. A third-party facilitator can often help the party accused of unjust behavior realize that even though they may not clearly see the injustice of their behavior, the needs of the relationship require them to adjust their behavior. Furthermore, a facilitator can help the offended party focus on proposals to improve the relationship and meet some of the offender's needs rather than spending all of their energy on criticizing the injustice they feel they are receiving. If a third-party facilitator is used, here are the steps I recommend be followed.

CONFLICT PARTNERSHIP THIRD-PARTY FACILITATION SKILLS

Note: Use all of the conflict partnership skills for third-party facilitation

PHASE ONE

Meet with Each Party Individually, if Possible

1. To learn about the conflict
2. To learn about the conflict parties

3. To ask critical questions, some of which might be:
   - What do you think the conflict is about?
   - What are your needs?
   - What are their needs?
   - What are some shared needs?
   - What does your relationship need?
   - What can you do to improve the relationship?
   - What *mis*perceptions do you think might be involved?
4. To introduce them to the conflict partnership process
   - Your questions introduce some of the important aspects of the process.
   - Encourage them to resist making demands and to focus on mutual-benefit options.
5. To clarify and get their agreement on the third-party role you will serve.
   - Encourage them to be thinking of mutual-benefit options and doables.

Note: Remember that there is nothing inherently positive about getting parties in conflict together if the process they will use is faulty. Meeting with them individually can help introduce a more effective process. It is not always possible to meet with the parties individually, but try.

PHASE TWO

Meeting with the Parties in Conflict

1. Preliminary matters.
   - If possible, choose a time and place conducive to effective conflict resolution.
   - Get agreement on your role as the facilitator.
   - Get any initial agreements on process you feel are important. For example:
     "Can we agree to let the other finish without interruption?"
     "Can we agree to try to avoid seeing only the negative in the other party?"
     "I hope you will go ahead and express your feelings,

but try to be listening for the important messages within those feelings, for something the two of you can do something about. Can we agree on that?"

2. Set a partnership atmosphere. Choose a wise opening based on what you have learned about the conflict and the parties involved. There is no one opening that is guaranteed to be perfect for all conflicts. At the very least, your opening should stress, in your own words, that the parties need each other to work the problem out effectively, and that you believe they can work together to find mutually beneficial steps to improve their relationship and to deal effectively with the conflict at hand. Remember to keep setting a partnership atmosphere throughout the facilitation.

3. Based on what you know about the conflict and the parties, choose your opening question and which person you will talk to first.
   • This is *very* important. It sets the tone for the entire process.
   • Don't just open the door to rehash the same old arguments.
   • Be aware of the perceived power of each party in choosing which goes first.
   • Try to choose and phrase your opening question in a way that promotes the overall atmosphere and specific skills of the conflict partnership process.

4. Clarify, clarify, clarify.
   • Clarification is one of the most critical contributions of a facilitator.
   • Be looking for any statements or expressions you see as needing clarification.
   • Always ask them to clarify what they heard the other party saying rather than your doing the clarifying for them. If they seem unable to clarify for themselves, you can *then* paraphrase what you heard them saying. But ask them to do it first.

5. Keep nurturing shared positive power.
   • Be conscious of any indications of disempowerment

or domination, and ask questions that help restore shared positive power.

- Don't be reluctant to remind them of their need to find their shared positive power if they are to improve their relationship and deal effectively with the conflict at hand.

6. Keep listening for shared needs.
7. Keep encouraging them to come up with mutually beneficial options.
8. Keep listening for doables.
9. Don't be the "answer" person; facilitate their empowerment.
10. Keep reminding them to talk to each other, not through you.
11. Keep quiet if they are doing well. When you intervene, have a reason for doing so.
12. Feelings will be expressed, sometimes angrily. If you are using the skills, the process can withstand these outbursts. Don't think you have to interrupt every time feelings are expressed loudly.
13. Get agreements along the way. This helps parties gain confidence, trust, and momentum.
14. When agreements are reached, make sure that the parties are clear on the specifics. Help them clarify specific individual responsibilities within the agreements.
15. Check back to make sure that the agreements are working.

APPENDIX B

Two Cases That Demonstrate the Conflict Partnership Process

CONFLICT ONE

Jon has six weeks of school left before completing his sophomore year in college. He is taking some courses in preparation for a curriculum in architecture, a fact that greatly pleases his father, who is a very successful architect. Jon, however, is not pleased. He feels as though his potential as a human being is stagnating, that he needs some time away from school and from many of the familiar patterns (Jon sees them as ruts) his life has always followed. He has decided on his own to drop out of school immediately, take incompletes in his courses for the spring semester, and move to an alternative holistic community in Hawaii for a period of time. The seventy members of the alternative community explore a more simple, natural life, growing their own organic food, developing alternative energy sources, building their own living quarters, and studying holistic philosophies.

Accompanying Jon on the trip will be Dana, a young woman who, in recent months, has become Jon's primary

265

companion. Fearful of his father's reaction, Jon has put off telling his parents about his decision. Finally, Jon realizes he must have a serious discussion with the family and decides to talk to his father tonight. His father is watching his favorite television show as Jon enters the den. We will listen in on the conversation. (Read the conversation all the way through, then go back and refer to the margin numbers as they are discussed in the explanations following the conversation.)

JON: Dad? Can I talk with you for a little bit?

DAD: Can't it wait, son? I've been waiting all week to see this show.

JON: It's really important, Dad.

(Dad is so engrossed in the television he doesn't hear Jon.)

1   JON: Dad? Can we talk after the show?

DAD: What? Oh . . . yeah. It'll be over in fifteen minutes. Let's talk then.

2   When the show is over, Jon asks Dad to turn off the television and invites him up to his room. Dad agrees and goes up to Jon's room.

3   JON: I've got something really exciting and important to talk with you about, Dad. I've been doing a lot of thinking and growing this year, giving a lot of serious consideration to my life, how I want to apply myself, and what I need to be the kind of person I want to be.

DAD: This really *is* serious, isn't it?

4   JON: It's exciting, too. I've made some decisions and I want to share them with you, get some of your ideas, and, you know, feel that you understand and hope the best for me.

DAD: Well, you've certainly got my interest up. Let's hear it.

5   JON: You know I've done well in school, and that I value an education. I also value things I can learn outside of

school. The architecture courses I've been taking are interesting, but I just don't think architecture is for me. I think I need—

DAD: Now wait a minute, son. You can't tell all that from just a few courses. You've always wanted to be an architect.

6   JON: Well, Dad, I wanted to *see* if I would be interested in architecture. I know *you* are very happy being an architect, and everybody knows you're one of the best. But, Dad, I think maybe *you* have always wanted me to be an architect more than *I* have wanted that, and I can understand that you would want that for me. I may even want my son to follow in my footsteps one day. But I believe each person has to follow his own path. Anyway, I've decided to explore some other possibilities to see where my interests and strengths lie.

DAD: You mean you want to change majors? Flip-flopping back and forth between majors isn't the way I brought you up. See things through to the end, Jon. I've always drummed that into you. I thought—

7   JON: You've also taught me to have the courage to speak my mind and make decisions. And I've made a good decision based on what I think is best for me right now. I've decided to work with a group of people in developing some alternative energy sources, experimenting with organic agriculture, and trying to get back to some of the basics of what life is all about.

DAD: What! That sounds like some sort of hippie commune!

8   JON: What do you mean by a hippie commune, Dad?

DAD: Well . . . you know! Kids who can't cut it in the real world and escape to some God-forsaken place and do whatever the hell they *want* to do!

JON: Then what we are going to do is definitely not a hippy commune. Let me tell you what it *really* is, okay? We are all in our twenties and are all interested in protecting the environment and working *with* the environment rather than just exploiting it for material gains. We will grow our own food, develop some solar and wind energy sources, design and build our own houses, and—

DAD: And have everybody sleeping with each other . . . and doing drugs!

9   JON: Dad? What did you hear me say?

DAD: You're going off half-cocked on some back-to-nature fantasy with a bunch of kids who want to drop out of the real world!

9   JON: Is that what I said? What did I *really* say, Dad?

DAD: (pausing, frustrated) Well, you said something about organic farming, and solar energy, and building your own houses . . . but c'mon, Jon, you know what those things mean.

JON: Do those things sound like a bunch of wild kids? These are people who are concerned about the world. They are intelligent people who care.

DAD: (pause) But it's all just so . . . sudden!

JON: Not for me, Dad. I've been thinking about this for a long time.

DAD: So you just made your decision without talking with me.

10   JON: Maybe I should have talked with you before, but I wanted to be sure of my own thoughts. And I guess I was a little worried about how you would react. But I have made the decision and I would like for you to give me some ideas about how to make the decision turn out as positively as possible.

DAD: How can you do this farming thing and go to school, too? Where is this place?

JON: It's in Hawaii, but—

DAD: Hawaii!

JON: It's a very progressive place for these kinds of things. And as for school, I've decided to stop for awhile and—

DAD: What! You can't do that! I won't have a son of mine dropping out of school!

9   JON: What do you mean dropping out?

DAD: Quitting school! You can't get anywhere in life without a college degree!

9   JON: Did you hear me say I was quitting for good?

DAD: Well . . . once you stop, most people never come back.

JON: But I'm not most people. I want to get my degree, but not until I can do it in something I really love, something I want to spend the rest of my life doing. I *will* come back to school, Dad, but I need at least a year to experience something else. I remember how you used to tell me about
11 the semester you took off and worked at odd jobs around the country. You said that was a great experience. That's what I'm going to make happen, too.

(Dad is quiet for a few seconds, deep in thought.)

DAD: Young kids out there without any rules . . . sex diseases are all over the place these days. And drugs . . .

JON: Dad, I can sit here and tell you all day that I would never touch drugs. I never have, and you know that. And as for sex . . . well, you and Mom have been so thorough about being careful, I'm probably more careful than ninety-nine percent of guys my age. Look, Dad, if you are going
12 to worry about these things, why don't you come out for a visit after about three months?

DAD: (surprised) Are you serious?

JON: Sure. You and Mom could both come. But not until after I've established myself on my own. But you're welcome to come for a short visit then.

(Dad begins to think more objectively about Jon's decision.)

DAD: I have to admit you seem to have thought this thing through. But your education, Jon . . . why can't you at least finish out this semester?

JON: I wanted to, but the group gathers in Hawaii on May
13 first. My exams aren't over until May fifteenth. If we can-
think of some options about school, I'd be willing to consider them.

DAD: You could wait to go until the fall.

JON: Maybe I could call the people in Hawaii and see if the
May first date could be delayed.

13 DAD: If you're hell-bent on going before the fall, you could
petition to take your exams early.

JON: Well, the idea about fall isn't really acceptable to me
because that would put me way behind all of the other
community members. And I don't like the thought of having a bunch of incompletes hanging over my head. Maybe
13 I *could* take my exams early. I'll check on it tomorrow.

DAD: Who are the others who'll make up this . . . this
community?

14 JON: Some are graduate students, some are working with
alternative energy groups, some are like me, undergradu-
ates who are searching for what they want to be and do.
I'm impressed with them. Here (Jon gives Dad some pic-
tures and biosketches of a few of the participants).

(Dad looks over the material.)

DAD: Hmmm. I guess they don't look so bad. How did
you find out about this place?

JON: From Dana.

DAD: That girl you've been dating? Wait a minute, son. Is
this some kind of romantic adventure you've got going?
Your mother and I have never even met this Dana.

JON: I know, and I feel bad about that. She's sort of . . .
different, I guess you'd say. She's not like any of the other
girls I've dated.

DAD: Different? Now that *really* makes me worry.

15 JON: Different in a good way, Dad. Maybe she could come
over for dinner this weekend.

DAD: Well, that's a start. Sure. Check with your mother on that.

(Dad is quiet, staring at the wall.)

16 JON: What are you thinking, Dad?

DAD: How I'm going to explain this to our closest friends. And the fact that I'm sure you're going to hit me up for the money to do all this.

JON: For once I'm not asking for a penny. All of us who were accepted get our airfare paid, and we all have paying jobs once we get there. Plus we sell some of the food we grow.

15   As for our friends, what would make you feel comfortable about that?

DAD: For you to write them a form letter.

JON: Okay . . . if you'll help me with it so I'll say things in a way they'll understand.

DAD: (after a long pause) You're sure I can't talk you out of this?

JON: It's a good decision, Dad. What would really make it even better would be for you to be excited about it, too.

DAD: That's asking too much. I'll try to *accept* it, but I don't think there's any way I could really get excited about it. I

17 mean, it's not something I'm doing *with* you.

17 JON: Well, there might be a way you could get more involved. Maybe we can come up with some ideas.

(They both think quietly.)

18 DAD: I just thought of something. Maybe I could give some ideas on the design of the houses, or maybe even a community meeting hall. You and I could work up some ideas for you to take with you.

JON: I like that! But it's pretty basic stuff for you, Dad. You're used to designing fancy office buildings.

DAD: It might be good to get back to some basic design work.

19   JON: That's one of the reasons I'm interested in this commu-
     nity. They really want to get back to basics. (pause) Dad?
     I've got to hit the old books, so could we go over what
20   we've decided? I'm going to check on taking the exams
     early; you're going to help me with the letter and some
     construction designs.

     DAD: And Dana is coming over for dinner Saturday if it's
     okay with your mother. And I'm going to hold you to
     your invitation for us to come visit. I think I'd also like a
     guarantee you'll come back and finish school in a year.

     JON: I promise I'll finish, but I'd like to leave the exact time
     open. It could be six months, or a year, or maybe eighteen
     months if things are really going well.

     DAD: A *year*, son . . . at the most.

     JON: I can't promise that. But let's keep in close touch about
     it as the year goes along. Just know that I am committed
     to finishing college.

     DAD: Well, I guess that's good enough. (pause) You know,
     son, this is the best talk we've had in years. You're growing
     up, Jon.

21   JON: Thanks, Dad. And I've learned something. I should
     go ahead and talk over a decision like this with you earlier.
     I shouldn't just be afraid you'll try to use your role as father
     to keep me from my dreams.

21   DAD: Well, if we can do it as well as we've done this one,
     I think we can discuss just about anything from now on.
     Now go hit those books.

ANALYSIS OF CONFLICT ONE

Following a format used earlier in this book, we will analyze
the conflict resolution process in the foregoing scenario by
referring to the numbers located in the left-hand margin.
Each number marks the use of a specific conflict partnership

skill and corresponds to the following material under the same number.

1. Jon wisely realized that the first step, creating the right atmosphere, would not be served by trying to force Dad to enter into dialogue during his favorite television show. Some of us might point out that Dad *should* choose his son's concerns over a television program, but it was better for Jon to make sure that Dad would be giving the matter his undivided attention. Jon's timing was appropriate. He made sure that Dad agreed to an uninterrupted time for serious discussion.

2. Jon's choice of his own room (the physical environment) helped in several ways. It got Dad away from the temptation of another television show, it assured privacy from unexpected interruptions by the rest of the family, and it gave Jon a little more confidence in confronting an issue he was feeling a bit uneasy about anyway.

3. Jon further set a good atmosphere by using a positive opening. He emphasized how exciting and positive his decision was; he did not fall into the familiar approach of emphasizing the probable negative response his Dad might have by saying something like, "Now I know you are probably going to be mad at me, Dad, but. . . ." Jon's opening also helped his own self power by stating his well-conceived reasons for what he was about to tell his dad.

4. In this one short sentence, Jon uses three important skills. He uses the skill of clarifying perceptions by letting Dad know that whatever disagreement Dad has with the decision Jon is about to state, the ensuing conflict is *not* over whether or not Jon is going to Hawaii. That decision has already been made. Jon's statement also reinforces a partnership atmosphere. By saying that he wants to listen to some of Dad's ideas, Jon employs the skill of developing mutual positive power, letting his dad know that Jon does not see the

situation as an I-versus-you battle but a "we" relationship pattern in which both parties can contribute positive ideas.

5. Here Jon helps to clarify perceptions again, this time
regarding Dad's perceptions of Jon as a good student
who values education and as a person who realizes important learning can take place both in school and in
life experiences outside formal education. The other
critical perception Jon helps clarify is the fact that he is
not finding architecture to be of great personal interest.

6. Jon shows a lot of positive self power in this series of
statements, clearly stating his own approach to choosing his life work, even though his choice may disappoint his father. Jon could have become defensive and
said, "You're trying to push me into architecture and I
resent it!"—a comment that would probably have
made it easy for Dad to come back with more combative statements. Instead, Jon was in charge of his
own reactions. Furthermore, Jon clarified perceptions
of the other party (his own perceptions of his father)
by realizing that fathers often hope their sons will follow in their footsteps. He even mentions a future commonality when he comments that when he is a father,
he may have a tendency to want his own son to follow in *his* footsteps.

7. When Dad made his "flip-flopping back and forth between majors" statement, Jon could have reacted negatively. Instead, he did not allow himself to get caught
up in such labels as flip-flopping and stated his goals
clearly rather than arguing. He also reached for the
positive power in the other party when he reminded
Dad that in his role as a father he had taught his son to
speak his mind and make decisions.

8. In effective conflict resolution, it is wise not to allow
loaded, emotional, stereotypical images to go unclarified. When Dad used the image of a hippie commune,
Jon again clarified perceptions by asking his father to
clarify what he meant. Once clarified, Jon then described the people in the alternative community rather

than debating what a hippie was or was not, or debating whether hippies were positive or negative. The conflict was *not* about hippies.

9. Jon clarified perceptions again by asking his father to repeat what Jon had said rather than saying, "Dad, you're twisting my words! I didn't say that!"

10. If people are trapped in the seesaw power pattern, they will rarely acknowledge any shortcoming on their own part. They fear that any admission of weakness will give the other party more power. Jon is obviously *not* using the negative, seesaw power pattern. He acknowledges that he probably should have talked about his decision before now. He then nurtures shared positive power again by asking for some ideas from Dad.

11. Jon again identifies a commonality he and his father share when he mentions Dad's semester off from college to work at odd jobs around the country. Jon also reaches for the person behind the role, not just allowing the relationship to be between father and son roles.

12. Rather than trying to win a debate over the issue of whether drugs and dangerous sex will run rampant at the alternative community, Jon identifies a possible doable when he suggests that his parents might come for a visit. That doable makes at least two important contributions. First, it has far more power to deal with Dad's "drugs and sex" perception than any amount of verbal debate could ever provide. Second, it involves Dad in a partnership approach to the alternative community in that he can actually share in Jon's experience.

13. Here Jon uses the skill of generating options. As we see, at least one of the options (taking exams early) turns out to be a doable that provides mutual benefits: both Dad and Jon feel better because Jon will not have to have a lot of incompletes hanging over his head, and it will be much better for Jon when he returns to school to have fully completed his sophomore year.

14. You will remember that one of the components of

clarifying perceptions of the conflict is the understanding of what the givens are in any situation or conflict. In other words, what are the real *facts*? Parties involved in conflicts should have their facts and supporting information ready. Jon has prepared well by bringing the photos and biosketches of the community participants with him to the meeting with his father.

15. Throughout the discussion, Jon has been aware of focusing on needs. His own needs have been understood and clarified, and he has focused on some of his father's needs to know about the people who will participate in the community, to be sure of his son's continued education, and, now, to know who Dana is. Thus, Jon suggests another doable (having Dana over for dinner), another small stepping-stone along the pathway to a better relationship with his father. In the second number 15 margin note, Jon focuses on Dad's needs again by asking him what would make him feel comfortable about telling their closest friends. As often happens in the conflict partnership approach, focusing on needs leads to a doable involving shared power (the joint writing of a form letter to the friends).

16. Earlier we spoke of being aware of nonverbal communication as a possible component of clarifying perceptions of ourselves and the other party. Here Jon notices Dad's nonverbals and asks what he is thinking rather than assuming Dad's nonverbals mean a particular thing Jon may want to interpret. Jon's sensitivity to Dad's nonverbals leads to the identification of one of Dad's concerns or needs (how to tell their closest friends) and then to the doable of sharing in the writing of the form letter.

17. In the first number 17 margin note we see Dad becoming further involved in the partnership process (partly as a result of the atmosphere Jon has set and maintained) as he states his need to be doing something *with* Jon. In the second number 17, Jon focuses on that need and invites Dad to generate options once again. It is important to note that even though Jon is

the one using the conflict partnership skills, his methods have positively influenced Dad to become a part of the process. Jon refrains from doing all of the work himself and invites his father to suggest options, a good example of sharing in the conflict resolution process with mutual positive power.

18. We now see how involved Dad is in the conflict partnership process. He comes up with an excellent doable (helping design some of the buildings)—one that uses his skills and positive power in partnership with Jon's needs and positive power. This is another example of how invitational the process can be. When one party employs the conflict partnership skills, the other party begins to see how mutually beneficial the process can be for the relationship, for the self, for dealing with future conflicts, and for improving the relationship for the future.

19. Jon recognizes another commonality, the importance of getting back to basics.

20. Jon employs a component of the skill of developing mutual-benefit proposals when he and his dad clarify specific responsibilities to make sure that they understand what they have agreed to do.

21. Both realize that the relationship has been improved for the future.

CONFLICT TWO

The Downtown Improvement Commission (DIC) is a group established by the Office of the Mayor to bring improvements to the crowded downtown section of a city of 300,000 citizens. The two most powerful members of the DIC, Mary Rolff and John Allen, have worked hard to obtain a large grant from the local Odal Foundation. Odal has just awarded the grant to the DIC with the stipulation that all of the grant be used for a single project so as to maximize quality rather than quantity.

Mary and her supporters on the DIC are arguing strongly for a daycare center to accommodate the working parents in the many office buildings downtown. John and his supporters are pushing just as hard for a small urban park to provide an attractive relief from the concrete jungle and an ideal place for the office workers to spend their lunch hour. Heated debates between the two factions have so monopolized and polarized the recent meetings of the DIC that the city newspapers have had a field day with the controversy. With all of the bad publicity, the DIC is on the verge of falling apart internally, the mayor is considering disbanning the DIC, and the entire city seems angry at the DIC for fomenting dissention rather than much-needed community unity in a city already troubled with severe factionalism.

The director of the DIC explodes during one meeting and tells Mary and John to get together and work out their conflict or there won't be a DIC to continue the generally acknowledged excellent work so far accomplished on other downtown projects. John and Mary meet one evening and follow their usual conquest style of dealing with conflict. We will eavesdrop on a portion of this first meeting.

> JOHN: If you weren't so bull-headed all the time, we could work this thing out.
>
> MARY: *Me* bull-headed? *You're* the one hell-bent on sacrificing the needs of our young children just so you can have a nice place to eat lunch!
>
> JOHN: I am not going to agree to spend this grant I worked so hard to get on a daycare center! And that's final!
>
> MARY: Well, I refuse to use the money for some fancy park! And *that's* final!
>
> (John stomps to the window and looks out. He decides he will come closer to getting what he wants if he tries to win Mary over with smooth talk, promising her something in

the future, which, of course, it is not in his power to give. He turns back to Mary.)

JOHN: (smiling) Look, Mary. You are a reasonable person. In fact, you are one of the most capable people I know. Let's talk sensibly about this. I'll make a compromise. You want your daycare center and I want my park. Let's build the park now and make the mayor happy, and I'll promise to get you another grant next year for the daycare center. Now I think that's a reasonable compromise, don't you?

MARY: You know, John, you're some piece of work, you really are. What do you take me for? But if you want to play that game, then let's do the daycare center now and I'll get you a grant for the park next year.

(Needless to say, John and Mary are getting nowhere fast. Urged on by one of you readers who is a good friend to Mary, Mary goes home and reads a book on the conflict partnership approach. When she and John meet again the next day, Mary uses the new approach. Let's see how she does.)

1   MARY: John, you and I have worked hard to make the DIC an excellent group. You and I have cooperated on numerous worthwhile projects in the past, and I believe we can do it again. We need each other if we are to keep DIC alive and effective in contributing to what I know we both have said many times is our major goal: improving the downtown area. Do you still agree that is our major goal?

JOHN: Of course I do. And the park is the best way to achieve that goal.

2   MARY: I accept the fact that you believe in the park, John. The park is a good idea and the daycare center is a good idea. But we don't have enough money to do both to the degree each of us thinks is needed. We've both stated that. So, since I am not willing to spend the grant for the park,

3   and you're not willing to spend the grant for the daycare center, maybe we can stop fighting and generate some other options.

4   JOHN: You mean both of us should give up what we want? Look, Mary, I don't know what you're trying to pull, but it won't work. I want that park and the mayor wants it. It's the best way to spend the grant.

5   MARY: What indication do you have that the mayor favors either plan?

JOHN: Well. . . . I just know she wants the park.

5   MARY: C'mon, John. Let's stick with what the mayor has actually said. Remember what she said to the two of us last week?

JOHN: She said that she's leaving it up to us. But I'm sure she favors the park.

6   MARY: And I'm sure she doesn't. So we can sit here and try to speak for the mayor, or we can realize that this is our decision to make and that we need to work together to keep the DIC viable.

JOHN: Okay, okay. So I don't really know what the mayor wants.

MARY: Nor do I. What we *do* know is that I think the city needs the daycare center and you think the city needs the park. The city probably needs both. But we won't get the grant if we don't come up with one, just one project we agree on, and the DIC will probably fall apart if we mess
7   up on this opportunity to show we can work together. Maybe we should put the park and the daycare center aside
8   for tonight and focus on the thing we both share as a crucial goal: the DIC and the improvement of the downtown area.

JOHN: I guess that is our common goal, alright.

9   MARY: There's something else we need each other for. We need to demonstrate that the DIC isn't made up of a bunch of people who can't get along.

JOHN: You're right about that. The papers are crucifying us, and so is the mayor.

10   MARY: Maybe we ought to find something the two of us can cooperate on, something the DIC already has the money to

fund. That way we can prove to each other that we really *can* work together, and everybody will see that the DIC isn't always bickering internally.

11 JOHN: Well, how about the Citizen of the Month idea that anonymous letter to the DIC suggested last week?

MARY: That's a good idea. Maybe we could coauthor a proposal and get the papers to interview both of us together?

JOHN: Let's do the proposal now.

12 (Mary and John work for an hour drafting the Citizen of the Month proposal.)

MARY: That's a great proposal, John. I can't believe I'm saying this, but (grinning) you aren't half bad to work with.

JOHN: (laughing) Thanks . . . I think. We did do well, didn't we?

13 MARY: Now let's see if we can do as well on the Odel grant.

JOHN: Uh oh. Round two of the fight, huh?

14 MARY: It doesn't have to be. Let's keep focusing on other options besides the daycare center and the park. What are some other possibilities for the Odel grant?

JOHN: Well, I guess we could resurface that idea we talked about last year but didn't have any money for. Remember? The shelter for the homeless? The homeless population has increased a lot in the past year.

MARY: That's an idea. Or how about a really attractive parking garage, with a lot of trees and flowers around it. People are screaming about the parking problems.

JOHN: Then there's the renovation of some of the older and really quite dangerous buildings. But that may be opening a hornet's nest since there's so many of them. (pause) But I don't like any of these ideas as much as the park.

15 MARY: And I still like the daycare center better. But at least now we know there *are* other possibilities. We don't have

to always see it as an "either yours or mine" issue. If we can come up with these ideas, ideas we both see as important and could work on together, then we don't have to accept the misperception that we are at an impasse. And we cranked out a dynamite proposal together on the Citizen of the Month thing.

16 JOHN: You know, you're right. That helped. (John suddenly snaps his fingers.) Hey! I just thought of something! One of the reasons Odel is willing to give DIC this grant is because they want the DIC to show internal cooperation and to be a model for other cooperative community endeavors. I wonder what would happen if we developed a plan for putting a really fantastic daycare center in the middle of the park area I've been talking about and then went to Odel *together* and asked for whatever additional monies might be needed?

17 MARY: That's a great idea! And if they wouldn't be willing
18 to give any more money, I'll bet we could merge our ideas for what I wanted the daycare center to be and what you wanted the park to be and still come up with a quality daycare center and a park around it that would fit into the existing grant.

JOHN: It would knock their socks off if the two major combatants came up with this plan together and made a joint presentation. The newspapers would give it wide coverage and the DIC would benefit enormously.

19 MARY: And the city would get a daycare center, a park, and a model for future cooperation. I like this!

20 JOHN: You know, it feels good to work *with* you for a change. I was beginning to think we would always be at each other's throats.

21 MARY: Well, now we know we can use a process that yields mutual benefits. When do you want to start working on our joint presentation?

JOHN: Let's go for it tonight. I had set aside four hours because I thought it would take that long to do battle with

you and win you over. Now, because of the way we've
done this, we've still got a lot of time left tonight.

ANALYSIS OF CONFLICT TWO

The following paragraphs correspond to the numbers found
in the dialogue.

1. Mary's new opening stresses the technique of learning
   from the past as she reminds John that they have been
   able to work together well in the past and can again.
   She also focuses on the important fact that conflict
   partners need each other to resolve conflicts effectively
   and to reach shared needs and goals.
2. Mary acknowledges the other party's beliefs and even
   affirms that John's idea has merit. She also states her
   own strong beliefs. She then clarifies the givens by
   stating that there is not enough money to do both the
   park and the daycare center to the degree envisioned
   and that neither Mary nor John is willing to support
   the other's pet idea.
3. Mary makes the critical point that because they have
   reached an impasse of their pet ideas, they should
   generate other options. Although John continues to
   follow his old patterns, Mary has at least focused on
   the need to generate other options, a skill they will
   eventually use to great mutual advantage.
4. John clings tightly to the conquest pattern. When only
   one party is using the conflict partnership approach,
   we often find that the other party resists at first. The
   one using conflict partnership needs to keep trusting in
   the process and continue to demonstrate its effectiveness for *all* parties.
5. Mary clarifies perceptions by asking John what indication he has of the mayor's position. In the second
   number 5 marginal note, she urges John to stick with
   the facts and not complicate matters by issue prolifera-
   tion or misrepresented statements. She then gets John

to clarify what the mayor had actually said at a recent meeting.

6. Mary keeps using "we" and stresses the mutual positive power she and John have as the people responsible for working together for the shared value of keeping the DIC viable.

7. Mary again clarifies the givens when she reminds John that the DIC is in trouble if they fail to work *together* on their problem ("we" again).

8. Here Mary makes a crucial contribution: she suggests that they put the two pet ideas aside because they are, at least for the present, creating an impasse, and once again suggests that together they generate options. Please note that she suggests basing the options on the shared value and goal of the DIC and improving the downtown area. She also keeps reaching for the positive potential in John, an approach that will eventually bear fruit for both parties.

9. Mary mentions another shared need and goal, the internal unity of the DIC.

10. Developing doables is managed effectively by Mary. She realizes that she and John need to lay at least one stepping-stone before they can build a pathway to an effective resolution of the current conflict *and* improve their relationship. She bases the prospect of a doable on the shared needs of the DIC and on their own need to earn each other's trust.

11. John finally begins to see the value of the process and comes up with an excellent doable. In the dialogue between margin notes 11 and 12, Mary affirms John's good idea (his positive power), thereby nurturing the belief that they don't have to use the old adversarial patterns to obtain mutual benefits.

12. The doable is accomplished and makes the important contributions for which doables are designed: creating positive momentum, mutual trust, and a stepping-stone along the pathway to dealing with the more troublesome issues.

13. Mary stresses the power of the doable they have just

completed by expressing the need to use the new-found cooperation in dealing with the Odel grant.

14. Mary stays in charge of herself and perseveres in her confidence in the conflict partnership process even though John's old patterns are still hovering in the air. She then urges them to generate options again. John has now realized the value of the conflict partnership process, and contributes some options.

15. Mary affirms their mutual positive power.

16. John can no longer doubt the value and power of the process. He has experienced it firsthand. He comes up with a mutual benefit proposal incorporating all of the things such a proposal should contain: mutual positive power, shared needs and goals, and mutual benefits.

17. Once again, Mary affirms John's positive power, something he probably needs because he is so accustomed to employing *negative* power. Throughout the discussion, Mary has consistently kept reaching for John's positive power until she and John both find it and use it to mutual benefit.

18. Mary realizes that Odel may not be willing to give additional funds, and therefore suggests another mutual-benefit proposal based on their steadily improving relationship: cutting back on the original preconceived answer each brought to the discussion and working together to design a project that would still meet shared needs and goals with quality.

19. Mary reinforces the shared needs and goals and the mutual benefits of the plan they have worked out together.

20. John has obviously learned from the conflict partnership process as applied to one conflict situation and sees hope for an improved future relationship.

21. Mary reaffirms that they now have the capability of using an effective process to deal with their relationship and conflicts therein. They get to work on putting the mutual-benefit proposal into action.

Index

Absolutes, 8, 9
Anger. *See also* Emotions
　dealing with, 237–240
　expressing, 238, 239–240
　receiving, 238–239
Apologies, 171–172
Arbitration, 10
Assumptions, 100
Atmosphere for conflict resolution.
　See Partnership atmosphere
Avoidance approach to conflict
　resolution, 16, 19–23
　reasons for ineffectiveness of,
　22–23

"Bandaid" approach to conflict
　resolution, 16, 26–28, 218
Bargaining approach to conflict
　resolution, 16, 23–26,
　136, 224
　problems with, 24–26
　values and needs in, 23, 25–26
Beliefs, moral or ethical, 52. *See also*
　Value conflicts; Values
Benefits, mutual, 65. *See also* Mutual-
　benefit agreements
"Buttons." *See* Vulnerabilities

Case studies of conflict partnership
　process
　Conflict One, 265–277
　Conflict Two, 277–285
Clarifying perceptions, 41, 89–125,
　241–242. *See also* Perceptions
　of conflict partner, 113–124, 125
　at first sign of conflict, 233–234
　obstructions to, 114–118
　of own needs, 101–103
　of own values, 106–108
　of past events, 171
　questions to ask, 91–95
　of self, 101–113, 125
Communication skills, 116–118
　timing and, 75
Communities, diversity within, 35
Components of conflicts, 93–95
　sorting out, 95–97
Compromise, bargaining approach
　and, 24
Concentration, timing and, 75
Conflict(s)
　clarifying perceptions of (*see*
　Clarifying perceptions)
　ingredients of, 33–61
　internal, 58–61, 97, 241

main ideas in understanding, 61
new view of, 3–10
positive aspects of, 7
words associated with, 4
Conflict partner(s)
    as caretakers, 228
    clarifying perceptions of,
        113–124, 125
    misperceptions of, 122–123
    needs of, 119–120, 134–140
    negative behavior of, 121–122
    options of, 192–194
    positive behavior of, 121–122
    positive power of, 156–158
    understanding experiences of,
        120–121
    who want their own way, 250–252
Conflict partnership process, 9–10
    basic principles of, 63–68
    case studies, 265–285
    conflict resolution as, 181–182
    eight essential steps in, 71–234
    focus of, 10
    goal of, 10
    keeping alive in relationships,
        232–234
    promoting, 83
    relationship-building and conflict
        resolution connected in, 65–67,
        232–233
    versus traditional conflict resolution,
        66–68
    "we" relationship in, 63–64
Conflict resolution. *See also* Conflict
        partnership process
    ineffective approaches to, 11–31
    levels of, 10
    as process, 181–182
    stepping stones to (*see* "Doables")
    traditional approach versus conflict
        partnership process, 66–68
    when other party does not want it,
        247–250
Conflict resolution skills. *See also*
        Conflict partnership process
    developing and applying, 155–156
    as relationship skills, 232
Confrontation, 242–246
Conquest approach to conflict resolution,
        16–19, 136
Control, use of power for, 51–52
Cultural differences, 78–79, 259–260

Delaying tactics, 219
Demands, 229
    replacing, with mutual-benefit
        agreements, 224–225
    unrealistic, 259
Denial of existence of conflict,
        240–242
Desires, 39–40, 128
Differences, 33–36. *See also* Diversity
    defining relationships through, 34
    feeling threatened by, 34
    using, in conflict resolution, 34
Difficult conflicts, 255–257, 258–260
    mutual-benefit agreements and,
        225, 227–228
Difficult people, dealing with,
        250–252
Dislike, versus injustice, 253
Dissolution of relationship, 10
Distractions, avoiding, 74, 78
Diversity, 33–36. *See also* Differences
    conflict as outgrowth of, 7–8
    positive value of, 34–36
Divorce settlements, 16–17
"Doables," 196
    defined, 204
    developing, 203–221
    eight criteria for, 206, 217
    examples of, 207–217
    importance of focusing on, 204–206
    mutual-benefit agreements and,
        225–228
    as steps, 220
    taking care in choosing, 218–221

Emotions, in conflict resolution,
        55–58. *See also* Anger
    approaches to dealing with, 55–58
    reluctance in expressing, 85
Empathy, 120, 136
Empowerment, 233–234
    location for conflict resolution and,
        76–77
    mutual, promoting, 83
    self power and, 153–155
Energy
    anger as, 237–238
    rechanneling, 110
Expectations, 42
    clarifying, 104–106
    positive, promoting, 82–83
    unclarified, 105–106

Facilitators, third-party, 257–263
conflict partnership skills for, 260–263
when to seek, 257–260
Factions, in bargaining approach, 23–24
Family conflicts
components of, 93–95
diversity within, 35
location of conflict resolution, 76–77
obstruction of needs in, 39
power conflicts in, 50–51
Fear of conflict, 7. *See also* Negative view
of conflict
Feelings. *See* Anger; Emotions
Fixed-image perceptions, 122
Forgiveness, power of, 180–181
Free-flowing optioning, 194–195
Friendships, diversity in, 35
Future. *See* Present-future

Ghost conflicts, 97–98
Givens, 228–230
Goals
clarifying, 103–104
conflicts over, 93
relationship versus personal, 104
short-term versus long-term,
103–104
Groundwork, establishing, 73–75
Growth, conflict as opportunity for, 7

Hope, creation of, 195
Humor, in free-flowing optioning, 195

Images. *See* Perceptions; Self-perceptions
Impasse, 224, 228
Initial comments. *See* Opening
statements
Injustices, conflicts involving,
252–255, 260
Intellectualization, 55, 57–58
Internal conflicts, 58–61, 241
causes of, 58–59
perceived as conflict between
parties, 97

Labor-management disputes, 103–104
Listening skills, 116–118
Location, for conflict resolution,
71, 76–80
guidelines for choosing, 76–80
nonthreatening, 76
partnership atmosphere and,
80, 86–87

Meanings, clarifying, 121
Mediation, 10
Methods, conflicts over, 93
Mishandling of conflict, examples of,
4–7
Misperceptions. *See also* Clarifying
perceptions; Perceptions
clarifying, 111
of conflict partner, 122–123
conflicts as result of, 41
Monologue pattern, 86
Mutual-benefit agreements, 222–234
difficult issues and, 225, 227–228
doables and, 225–228
as endings and beginnings, 232
as givens, 228–231
Mutual-benefit options, 72

Need(s), 8, 127–146
in bargaining approach, 23, 25–26
of conflict partner, 111, 119–120,
134–140, 146
defined, 36, 101
versus desires, 39–40, 128
differences in, 33
effects of ignoring, 36–38
effects of obstructing satisfaction of,
38–39
incompatibility of, 40–41, 258–259
meeting, through conflict
resolution, 10
of others, importance of
understanding, 37
own, clarifying, 101–103,
129–134
own, ignoring, 37–38
personal, 128–134, 140–143, 146
of relationship, 38, 140–143, 146
relative value of, 25–26
shared, 143–146, 158
Negative view of conflict, 4, 7
Negotiation(s)
setting time for, 75
traditional, 10
Nonverbal communication, 117

Opening statements, 71, 80–87
atmosphere and, 80
basic functions of, 81–82
examples, 81–85
general, 82–84, 86

lengthy, 86
specific, 84–86
Options. *See also* Free-flowing optioning
of conflict partner, 192–194
generating, 183–201, 207
imaging, 191–192
key, identifying, 196–197, 207
moving beyond preconceived answers
in, 187–190
past experience and, 197–201
preparation phase for, 183–186
seeking commonalities in,
187–188, 195
turning into doables, 213

Partnership atmosphere
creating, 71–87
opening statements and, 80–81
Past
impedance of conflict resolution by,
162–165
learning from, 165–180
mistakes of, 163
mutually wounding, 259
negative use of, 162
patterns, holding on to, 163–164
romanticizing, 165
steps in learning from, 175–176
three skills for learning from,
175–176
understanding part played by,
171–180
viable options and, 197–201
Perceptions, 7–9, 41–49, 97. *See also*
Clarifying perceptions
of conflict partner, 118–119
differences in, conflicts arising from,
42–49
fixed-image, 122
formation of, 89–90
of incompatibility of needs, 40
intentional distortions of, 45–47
negative, 45–47
of other party, conflicts arising from,
44–47
rigidity of, 44–45
of self, 42–44, 101–113, 125, 152–153
of situations, conflicts involving,
47–48
of threat, conflicts arising from,
48–49
transforming, 7–9

Perpetuation of conflict, 108
Personal preparation. *See* Preparation,
personal
Physiological warning signals,
109–111
Place. *See* Location, for conflict
resolution
Power, 50–52
defined, 50, 148
of forgiveness, 180–181
negative, 148–150, 156–157, 224
positive, shared, 147–159, 196–197,
213, 221, 233
roles and, 29
use of, 52
Preferences
conflicts over, 52–53, 92–93
versus values or principles, 52–54,
92–93
Preparation, personal, 71–72
partnership atmosphere and,
80, 86–87
Present-future
focusing on, 166–170, 180–182
imaging, 182, 191–192
Principles, 52–55
conflicts involving, 52–55
own, clarifying perceptions of,
106–108
Priorities, identifying, 96–97
Process. *See* Conflict partnership
process

Questions, asking, 117–118
Quick-fixer approach to conflict
resolution. *See* "Bandaid"
approach to conflict resolution

Reality, perception of, 41
Reforms, right-angle, 219
Relationship(s). *See also* Conflict
partner(s)
in conflict partnership process,
63–65
conflicts in context of, 90–91
dealing with needs of, 38, 140–143,
146 [*see also* Need(s)]
defining through differences, 34
goals for, clarifying, 103–104
improving, through conflict
partnership process, 34, 64–65

Relationship(s) *(cont.)*
    long-term, clarification of, 8–9
    overall, conflicts in context of,
        64, 81, 90
    self-perceptions and, 43
    strengths of, focusing on, 83
    versus values, importance of, 98–99
Relationship skills
    conflict partnership skills as, 232
    developing and using, 155–156
Relaxation, 110
Resolvability of conflicts, 255–256
Responsibilities, clarifying, 231
Role(s), 28–29
    in handling conflicts, 111–113
    seeing people in terms of, 28
Role-player approach to conflict
        resolution, 16, 28–31
    negative effects of, 30–31

Self-image. *See* Self-perceptions
Self-interests, 8–9
Self-perceptions
    clarifying, 101–113, 125
    conflicts arising from, 42–44
    positive self power and, 152–153
Sensing, 117
Situations, conflicts involving
        perceptions of, 47–48
Small steps. *See* "Doables"
Socioeconomic status, and location of
        conflict resolution, 78–80
Specific situations, opening statements
        applicable to, 84–86
Status, 29
Stereotypes/stereotyping, 114–116, 157
Submission, 10

Temporary agreements, 220–221
Third-party facilitators. *See* Facilitators,
        third-party
Threat, conflicts arising from perceptions
        of, 48–49

Timing, 71–76
    importance of, 76
    partnership atmosphere and,
        80, 86–87
Tradition, 164–165
Trust, 104–106, 226
    building, with "doables," 221

Value conflicts, 52–55, 92–93, 98–101
    options in dealing with, 99–100
Values, 8, 52–55
    in bargaining approach, 23, 25–26
    clarifying, 43–44, 55, 99, 106–108
    differences in, 33
    versus preferences, 92–93
    self power and, 153
    violations of, 253
Visualization
    clarifying needs through, 129
    in free-flowing optioning, 195
    of improved present-future
        relationship, 182
    of options, 191–192, 195
    relaxation through, 110
Voices, internal, 58–59
Volatile aspects of conflicts, identifying,
        96–97
Vulnerabilities
    avoiding exploiting of, 123–124
    of conflict partner, 123–124
    own, recognizing and dealing with,
        108–111

"We" relationship, in conflict
        partnership, 63–64, 72
    location promoting, 77–78
Wisdom-of-the-ages syndrome, 164–165
Workplace conflicts
    confrontation in, 242–246
    conquest approach in, 17, 19
    over goals or methods, 93
    location of conflict resolution and,
        77, 78
    power in, 50